Digital

Transformation

with Business Process Management

BPM Transformation and Real-World Execution

Foreword by Nathaniel Palmer

Published in association with the
Workflow Management Coalition

Workflow Management Coalition

WfM C

Excellence in Practice Series

Future Strategies Inc.
Lighthouse Point, Florida, USA

Digital Transformation with Business Process Management BPM Strategy and Real-World Execution

Copyright © 2017 by Future Strategies Inc.
ISBN13: 978-0-9863214-5-0

Published by Future Strategies Inc., Book Division
3640 North Federal Highway, Lighthouse Point FL 33064 USA
954.782.3376 / 954.719.3746 fax
www.FutStrat.com email: books@FutStrat.com

For bulk orders, resellers, academic orders and extracts, please contact the publisher.

Digital Transformation with Business Process Management: BPM Transformation and Real-World Execution

p. cm.
Includes bibliographical references and appendices.

1. Business Process Management. 2. Organizational Change. 3. Technological Innovation. 4. Information Technology. 5. Total Quality Management. 6. Management Information Systems. 7. Office Practice Automation. 8. Knowledge Management. 9. Workflow. 10. Process Analysis

Fischer, Layna. (ed)

Table of Contents

Section 3: Appendix

Digital Edition: BPM-BOOKS.com

Digital BENEFITS:
Enjoy immediate PDF download (13 MB), live URLs, searchable text, graphics and charts in color. No shipping charges. No taxes.
Delivered in unzipped PDF; mobile-device friendly

BPM as the Platform for Digital Transformation

DIGITAL IS BIGGER THAN MOBILE

2017 marks the 10th anniversary of the iPhone, and, with it, perhaps the single greatest step towards digital disruption. Over the last decade, we have seen an extraordinary shift in customer expectations – which has ultimately created the need for digital transformation. How digital are your processes today? Many will answer this in terms of their mobile strategy, yet most will have missed the point. It is not the iPhone which excited consumers and drove innovation – it was a *catalyst* for digital disruption, but not an end-game. Rather, that which drives customer demand for digitization is the promise of (and expectation for) instant gratification.

If you cannot provide what I want immediately (an answer, a ride, a drone-delivered beer), I will quickly find someone who can. The value you offer to me erodes the longer it takes you to satisfy my desire, and the business value I represent to you drops just as fast, as I am become increasingly likely to move on to your competitor.

Today in 2017, the greatest catalyst for digital disruption is not mobility, it is *conversations*. The most emblematic and palpable devices representing digital disruption are not the iPhone or iPad, it is the *Amazon Echo* or *Google Home*. To be certain, as devices go they are relatively pedestrian; merely a speaker and a microphone. Certainly, they are nothing as transformative or ground-breaking as the iPhone was at the time. But speak; you shall be heard. What drives this innovation is the cognitive capability offered by Amazon's *Alexa* or *Google Assistant*. These translate verbal commands into discrete results; conversations instead of taps onto a tiny screen. Soon these conversations will be heard across an infinite spectrum of enabled devices, and the way our customers will expect to interact with be not through taps and clicks, but conversations.

WITHOUT BPM IT'S ALL TALK AND NO ACTION

Does this sound like Business Process Management (BPM)? Perhaps not the way BPM has been leveraged for the last decade. Yet in the era of digital transformation, BPM will indeed follow a conversational model. This is because the best-equipped platform for enabling any business and consumer to conduct business through conversations is in fact BPM. What BPM provides is not only the means to digitize customer-centric processes, but the correct operations and business rules needed to support any customer transaction.

Today, Alexa can add an item to a shopping list, but the transaction essentially stops there. Customers will quickly grow impatient with this level of capability, and we will demand the ability to complete the transaction; confirm prices, schedule services, negotiate terms, reschedule a delivery. There are all things which today are simply best handled through conversations. Is this not what AI-enabled commerce promised to deliver? Yes, but artificial intelligence (AI) is merely the interface (when it has a voice in front of it). How it enables *digital* transformation is via BPM.

AI AS A PROCESS INTERFACE

Clearly digital transformation involves more matters than managing customer interaction. How might routine work change under this model? Consider how you received work today, with an alert sent via email or text. Your next step is review the task and figure out what's next, but instead imagine an AI assistant who parses and summarizes the task, and asks for response (i.e., interacting just as you would with Alexa). The task might be an exception requiring approval, and within the summary is context from the decision logic (e.g., business rules) which outlines the circumstances. It may seem farfetched to imagine Alexa or Google Assistant being integrated with your internal core systems. Indeed, tight-coupling would be awkward at best, yet for a BPM environment it would be no more exotic than exposing interaction via an iPhone or other mobile device. What the growing spectrum of AI engines provide is the ability to respond in a natural language statement as you would any assistant, bridging the gap by interacting with the BPMS. You can ask questions for further drilldown or require to be told when something requires your undivided attention. This highlights a critical principle of the future of both software and digital transformation; to re-envision the structure of the task to be not a single, discrete unit of work, and to remove the distinction between what supports a task and the task itself.

Of course, all work can be done via voice prompt, or for that matter text or email. Yet many tasks can be, and the ability to have work truly follow the worker, for both convenience and expediency, underscoring the value of separating how work is performed from the work itself. AI is merely an abstraction of the interface, and the business logic that comprises the rules and process definition remains within the BPM environment. Core systems remain intact, processes are followed and reported on, yet this abstraction of the interface into conversation components greatly simplifies the interaction between participants. Beyond simply supporting verbal commands, the processes may extend (by leveraging both BPM and AI system capabilities) to proactively chasing down the other participants and asking qualifying questions until the work is successfully completed, based on criteria defined within configurable rules.

BPM AND INTELLIGENT AUTOMATION

Today process automation (sans BPM) still looks a lot the same investments in industrial automation for the last 40+ years; designed for optimal efficiency and consistency. Industrial engineers designed the ideal routes to move objects in the most efficient way possible. Yet the challenge we face is that fixed pathways are not consistent with the way we work as humans. We do care about what's in the package, we do care about context. This is fundamental to digital transformation.

In a conversational model, we cannot fully script out in advance the sequence of steps and end-to-end processes without knowing the exact context of any given task we will be performing. Leveraging BPM over other modes of process automation expands the range of what can be automated or otherwise managed. It is the combination of process, rules and data which frame today's BPM platforms which, in turn, enables "intelligent automation."

Today's BPM platforms deliver the ability to manage work while dynamically adapting the steps of a process according to an awareness and understanding of content, data, and business events that unfold. This is the basis of intelligent automation, enabling data-driven processes adapting dynamically to the context of the work, delivering the efficiency of automation while leveraging rules and policies to steer the pathway towards the optimal outcome. For these reasons, BPM is the ideal platform for digital transformation. Not old wine in new bottles, but the critical leverage point for capitalizing on digital disruption.

Nathaniel Palmer, WfMC Executive Director

Introduction:
Digital Transformation with Business Process Management

Layna Fischer, Future Strategies Inc.

BPM is essential to a company's survival in today's hyper-speed business environment. The goal of **Digital Transformation** is to help empower enterprises to compete at the highest level in any marketplace.

This book provides compelling award-wining case studies contributed by those who have been through the full BPM experience. The case studies describe the processes involved to generate successful ROIs and competitive advantages.

Digital transformation describes the changes associated with the application of digital technology in all aspects of human society. Digital transformation may be thought of as the third stage of embracing digital technologies: from digital competence to digital usage to digital transformation, with usage and transformative ability informing digital literacy. The transformation stage means that digital usages inherently enable new types of innovation and creativity in a particular domain, rather than simply enhance and support the traditional methods.[1]

These industry thought-leaders together with the leading-edge case studies will help you understand the meaning and impact of Digital Transformation and how you can leverage that transformation; likely using BPM you already have. Learn how to extend that into core processes that run the business and thus engage more meaningfully with your customers. The authors discuss the impact of emerging technologies, the mandate for greater transparency and how the ongoing aftershocks of globalization have collectively impacted predictability within the business enterprise.

Section 1: Digital Transformation

FOREWORD: BPM AS THE PLATFORM FOR DIGITAL TRANSFORMATION

Nathaniel Palmer, WfMC, USA

Today's BPM platforms deliver the ability to manage work while dynamically adapting the steps of a process according to an awareness and understanding of content, data, and business events that unfold. This is the basis of intelligent automation, enabling data-driven processes adapting dynamically to the context of the work, delivering the efficiency of automation while leveraging rules and policies to steer the pathway towards the optimal outcome. For these reasons, BPM is the ideal platform for digital transformation. Not old wine in new bottles, but the critical leverage point for capitalizing on digital disruption.

---

[1] https://en.wikipedia.org/wiki/Digital_transformation

TRANSFORM CUSTOMER EXPERIENCE AND OPERATIONAL EXCELLENCE BY GOING DIGITAL OUTSIDE *AND* INSIDE

Connie Moore, Digital Clarity Group

The amount of information generated each day within businesses and government is enormous. It continues to outstrip the abilities of workers to process incoming requests and information from customers and prospects, and for sales, service, support and finance to fulfill those requests internally.

Connie Moore examines how this unending deluge of structured and unstructured information pushes organizations to ditch their old, outdated ways of working. In place of old ways, they must embrace a plethora of channels to capture the ever-rising amounts and types of data submitted by customers in an effort to become fully digital on the *outside*.

At the same time, enterprises are concerned with internal efficiency and advances in operational excellence in their rapidly changing industries. In response, they are putting their efforts behind new systems that transform digital operations, streamline internal processes, reduce the information glut, integrate business applications with information stores and go digital *inside*.

IOT WITH IBPM & DCM FOR BATTLEFIELD DIGITAL TRANSFORMATION

Kerry M. Finn, Raytheon Corporation, USA, Dr. Setrag Khoshafian, PegaSystems Inc., USA

Aspects of business process management (BPM) have been around for many years, with a known value statement in terms of business efficiency and cross-functional life-cycle improvements. The essential concept is that when a business can agree on and build a common model for key business processes that span functional organizations, followed by supporting organizational, user process and technology changes, then very significant life-cycle improvements in cost, cycle time and manpower can be achieved beyond the scope of one business function or organization. The evolution of intelligent Business Process Management (iBPM) as workflow automation shifts to its 4th generation provides a powerful tools suite that enables dynamic processes that accommodate agility and change through a common and integrated suite of DevOps-inspired automation and time to market deployment of workflow solutions.

The paper spans the complete spectrum of digital technologies as they are leveraged in Battlefield planning and operations, including mobile, social collaboration, cloud, analytics, IoT, and especially digitized theater value streams through iBPM and Dynamic Case Management (DCM). The authors provide frameworks to accelerate process responsiveness, visibility, and transparency with continuous optimizations. They also address the digital transformation maturity assessment frameworks for battlefield responsiveness to accommodate tactical networks.

BPM FARMING: REAP BENEFITS BY NURTURING YOUR EXISTING PLATFORMS

Kay Winkler, NSI Soluciones, Panama

BPM *everywhere* indeed! The third wave of business process management has come and receded, having left an irreversible imprint on today's technological landscape and business practices. The Internet of Things (IoT) enables business processes to extend services closer to our customers than ever before, while even more business applications sport BPM capabilities of some sort or another. Chances are that you have multiple workflow tools and BPMS set up in your organization. Thus, likely having an immense arsenal of technologies at your disposal to automate business processes, your stakes are high to harness the power of existing technologies, while avoiding the pitfalls of redundancies, information silos and misuse of applications whose main purpose is different to BPM.

The author details the key questions a company needs to address when desiring to keep using its existing BPM while improving current and creating new process solutions. He explains how to achieve business transformation, whereby all pieces of a larger and holistic strategy must fit perfectly.

CREATING DIGITAL THREADS, DRIVING LEAN STARTUP MODELS

Neil Ward-Dutton, MWD Advisors, UK

Digital transformation is a subject on every executive's lips; no matter what industry they're in. Organizations from sectors as diverse as financial services, retail, utilities and logistics see the threats posed by both new digital natives entering their marketplaces, by more traditional competitors stealing a march on them with new digitally-powered services and experiences, and even by out-of-sector players using digital channels to launch competitive products and services. However, digital technologies also hold the promise of giving you ways to protect your company against these threats, at the same time as improving the experiences that your organization can deliver to customers; improving your operational efficiency and agility and driving more innovation into your products and services.

In this paper, the author digs into several aspects of the concept of digital transformation and show the strategic role that IT has to play in delivering those aspects. He then goes on to show the extent to which modern business process application platforms fit the technology platform requirements that spring from serious digital transformation efforts.

IMPROVE, AUTOMATE, DIGITIZE

Frank Kowalkowski, Knowledge Consultants, Inc., USA

Have you ever wondered why organizations spend a lot of money, get involved with large projects for improvement or transformation, get outside help, and yet, *still* don't realize the value they expected? Then, several years later, things seem to get on track or they get worse. Did the management learn anything? Every time a new technology, method or other 'hot thing' comes out, organizations try to take advantage of it before the competition. The author looks at new advances in digitization, process automation and myriad other technologies pushing their way into the business space.

He points out that there are organizations that already have a staff of 1000 or more analysts doing analytics on data. Often this is not automatically captured data but is data that supports decision-making by humans. This is true especially in health care and government. The digital parts are usually not operationally integrated into processes but are linked to business needs that require support by human operators of the processes.

Mr Kowalkowski details orderly ways to proceed with integrating digitization, transformation and BPM efforts. The basic idea is to start with accurate processes at the *beginning* of a transformation rather than jumping into the new technology immediately. At the same time management needs to know if the value proposition they read about is realistic for their organizations.

A METHODOLOGY FOR HUMAN BPM PROCESSES

Keith D Swenson, Fujitsu America, Usa

We often think of digital transformation in terms of machines and data flows. As we make everything digital, what is it that we are transforming? There is little to gain from digitizing things that are already automated.

The real benefit comes from transforming things that are not automated; things that today are human processes. The goal cannot be to simply automate earlier manual processes. Many processes are done by humans today because they cannot be automated by the traditional means. Humans have a natural decision-making ability that far exceeds the capability of pre-defined rules. The important question in front of us is how to make a digital organization that works symbiotically with people. Not replacing, but enhancing, their work.

In this chapter, Mr Swenson offers a method to take a human information worker process and to properly implement a case process that support the worker to get more done, to be more efficient and more accurate.

Section 2: BPM Execution

Award-winning Case Studies

ARAYMOND, BRAZIL

Nominated by Lecom S/A, Brazil

A multinational French company with extensive presence in Brazil, ARaymond Brazil adopted a Business Process Management suite for increasing efficiency and control of its internal processes, ensuring a sustainable growth in the country. Created in 1865, ARaymond has, for several generations, developed manufactured and marketed fastening and assembly solutions.

The Brazilian branch, ARaymond Brazil, started operating 19 years ago and is currently a national reference in the auto parts sector, working with most automakers in the country, besides being an important supplier for all South America. A few years ago the company identified the need to improve its internal processes in order to support operation growth. Based on that, the company started a project to automate some of its processes with a technological suite. An agile BPM methodology was used, enabling delivery with quality in short cycles of process analysis, redesign, prototyping and validation by end users.

DIE MOBILIAR, INSURANCE COMPANY AG, SWITZERLAND

Nominated by ISIS Papyrus Europe AG, Austria

The Swiss insurance company *Die Mobiliar* is the oldest private insurance organization in Switzerland. As a multiline insurer, offering a full range of insurance and pension products and services, *Die Mobiliar* needs to handle a huge quantity of documents, exchanged with approximately 1.7 million customers. Therefore, the "Mobiliar Korrespondenz System" MKS (Mobiliar Correspondence System) for ad hoc generation of well-designed and rich content documents is vital for *Die Mobiliar*.

Each insurance document is designed and delivered in high quality by the document generation processes executed in a huge and manifold working environment. Documents are composed from building blocks following insurance regulations. Moreover, the data filled into a certain document is retrieved on the fly from diverse data sources. These complex business processes are handled in a quick and exact way by the MKS built on the Papyrus Platform and its ACM (Adaptive Case Management) and BPM (Business Process Management) capabilities. The combination of these two technologies enables flexibility from design time to run time of the document generation process.

FUJIREBIO DIAGNOSTICS, USA

Nominated by Wonderware, India

Fujirebio Diagnostics, Inc. (FDI) is a premier diagnostics company and the industry leader in biomarker assays. We specialize in the clinical development, manufacturing, and commercialization of in-vitro diagnostic products for the management of human disease states with an emphasis in oncology.

FDI personnel identified a major opportunity to save time and paper by automating the acquisition of equipment data and generating electronic reports for review and approval.

With direction from FDI's executive management driving a strategic "Electronic Initiative" as a vision for future systems, a project team was assembled to define and implement a system capable of addressing a complex set of user requirements to streamline our existing paper based GMP record system and manual data logging process with an electronic system.

A comprehensive Project Management Plan was then developed to drive the ensuing project to completion by incorporating FDI's System Development Life Cycle (SDLC) procedures to ensure that all deliverables were generated and the project completed in accordance with company requirements to comply with FDA regulations.

INTA, ARGENTINA

Nominated by PECTRA Technology Inc., USA

In order to optimize institutional management, INTA (National Institute of Agricultural Technology) developed the "Administration Modernization" project which included implementation of a Business Process Management System (BPMS) parallel to modification of internal regulations and structure in order to reduce the complexity of processes, while maintaining legal protection and improving the information system. More than five years after the implementation of the BPMS, INTA's National Directorate for Information Systems, Communication, and Quality reports multiple benefits: greater adoption of BPMS (rising from 1 to 30 implemented processes); 1400% growth in number of users and the incorporation of 15 regional centers, 5 research sites, 50 research stations, 16 institutes, and more than 300 extension units; greater employee satisfaction (99%) due to the reduction of administrative and manual tasks—mostly tracking the status of internal procedures.

The project made it possible to integrate and digitize the information from multiple applications and manual procedures. A BPMS Center of Excellence (CoE) was created and it continues optimizing and automating processes. Reports and control panels for all processes were configured.

Today the BPMS implemented at INTA manages more than 7,500 daily automated process transactions that manage funds of up to $700 billion and involve internal and external organization users, showing improvements in time management, organizational transparency, and ease of access to the information.

MINISTRY OF INTERIOR, COLOMBIA

Nominated by AuraPortal, Spain

The platform meets the needs of legal representatives from over 5000 religious entities, which according to the figures estimated by the Interior's Public Information Bureau, agglomerate over 10 million parishioners.

The Ministry's religious entity process was confusing for the general public. This situation was exploited by unscrupulous people who acted as intermediaries in managing the process and charged very high rates for their services. Furthermore, it was difficult maintaining updated information in the public record which led to circumstances of misinformation and duplication problems.

The Religious Affairs processes were analyzed, developed, tested and put into service on time; and in March 2015 the Ministry was able to offer the free online certificate of recognition of legal status to non-Catholic religious entities.

Both the Ministry and citizens are pleased with the results. Now, thanks to the automation of these processes, requested Legal Entity recognition certificates are issued within a few minutes. The certificates are sent via e-mail free of charge. This constitutes an important alignment with the Ministry's mission of transparency, effectiveness and efficiency, hereby providing the citizens optimal services.

NATIONAL BANK OF KENYA

Nominated by Newgen Software Technologies Ltd, India

National Bank of Kenya is one of the largest banks in the country providing financial services to all the sectors of the economy. The bank needed a platform to include digitization tools and provide statistical data on stock, incoming and shredded documents. Previously, manual and paper-based transaction processing/data entry was done in the branches. Customers had to wait in long queues. There was no tracking and monitoring of files.

National Bank of Kenya was facing several business challenges such as: lack of process standardization because as the processes were not centralized, all the business processes were working in silos. Manual intervention in business processes was slowing things down and there was no process visibility and auditability. To centralize and streamline the business processes, the bank successfully implement a product suite for automation of Business Process and Document Management System.

SANTOS CITY HALL, BRAZIL

Nominated by Lecom S/A, Brazil

Santos is a municipality in São Paulo, the richest state of Brazil. In 2014, the City Hall began a program called "Digital Processes", aiming at improving its internal processes. One year after implementation, the program already presents significant numbers, with countless operational and financial benefits. The initiative of Santos City Hall has been widely spread in Brazil and has become a significant benchmark for Brazilian federal, state and municipal government entities.

With a population of 433,200 inhabitants in 2015, Santos is currently ranked sixth place in Human Development Index (HDI) among the municipalities of Brazil, which evidences its quality of life and economic development higher than the national standard. Its GDP per capita is double that of São Paulo state.

The Digital Processes program was based on the application of an Agile BPM methodology, with short cycles (sprints) of process redesign, prototyping and delivery.

One year from initial implementation, there are already 39 processes in place and 53 under construction. Development in sprints helped to minimize users' resistance and showed great results in a short period of time. It gave power to the program team and motivated Santos City Hall to move forward with its implementation.

SEGUROS UNIVERSAL, DOMINICAN REPUBLIC

Nominated by Bizagi, UK

Founded in 1964, Seguros Universal ("Universal") is an insurance company based in the Dominican Republic. Part of Grupo Universal, the organization offers a wide range of products from personal cover for fire, health and accident, through to company pension and liability plans. Universal also supports the insurance needs of retail companies and banks.

In 2013-14, Universal embarked on a BPM initiative to automate its Vehicle Insurance Claims process. Utilized by three subsidiaries (Seguros Universal, Propartes y Asistencia Universal) of the Group and nearly 500 end users, this is considered the most complex of all processes within the organization. Today, "BPM Auto" underpins the end-to-end process, complete with comprehensive and robust case management and analytics.

A key aim of the BPM system was to reduce the amount of parts returned in the claims process: which it has achieved by 30%. Additionally, BPM has given every participant in the process access to timely and accurate information related to claims, delivering a faster, more productive and error-free process that continues Universal´s reputation for service excellence. The BPM initiative is the first of its kind in the Dominican Republic, testifying to Universal´s commitment not only to innovation, but giving the 50-year old company a significant competitive edge.

Win an Award for *your* BPM project

The annual WfMC **Awards for Global Excellence in BPM** are the ideal way to be recognized by the industry worldwide, to publicly acknowledge and recognize the efforts of your team and to inject passion into your BPM projects. The prestigious annual Awards are highly coveted by organizations that seek recognition for their achievements.

Get recognized for your vision and your team's superb efforts by entering the Global Excellence Awards

Co-sponsored by WfMC and BPM.com, and coordinated by Future Strategies Inc., these prestigious awards recognize user organizations worldwide that have demonstrably excelled in implementing innovative Business Process Management solutions. We work with leading industry analysts such as Forrester and Gartner who use these case studies to analyze BPM technology users and suppliers, illustrate trends, industry growth, ROI and more.

General information and guidelines for submissions, see **http://bpm-awards.org**

Section 1
Transformation

Section 4
Transformation

Transform Customer Experience and Operational Excellence By Going Digital Outside *and* Inside

Connie Moore, Digital Clarity Group

ORGANIZATIONS STRUGGLE TO KEEP PACE WITH THE GROWTH OF INFORMATION

The amount of information generated each day within businesses and government is enormous. It continues to outstrip the abilities of workers to process incoming requests and information from customers and prospects, and for sales, service, support and finance to fulfill those requests internally.

Need proof? Just consider:

- Ninety percent of the world's data has been generated over the last two years
- More information is created every two days than was created between 0 BCE to 2003
- The average amount of information managed daily by workers equals:
  - 500 e-mails
  - 5 faxes
  - 100 documents
  - 50 images
  - 40 social interactions
  - 10 contracts
  - 10 videos

This unending deluge of structured and unstructured information pushes organizations to ditch their old, outdated ways of working. In place of old ways, they must embrace a plethora of channels to capture the ever-rising amounts and types of data submitted by customers in an effort to become fully digital on the *outside*.

At the same time, enterprises are concerned with internal efficiency and advances in operational excellence in their rapidly changing industries. In response, they are putting their efforts behind new systems that transform digital operations, streamline internal processes, reduce the information glut, integrate business applications with information stores and go digital *inside*.

> The ever-increasing deluge of information pushes organizations to ditch their old, outdated ways of working and become fully digital—across the organization from the outside to the inside and back again—to deliver value to the customer.

THE MATURITY OF DIGITAL INSIDE AND OUTSIDE IS UNBALANCED IN MOST FIRMS

Because the digital world and customer behaviors are moving so quickly, senior executives in most organizations (rightly) feel compelled to do something immediately to remedy digital weaknesses and convert them into strengths. (For insights into weaknesses and strengths, see Table 1.)

Table 1: Turn Digital Outside and Inside Weaknesses into Strengths

Weak Digital Outside	Weak Digital Inside
• Customer journey is often broken, leading to customer frustration, unfinished transactions and abandoned processes • Customer expectations are unmet, potentially leading to lost customers • Customer interactions are not customer-friendly, as compared with competitors • Information is siloed and difficult to access	• Processes are viewed from an internal perspective, with customers an afterthought • Metrics are usually internal measurements • Work and information is often lost in handoffs between silos and workers • Processes are often inefficient and outdated—leading to waste, inefficiency, errors and poor quality, which may be apparent to customers
Strong Digital Outside	**Strong Digital Inside**
• The customer is at the center of interactions • Customers are supported throughout their journeys • Customers can choose the channels they like at any given time • Customers have ready access to many information types • Customers can be supported by people (call center, bricks and mortar) or engage in self-service (voice response, virtual assistant, mobile apps) • Mobile customers are supported with the same quality of service as stationary customers	• Greater efficiency and productivity improves profits and lowers the cost to customers • Processes start from the customer's perspective (based on Lean) • Greater quality and lowered defects helps to improve customer satisfaction and lower costs • Smooth handoffs (with audit trails) between workers and departments keep work from falling into the cracks • Greater transparency leads to more accountability and better service • Easy to see the status of work in progress, providing greater insight to customers • Content is automated, under control, easy to locate and flows smoothly across departments, making it easier to serve customers

After investigating their options, executives typically embrace business transformation either *outside* or *inside* the organization to stay ahead of the competition or catch up with competitors.[i] Taken together, digital outside and digital inside are two sides of the same coin, although many enterprises mistakenly focus on, or only see, one side of the coin as they embark on digital transformation.

- **Digital outside.** Many firms start by doubling down on the customer experience. They do this because many of their customers engage both digitally and physically whenever and however they choose—often switching channels as circumstances change—while expecting the same level of service across all channels. Plus, these customers and prospects expect their providers to have all the relevant data, documents, images, forms, and other information needed to service their requests, no matter which channel they are using at any given time. And these customers expect their suppliers to anticipate their needs and delight them during "moments of truth" when they re-decide whether to continue doing business with the firm.

- **Digital inside.** Many other firms start their digital journey by focusing their transformation strategies on internal operations. These organizations seek a big jump in quality of service or products, greater efficiency gains that translate to higher profits, lowered risk of being non-compliant or even improvements in hard-to-measure initiatives, like greater collaboration that leads to more innovative, competitive products. Some organizations are also making internal-only processes available to customers to increase the level of self-management that customers can undertake.

While senior executives see an urgent need to simultaneously pursue digital outside for customer experience and digital inside for operational excellence, most organizations find it extremely difficult to focus on both sides of the coin at the same time. Doing both at once is often cost-prohibitive, inherently risky, and requires more executive leadership bandwidth and organizational change than many companies are willing to bear.

As a result, most senior executives choose one or the other approach when getting started, but usually not both. Which of the two digital worlds to start with first— digital outside or digital inside-- depends on many factors, including the organization's business strategy, industry, customers, partners, competitors, workforce, culture and technology.

But, it's an illusion to think that the organization can decide to focus on digital outside exclusively and put digital inside on a shelf—or vice versa. That's because the six key steps for delighting customers in a digital outside world are directly and strategically connected to the six key business functions inside organizations for delivering on those promises. (See Figure 1.)

For example, as customers go from learning about products and services (step 1), to buying products (step 2), to getting products and services (step 3) through the digital outside, they are also knowingly or unknowingly coupled to the digital inside business processes and functions of marketing, sales, and distribution. The pattern in steps 1-3 continues as digital outside customers experience the digital inside business functions of service, finance and support while engaging with the organization's digital inside activities, specifically: use the product (step 4), pay for the services (step 5) and maintain the product over time (step 6.)

It's an illusion to think that the organization can decide to focus on digital outside exclusively and put digital inside on a shelf—or vice versa.

**Figure 1: Customer Actions in Digital Outside Mirror
Employee Actions in Digital Inside**

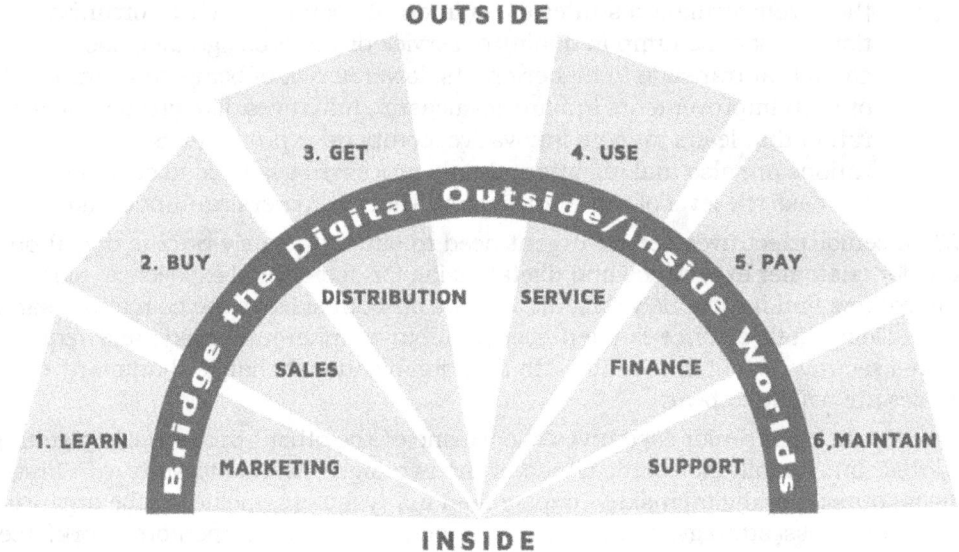

OUTSIDE

3. GET   4. USE

Bridge the Digital Outside/Inside Worlds

2. BUY   5. PAY

DISTRIBUTION   SERVICE

SALES   FINANCE

1. LEARN   6, MAINTAIN

MARKETING   SUPPORT

INSIDE

As Customers Become IT-Savvy, Digital Inside Sheds Its Mystery

Compared with ten years ago, the whole world—business, society, government, education, non-profits—seems to have inverted. Businesses used to be digital treasure troves, with their supercomputers, servers, LANs and phalanxes of laptops collecting, storing and creating vast amounts of information under lock and key. But consumers now store *their own* vast amounts of data, documents, photos, videos, music and other media in the cloud, on their home networks, and on their multiple laptops, tablets, smart phone and smart electronics.

The result? Automation that used to confuse, overwhelm and intimidate customers when they went to their bank branch or to renew a driver's license no longer seems so mysterious—the playing field between customers' understanding consumer technology and understanding the digital outside and inside has been leveled.

And customers are quite willing to challenge companies on why they operate so inefficiently. Let's face it—the reins of power have shifted from businesses and government agencies to customers, who are very willing to march to a competitor or post a negative review to Yelp and Qype—or, conversely, reward the really good companies on Angie's List.

For example:

- Nothing upsets a customer more than to be passed from one customer service rep to another and yet another, only to be asked repetitively for name, address, e-mail, phone number and account number. Hanging up in frustration after talking to five or six people in an hour, they think, why doesn't this firm get its CRM and database act together and solve my problem?
- When a mail-order customer receives a form along with a product delivery, and is asked to complete the form, cut it on the dotted line and mail

the slip back to the company for future re-orders, she thinks, is this business really a forward-thinking company that I want to buy from?

Customers now have strong opinions and rising expectations for the channels they use and types of information they exchange with companies and government agencies. The gamut of tools in use at any given time can run from web sites, to texting and emailing, to social media and embedded software (Internet of Things, anyone?).

Similarly, the analog and digital information used by customers can range from the traditional (faxes, paper forms, PDFs, RFT documents, bar codes, output from business applications like ERP, HRM and CRM) to more complex content (digital photos, videos, audio, CAD files and QR codes) to advanced information types (3D print files, medical diagnostics, video chats, and advanced analytics reports). To be competitive, organizations must offer an ever-expanding variety of channels and information types to these tech savvy customers, who expect the companies they deal with to be *fully digital on the outside and inside.*

BOTH DIGITAL OUTSIDE AND INSIDE MUST BE CUSTOMER-CENTRIC

Digital outside happens when a company doubles down on providing exceptional interactions with customers—supporting the customer's journey across all the channels used throughout a series of interactions—and delighting the customer in the process. Importantly, traditional channels can, and should, still be used to support customers, including brick and mortar locations, mail processing centers, fax servers, a direct sales force with mobile applications, CRM and call centers. These are tried-and-true ways of liaising with customers and may provide the best support for an older generation of customers.

But most customers expect much more than that. To be fully digital outside, organizations also need a constantly expanding combination of channels, metadata, and information management platforms, including: speech IVR and speech recognition, video chat, web chat, collaborative browsing, social media, email response management, knowledge management, virtual assistants, "how to" video services, smart messaging service, mobile apps, and smart video.[ii]

Many firms mistakenly believe that omni-channel is the silver bullet to a transformed digital outside, allowing customers to move seamlessly across channels as their situations change. But that is only the tip of the iceberg. Customers also need, expect and demand high levels of service and quality when requesting and receiving information from the supplier and providing new inputs. Without information management technologies like data warehousing, MDM, product information management, analytics, and enterprise content management (ECM) platforms—with metadata, integrated repositories, enterprise search and content analytics—only a portion of the customer expectations will be met. (See Figure 2.)

Figure 2: Strong Digital Outside Is Compromised By A Weak Digital Inside

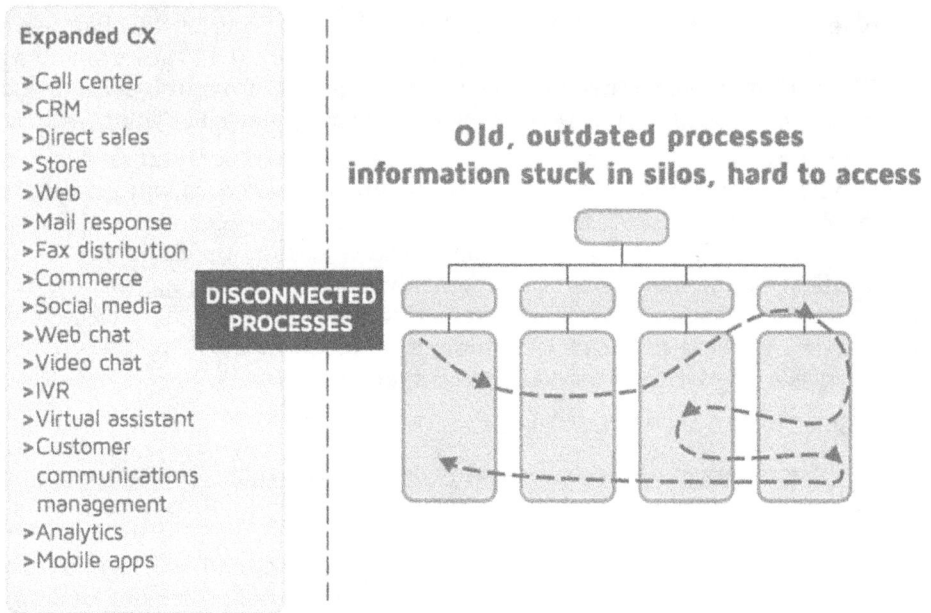

Unless an organization's internal processes are also optimized and designed from the customer's vantage point, and fully and holistically integrated with the company's digital outside, there's a high risk that customer expectations will be raised by digital outside initiatives, only to have them dashed when an internal process fails or information is unobtainable or unusable. Examples of raised/dashed expectations could be when the customer has a delightful experience ordering a product in the firm's digital outside but doesn't receive items that were ordered, receives damaged items that are difficult to return, experiences billing problems or has trouble getting the product to work properly.

Incorporate Customer Centricity Into Digital Inside

Replacing outdated, archaic business processes within business siloes with newly conceived, end-to-end, cross-functional business processes that span the organization is not a new idea. Companies have been embarking on process improvement efforts for years—particularly after large enterprise suites came on the scene in the late 1990s. Six Sigma experts and Lean practitioners frequently lead process improvement projects fueled by a strong business focus on strategic end-to-end processes like supply chain, procure to pay, order to cash, and hire to retire.

It's not just that a large number of today's processes are archaic, it's also that the way we do business has changed rapidly because of digital disruption. As a result, our processes, information management approaches, and the methods we use to improve them need to match the pace of change in the digital marketplace. For example, consider the many decades that consumers used the plain old telephone service (POTS). Eventually, wireless home phones hit the sleepy telephone market, followed by wireless phones and personal digital assistants. Then, changes to both technology and consumer behavior started accelerating and then skyrocketing with the introduction of smart phones, tablets, texting, social media, mobile applications, iTunes, location services, mobile commerce . . . the list goes on. This drumbeat of accelerated change makes it challenging yet crucial for digital outside and digital inside teams charged with transformation to keep pace with their B2B, B2C, G2B and G2C customers and constituents.

Companies have gotten huge business advantages from these business-process improvement projects, like increased productivity, improved quality, greater efficiency, working collaboratively across business units and overall operational excellence. (Toyota and GE are great examples of a relentless focus on operational excellence.) But too often, process initiatives take a strong internal focus, leaving customer experience issues far behind. Usually this is because process practitioners often work for the COO or CFO, who, by job definition, has internal portfolios. This happens despite the fact that both Lean and Six Sigma—the methodologies typically employed for process initiatives—explicitly prescribe designing processes from the customer's viewpoint.

Companies that focus exclusively on *digital inside* have opposite outcomes from companies that exclusively pursue *digital outside*. Customers may experience frustrating or uneven support when engaging with the organization, whether through digital channels, within a store, or face-to-face with a sales rep, but may be delighted with the company once they buy products or services. That's because the organization's business processes have been redesigned with quality, excellence, high throughput and increased productivity in mind.

That redesign may include adopting BPM software for automating business processes; implementing enterprise content management (ECM) to manage all unstructured content in digital forms; using analytics to measure the effectiveness of processes, content and interactions; implementing the latest collaboration software for internal communications and coordination; and deploying large-scale enterprise suites to leverage the best practices codified in those solutions. But still, despite this investment, the company can only get so much advantage because digital outside is out of balance with digital inside. (See Figure 3.)

Figure 3: Strong Digital Inside Gets Diminished By A Weak Digital Outside

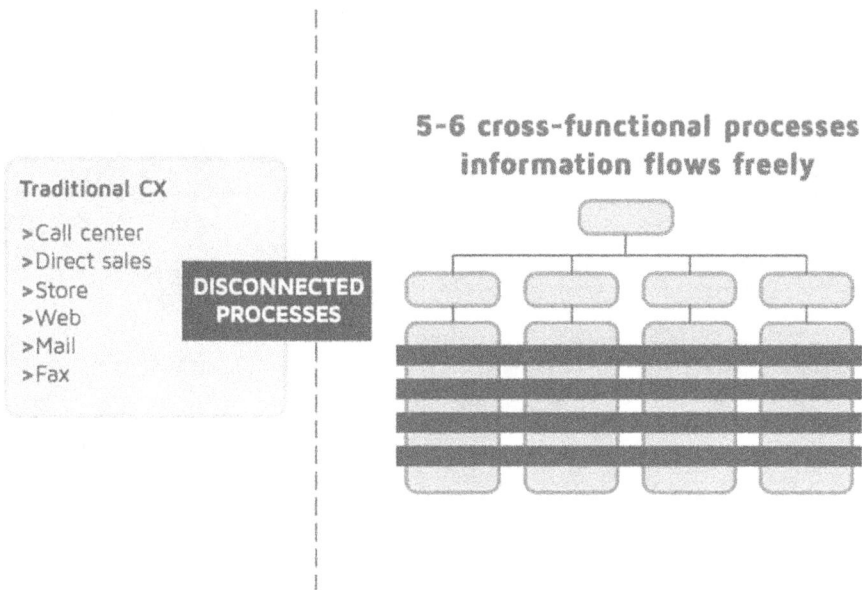

Reach for Digital Outside and Inside To Transform the Business

Ultimately, business transformation requires a delicate balancing act; combining both digital outside with digital inside to support a seamless end-to-end process. There is no way to separate the two worlds for very long and still transform the business, particularly since the goalposts for transformation keep getting higher and higher. Thus, business transformation must focus on re-inventing customer interactions, implementing streamlined cross-functional processes that put the customer first and adopting fundamentally re-imagined and redesigned business models. It also requires a substantial investment in digital technology, running the gamut from software for new customer care channels to BPM, ECM, analytics and enterprise suites for operational excellence.

> Business transformation must focus on re-inventing customer interactions, implementing streamlined cross-functional processes that put the customer first and adopting fundamentally re-imagined and redesigned business models.

This is a tall order for most organizations, but some name-brand companies excel at transforming the digital outside and digital inside at the same time. (See Figure 4.) For example, take three well-known examples: Amazon, Apple and Costco. Smaller, lesser-known companies are pursuing similar transformation efforts too. For example, a UK building society is pursuing transformation across the board, championed by the CEO and board of directors. This five-year project requires a complete overhaul of most systems, including installing a new mortgage platform, a new customer platform, telephony, data warehousing, analytics, web content management and workflow. Two years into the project, the executives are highly motivated and feel compelled to stay the course because they believe in the company's vision and know their competitors are on similar paths. (See Figure 4.)

**Figure 4: Strong Digital Outside and Inside Is
The Winning Combination for Transformation**

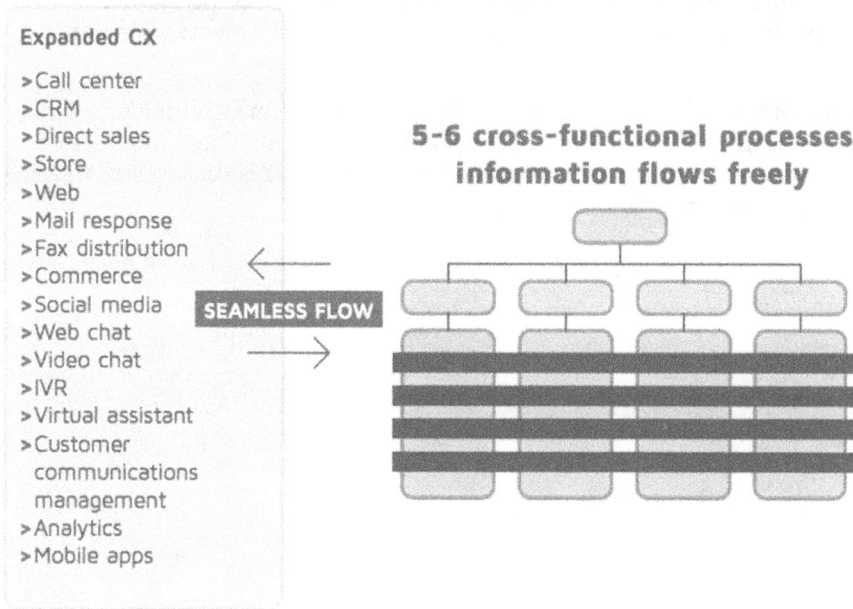

Expanded CX

> Call center
> CRM
> Direct sales
> Store
> Web
> Mail response
> Fax distribution
> Commerce
> Social media
> Web chat
> Video chat
> IVR
> Virtual assistant
> Customer
communications
management
> Analytics
> Mobile apps

SEAMLESS FLOW

**5-6 cross-functional processes
information flows freely**

Firms should consider different avenues when embarking on business transformation. For example:

- Senior executives could select a single strategic process that would be digital outside and inside if it were re-invented as a cross-functional process that flows seamlessly between customer behaviors and internal functions. If so, it might be smartest to focus on that single process first, tackling digital outside and inside at the same time. (Supply chain management is a good example of such a process.)

- Or, senior executives may be most concerned that competitors are pursuing complete transformation with high intensity (along the lines of the building society described above). If that is the case, the organization may need to embark on a multi-year process for re-imagining its digital outside and inside.

There is no one perfect answer, but many companies have successfully transformed their businesses by going digital inside *and* outside. The trick is to develop a digital strategy; build your core competencies in emerging technologies, information management, and process transformation; and then start creating your organization's vision for the future, keeping in mind that customers ultimately don't know or care where or how the work is done—they just want unparalleled service at an unbeatable price. By going digital outside and inside, organizations have it within their grasp to deliver on that promise.

[i] For insights about who drives business transformation, see "Who Drives Customer Experience: The CIO, The CMO, or Fill-In-The-Blank?" http://www.digitalclaritygroup.com/customer-experience-cio-cmo/

[ii] For a more detailed explanation of these customer care channels, see the "Is Your Organization Ready to Take the Leap Towards Customer Care?" http://www.digitalclaritygroup.com/is-your-organization-ready-to-take-the-leap-towards-customer-care/

IoT with iBPM & DCM for Battlefield Digital Transformation

Kerry M. Finn, Raytheon Corporation, USA
Dr. Setrag Khoshafian, PegaSystems Inc., USA

INTRODUCTION

Aspects of business process management (BPM) have been around for many years, with a known value statement in terms of business efficiency and cross-functional life-cycle improvements. The essential concept is that when a business can agree on and build a common model for key business processes that span functional organizations, followed by supporting organizational, user process and technology changes, then very significant life-cycle improvements in cost, cycle time and manpower can be achieved beyond the scope of one business function or organization. The evolution of intelligent Business Process Management (iBPM) as workflow automation shifts to its 4th generation provides a powerful tools suite that enables dynamic processes that accommodate agility and change through a common and integrated suite of DevOps-inspired automation and time to market deployment of workflow solutions.

This paper will highlight the key Command, Control, Communication, Computers, Cyber, Intelligence, Surveillance and Reconnaissance (C5ISR) battlefield management challenges, limitations and opportunities within a tactical network supporting an adaptable end-to-end connected theater for the warfighters. However, to fully realize the more pragmatic, collaborative and operational optimization of battlefield planning and operations – especially logistics and battlefield planning – what is needed are end-to-end capabilities and value streams planning and operations needed to win complex international missions. The paper will present the end-to-end process fusion capabilities in a tactical network that are needed for a 360-degree view of the Battlefield planning and operations. More importantly, it presents the Internet of Things (IoT) sensor data in support of situational awareness and mission over-watch as well as increasing robotics operations (from drones to software) needed to become essential data analytics in support of intelligent systems for surveillance and reconnaissance of dynamic processes and cases for planning and operations. In many logistical and battlefield planning and operations the speed of insight to action need to be accelerated – approaching real-time responsiveness in the context of holistic processes as much as possible.

The paper will span the complete spectrum of digital technologies as they are leveraged in Battlefield planning and operations, including mobile, social collaboration, cloud, analytics, IoT, and especially digitized theater value streams through iBPM and Dynamic Case Management (DCM). We will provide frameworks to accelerate process responsiveness, visibility, and transparency with continuous optimizations. It will also address the digital transformation maturity assessment frameworks for battlefield responsiveness to accommodate tactical networks.

The paper is organized as follows: Section 2 highlights the C5ISR Battlefield Challenges; what are the problems being addressed by the paper? Section 3 provides an overview of the Digital Transformation Platform: the essential technology that enables addressing those challenges. Section 4 describes the most important digitization trend – Internet of Things (IoT) – and how it relates to Battlefield connectivity. There are many heterogeneous sources of data in Battlefields. Section 5 discusses the fusion of data from multiple sources. The discussion regarding Leveraging the Digital Transformation Platform – especially the digitization of end-to-end value streams in Section 6 delves deeper into optimizing Battlefield operations. Section 7 expands upon DX Competency Centers and Maturity Model. Section 8 is the conclusion that wraps it up.

C5ISR THE BATTLEFIELD CHALLENGES

During the early portion of the 21st century, the Western military-industrial complex went through a dramatic era of consolidation resulting in variety of incongruous and incompatible Aerospace & Defense (A&D) contractor-built "Things" (e.g. sensors, devices, military vehicles). These military *Things* represent critical battlefield capabilities defined as Command, Control, Communication, Computer, Combat Systems, Intelligence, Surveillance and Reconnaissance (C5ISR) supporting military Net-Centric Operations[1]. While the military has been a driver in connected and machine-to-machine communications such as radio frequency identification, more commonly known as RFID, it has been slow to adopt disruptive and emerging technologies like the "Internet of Things" (IoT) and "intelligent Business Process Management" (iBPM). Emerging technologies like IoT and iBPM can help knit C5ISR incompatible mission capabilities, vehicles, drones and sensors into a situational aware, adaptable, composable and interoperable warfighter-focused battlefield.

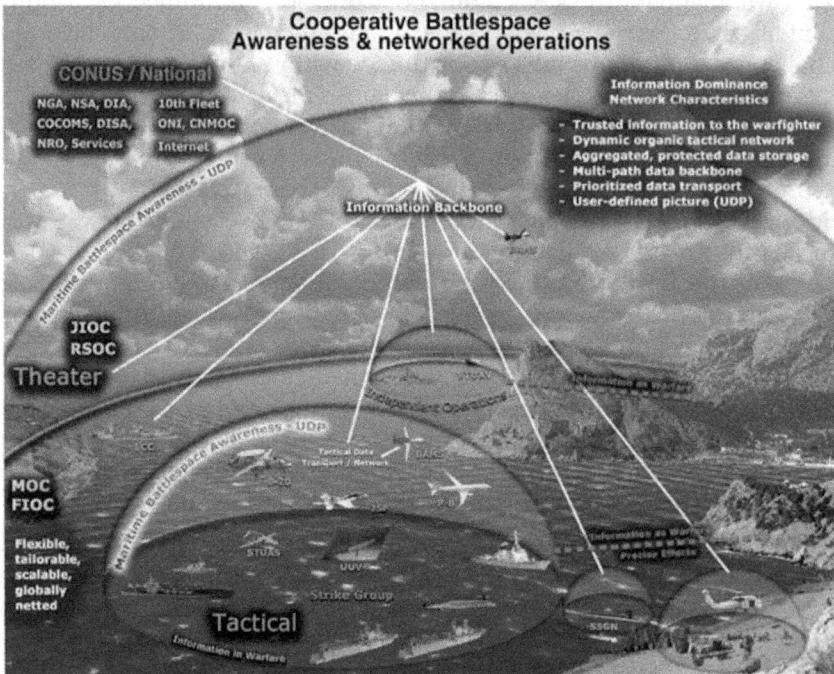

Figure 1 Warfighter Theater of Operations Operational Viewpoint 1 (OV-1)[2]

---

[1] http://disa.mil/news/pressreleases/2010/nces_foc_102010.html
[2] http://docplayer.net/docs-images/29/13896695/images/10-0.jpg

Failure to integrate protection capabilities and provide adaptive solutions to protection will be detrimental to forces operating in the future operational environment. Protecting U.S. military forces has never been as complex a mission as it is in today's adversarial environment. Current and future adversaries will employ techniques such as rockets, artillery, and mortars, cruise and ballistic missiles, rotary and fixed wing aircraft, terrorist activity, weapons of mass destruction, insurgent activity, unmanned aircraft systems, electronic warfare, infrared electro-optical, radio frequency, directed energy weapons and improvised explosive devices. This environment will likely intensify as adversaries prove adaptive to our capabilities.[3]

C5ISR (e.g. communication, cyber, reconnaissance) provides the DoD with key high-level mission capabilities supporting military objectives like increasing warfighter effectiveness with diverse adversaries while at the same time increasing the adoption of new technologies (e.g. IoT and iBPM) and reducing overall cost of the military. Military mission architecture and mission capabilities provide a blueprint of military battlefield operations that provides clarity through a common language and understanding of the warfighter capabilities used to align strategic and transformational objectives and tactical demands for the DoD. This is very similar to how corporations use business architecture and business capabilities (e.g. business capability map) today to link between two complex, yet disparate, environments: business architecture and IT technical architecture.

Architecturally, emerging technologies like IoT and iBPM capabilities epitomize the double edge sword for mission capability architecture, as they are architected around the concept of "Everything" is connected to "Everything" through the internet. Though vital for its success, the security and communication architectures of these connected Things is vulnerable and constantly under threat. Everything is becoming a sensor-drone type "Thing" for the battlefield, from communication devices, joint coalition forces, appliances, vehicles, aircraft, to the clothes the warfighters are wearing and the devices they carry and wear.

Additionally, C5ISR (e.g. communication, cyber, reconnaissance) framework provides the DoD with a high-level battlefield mission viewpoint of capabilities (e.g. the militaries operational mission or business capabilities) that guide A&D contractor product development to integrate within a tactical warfighter battlefield network. Another DoD framework is the Department of Defense Architecture Framework (DODAF) that provides the DoD with a common warfighter-focused architectural viewpoint of the C5ISR mission capabilities for acquisition of A&D products and platforms that must align with the security and communication needs as well as the challenges and limitations of a tactical warfighter network. The *Figure 1 Warfighter Theater of Operations Operational Viewpoint 1 (OV-1)* provides a C5ISR-inspired viewpoint of an international joint coalition forces battlefield that includes multiple allied mobile ground forces, surface ships, aircrafts, weaponry, satellites, UAVs and a variety of unmanned airborne electronic warfare technology solutions.

The military concept of decision cycles places connected information and process flow at the heart of all activities from joint-force planning and logistics to intelligence. In some cases, information's importance and impact is so great that it is classified in the same category as artillery—and as a deadly long-range weapon. Access to information anytime, anyplace to anything is central to all "In Theater" activities and processes shown in *Figure 1 Warfighter Theater of Operations Operational Viewpoint 1 (OV-1)* the Department of Defense (DoD) is naturally eager for

---

[3] www.tradoc.army.mil/tpubs/pams/p525-7-1.doc

technology that improves workflow automation, communication, routing, situational awareness and processing information in a tactical bandwidth environment. C5ISR (e.g. communication, cyber, reconnaissance) mission capabilities as specific technologies for the modern warfighter must provide secure access to distributed information through tactical data links that adapt to a variety of communication protocols in support of critical data and voice communication needs for C5ISR (e.g. communication, cyber, reconnaissance) specific operation technologies. The channel of communication is structured to be highly reliable, real-time, secure (encrypted) and ruggedized for extreme environmental conditions.

DIGITAL TRANSFORMATION PLATFORM

The previous section provided an overview of the C5ISR Battlefield Challenges. The core technology that enables addressing these challenges in the context of robust methodologies and competency centers is the Digital Transformation Platform[4]. Connecting operations in mission-critical tactical networks and overall orchestration of coalition forces, warfighters, connected assets and end-to-end objectives in theater operations needs the capabilities of a robust digital transformation platform. More specifically, here are some of the specific capabilities of the Digital Transformation Platform for connecting tactical (e.g. unpredictable bandwidth) Battlefields:

- *Digitized and Automated Value Streams with Processes:* Ability to easily model capability viewpoints (e.g. DODAF) and execute end-to-end value streams: involving Connected Battlefields (IoT), Theater of Operations, Logistics, Field Support, and the out-of-theater supply chain depots. These Value Streams typically involve digitized processes to orchestrate the work and tasks with complete visibility and mission activity monitoring of operations. This is illustrated in *Figure 4: Coalition Theater Battlefield Planning - Value Stream* where each stage or milestone in the value streams is automated through process fragments, with Things, Robots, and human resources collaborating towards resolution.
- *Business Rules:* Rich collection of Policies or Business Rules: including easy-to-author and change rules for regulatory compliance, tax calculations, revenue calculations, constraints, risk rules, service levels, to name a few. Usually experts or knowledge workers author these rules and they can now be actively participating in both authoring and changes the rules that are then readily digitized.
- *Structured Processes and Dynamic Cases:* The Digital Transformation Platform supports modeling and immediate execution of structured flow-chart or workflow processes. In addition, various processes including planned and unplanned tasks can be organized in *dynamic* case hierarchies. A case is a higher-level construct that can organize work automation tasks and potentially involve various units to complete and resolve a case. A dynamic case automates the value stream in stages or milestones, offering complete visibility and control to the production managers.
- *Analytics:* Battlefields are speaking. Sensors in theater operations are generating enormous amounts of data. A digital transformation platform also includes predictive modeling capabilities to extract or mine

---

[4] *iBPM: The Next Wave.* http://e.pega.com/ibpms

executable models from the Battlefield data and then operationalize them within the aforementioned-digitized value streams. The combination of business rules (typically human-authored) with analytics (typically through machine learning) is very powerful and results in optimized Next Best Actions for warfighter operations; actions that are intelligent, responsive, and contextual.

- *Big Data:* The event data and Battlefield operations and sensor data can be aggregated in Big Data databases to subsequently discover and operationalize recommendations based on the patterns detected in the Big Data repositories. Big Data are usually characterized through Volume, Velocity, and Variety; definite characteristics of Battlefield data.
- *Event Processing:* Battlefields constantly generate events on their status. Event rules and event correlation strategies can be used to decide when and how to respond to these events; for example, elevated hostile threat levels detected by multiple blue-force tracking sensors within a prescribed area or temporal window. These event correlation rules can then activate and instantiate processes to respond to the events.
- *Intelligent Integration:* The Digital Transformation Platform also needs flexible and intelligent integration with Systems of Record. This is a Modernization, Digitization and Innovation Platform on top of existing legacies that can adapt to the tactical unpredictable network bandwidth. Thus, it wraps, renews, and modernizes military operational technologies while leveraging legacy data as needed and just-in-time, using a plethora of integration technologies.
- *Work Automation:* The Digital Transformation Platform for optimized Battlefield operations is first and foremost a work automation platform. This means it can involve Blue Force Tracking devices as participants in end-to-end digitized coalition theater operations. It also means it can do skills and tactical network limitations-based routing to assign tasks to the most accessible and available qualified warfighter whether in the field or in the control and command office. Military specialists can have complete visibility and control of the end-to-end digitized and automated value streams: whether monitoring mission operations, adapting battlefield plans or improving overall operations.
- *Mobile Applications:* The Digital Transformation Platform supports the generation of responsive warfighter User Experiences; design once and deploy everywhere, browsers, smartphones or tablets. Furthermore, UX designers can easily build and deploy mobile applications or mash-up with the battlefield operation's existing mobile applications.
- *Cloud-Ready and Flexibility from On Premise to Cloud:* The Digital Transformation Platform is Cloud-enabled and allows various digitized value-stream Battlefield operations be deployed on the public cloud, private clouds or hybrids. Sometimes organizations do their development and testing on public cloud and then the deployment on premise due to security considerations. This flexibility and agility in private, public and hybrid cloud options is essential in modernizing Well operations.

Despite the unpredictable and limited conditions of the tactical network, in general, Battlefields are becoming increasingly more agile and connected. In this context, connectivity is achieved through connected assets, also known as Internet of Things (IoT). The next section delves deeper into IoT and Connectivity for Battlefields, especially in the context of the Digital Transformation Platform.

IoT and Connectivity for Battlefields

The opportunities are tremendous to optimize coalition forces within tactical network operations and communications in Battlefields through unpredictable and bandwidth-limited connected devices The Digital Transformation (DX) platform can leverage these unpredictable connected assets: ISR, Vehicles, Weaponry, warfighter with wearables, and other categories of mission connected devices.

- *Assets are increasingly connected* and digitized: The status of Battlefield potentially remote assets can be viewed, analyzed and diagnosed. Furthermore, often the servicing can be done remotely by updating software through connectivity or through "digital twin" visibility and interaction.
- *Battlefield technicians are connected and mobile*: they can be tracked, accessed through mobile devices, as well as connected vehicles for geolocationing. Furthermore, analytics may be used to provide the closest skilled Battlefield service technician for a specific context such as specialized skill or specific part.
- *Battlefield Dispatchers* are also connected not only to the Battlefield resources but also to the IT applications of distribution or warehouses. Here again, analytics can be used for the next best servicing action for the particular customer in the Battlefield.
- *Logistics and on-time delivery* that guarantees optimization of the service level agreements for end-to-end delivery of the connected or tracked assets. Furthermore, with IoT, Battlefield operators are finding new ways to optimize inventory levels and improve efficiencies and quality of parts needed in Battlefield service.
- *Augmented Reality:* This is an emerging technology that is helping field service procedures become more successful through direct interaction with the connected product. Smart phones, smart tables or wearables can be used to provide intelligent instructions. Videos may be overlaid on the physical device, helping the Battlefield service technician be more productive and precise.

Having this spectrum of connectivity limitations and options within the tactical operational network, the potential of real-time action becomes a reality. As we have discussed elsewhere there are four essential options for *insight* into *action* with IoT:

❶ *Things – including Battlefield assets - as participants in processes within dynamic cases*

Traditionally, the participants in mission-process management were warfighters (roles, skills, teams, etc.), systems (back-end applications or services), and coalition partners (for international encounters). With the *Internet of Things* and the *Process of Everything*, Things (including robots as military in-theater assets) are also participants in processes.

Things such as Aerospace and Defense (A&D) manufactured or manufacturing devices are becoming increasingly intelligent, self-aware, self-healing and self-governing. Thus, maintenance of dynamic cases will include the Thing category of participants.

❷ Dynamic cases instantiated from thing events

One of the most pervasive use cases for IoT with a Digital Transformation Platform is the instantiation of an adverse event case when sensing (through IoT sensors) a failure or critical issue with the device. There are two complementary scenarios here:

- An Event Due to what is being sensed through the connected assets: what the connected asset is sensing
- An Event Due to a potential issue with the connected asset: the actual device and operation of the connected asset

The intelligent Thing autonomously senses and then either directly, or through a brokering layer, activates an exception case (as discussed earlier). This typically includes monitoring by the command and control center and dispatching military technicians to respond and resolve the theater (e.g. active and/or inactive) problem. Within the processes executing in the exception case tasks and activities will be assigned to people as well as Things or robots. The dynamic case for Digital Prescriptive Maintenance orchestrates the people, the suppliers, the A&D manufacturers as well as out-of-theater (e.g. inactive) operations such as depot management.

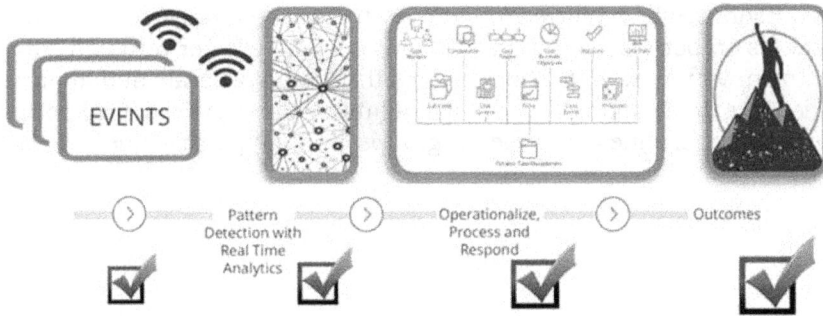

Figure 2: Events to Exception Case to Outcomes

❸ Complex event correlation in real-time for Optimized Battlefield Operations

The previous use case explained an adverse event or state (e.g. hostile advisory) that was sensed (potentially analyzed at the edge or the device) to instantiate a Battlefield case. Often it is not just an individual event but also a stream of events that indicate a potential problem that need to be addressed through maintenance cases. Sometimes you need to detect patterns involving multiple events over a time period, potentially from different sources in the Battlefield.

The correlation of these events in a temporal window is a common advisory response use case. The correlation needs to happen real-time. For example, if two temperature peaks occurred within five minutes, it could indicate a serious problem that must be addressed with an exception case for appropriate advisory response. The event correlations will be digitized through decisioning rules and the prescriptive action will be handled through instantiating the maintenance case.

❹ *Predictive and Big Data analytics for Battlefield Operations*

Battlefield assets are generating enormous amounts of information in secure mission critical networks. As more mission-critical equipment and manufactured devices come on-line through connectivity (IoT), the amount of data these devices generate will far exceed what the military has experienced thus far. Big Data will increasingly become Thing Data.

Just having this raw data is not enough. This information can be mined and analyzed to better understand the device's behavioral characteristics and potential issues to maintain it intelligently. Unlike the previous scenario of real-time correlation of events, the data is aggregated over time and subsequently visualized and analyzed using predictive analytics models.

There are many sources of data in Battlefield operations; movement of forces; aerial, land and sea reconnaissance and, increasingly, sensor data from connected and disconnected assets. To mine the insight, sometimes in real-time, and then take action, the aggregation and fusion of heterogeneously-sourced data are critical. This is discussed in the next section, Section 5.

BATTLEFIELD DATA FUSION

The turbulent seas of the North Atlantic in 1941 are a surprising place to find an explanation for the military's access to information need of the Internet of Things through intelligent Business Process Management.

"But in that pitched battle between Allied merchant ships and German U-boats, information was the key to victory. Codebreaking and aircraft from escort carriers were the sensors, feeding information into centralized command centers, where decision makers on both sides routed submarine 'wolf packs' or rerouted convoys of merchantmen. Victory went to those groups that could generate and analyze more information in a timely manner and, then, adjust not just their tactical posture but their logistical supply lines, intelligence groups, and support facilities."[5]

---

[5] The past, present and future of the IoT in the Military – Deloitte University Press

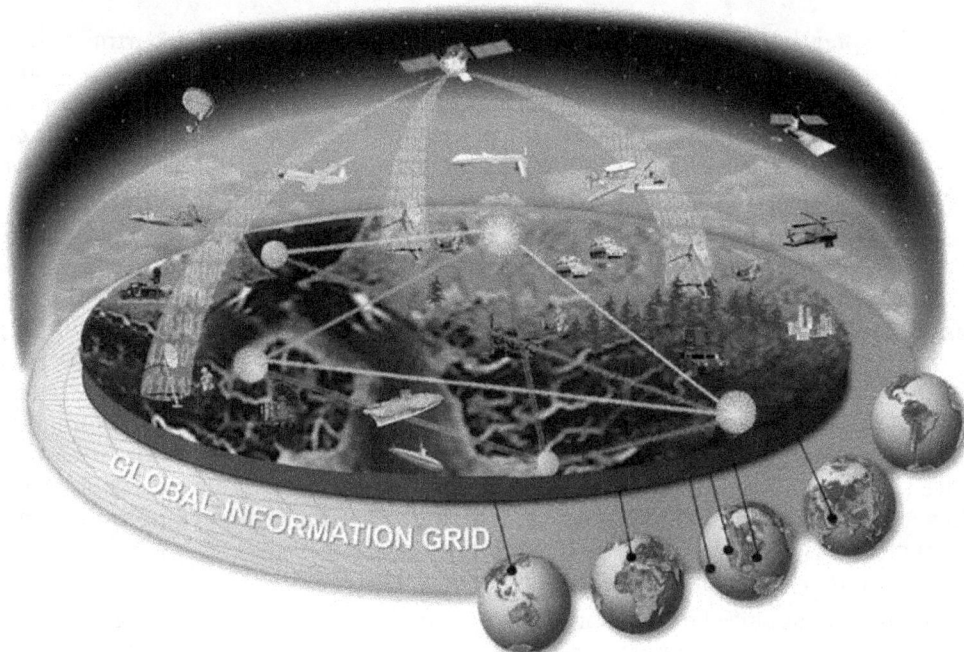

Figure 3: Global Information Grid - Operational Viewpoint - 1[6]

Today, and as during World War II, it is hard to overstate the importance of secure access to tactical battlefield information to military commanders everywhere. For many, Air Force weapon and support systems employing sensors, performance requirements can be met only when data from multiple sensors or time sequenced measurements from a single sensor are combined.[7]

This process of combining data for all military branches (not just the Air Force) has been called sensor correlation and fusion, or simply data fusion. At the core of the is the "Global Information Grid" which represents a Battlefield Data Fusion architecture for all branches of the military accessing a variety of C5ISR technologies communicating and collaboration international coalition forces shared "Information" in an allied expeditionary theater of operations. In order to support coalition forces expeditionary sharing of battlefield data, information and processes must be fused together. Battlefield Data Fusion starts with automation of common end-to-end mission workflow process as well as data integration of multiple and disparate data sources and knowledge representing the same real-world battlefield object into a consistent, accurate, and useful military operations representation.

A recent survey of DoD supply logistics managers identified ineffective data management as the primary risk to their supply chains. This lack of information directly results in equipment shortages on the one hand and waste of excess equipment on the other. The DoD recognizes these inefficiencies and has long worked to improve them. As far back as 2005, the Defense Logistics Agency argued for the military's adoption of RFID as a standard for supply-chain tracking. The potential benefits seemed obvious; better awareness of equipment location and status, faster, more accurate deliveries of needed supplies; and, of course, less manpower wasted on dreaded inventories. However, even as an early adopter, the DoD has struggled to

---

6   http://www.dmgfederal.com/implementing-configuration-management-using-enterprise-architecture/

7 New World Vistas – Air and Space Power for the 21st Century – Sensor Volume

win widespread acceptance for RFID. Largely this is because the department has had difficulty demonstrating the return on investment for the subordinate commanders who bear the time and cost burden of implementing RFID.[8] Without a clear picture of how they will benefit, DoD leaders are reluctant to invest scarce resources in these technologies; an important point why the DoD hesitates to adopt emerging technologies like IoT and IBPM.

Battlefield data fusion through a common set of automated workflow processes are often categorized as low, intermediate or high, depending on the network echelon and/or the processing stage at which fusion takes place. Low level data fusion combines several sources of raw sensor data to produce new raw data. The expectation is that fused data and the mission-intelligent knowledge at all echelons of the tactical network is more informative and synthetic than the original inputs. There are also battlefield data fusion domains and echelons of classification as command-control, geospatial, decision, position, communications, data and sensors which all have their unique attributes and challenges in the theater of battle. Understanding these unique battlefield data fusion tactical network and echelon complexities and characteristics helps to understand the lack of investment that stifles the military's ability to emerging technology adoption.

In Theater, most battlefield sensors have operated in a somewhat stove-piped manner, with information going to a single operator or otherwise being kept separate from other sensors. Any mixing of that data into an operational picture takes place at a fixed site such as a command post.

The armed forces are now looking for ways to combine data, closer to the action and regardless of the operational environment, from multiple sources through common warfighter mission process automation of data fusing from satellites, unmanned aerial vehicles, ground sensors and radar. With the military adding more sensors in battlefield scenarios, one of its next goals is to accelerate "Battlefield Data Fusion" through automating common workflow processes while combining data from multiple, sometime disparate, sensor systems and create a near-real time operational picture that can be viewed from multiple military operational viewpoints. Multi-sensor data fusion is an emerging technology applied to DoD areas such as automated target recognition, battlefield surveillance, and guidance and control of autonomous vehicles, and to non-DoD applications such as monitoring of complex machinery, medical diagnosis, and smart buildings. Techniques for multi-sensor data fusion are drawn from a wide range of areas including artificial intelligence, pattern recognition, statistical estimation, and other areas.[9]

Strategic DODAF viewpoints of key C5ISR mission capabilities help visualize a battlefield "Data Fusion" digital transformation that can be achieved through disruptive technologies like IoT and iBPM tools and platforms.

Digitizing and Optimizing Battlefield Operations

Business architecture, in general, and value-stream mapping to business capabilities have injected clarity into the complex business/IT transformation puzzle. The business capability provides the link between two complex, yet disparate, environments; business architecture and IT architecture.[10] The same can be said for DoD battlefield mission architecture (e.g. the business of the military) as well. At the

---

[8] The past, present and future of the IoT in the Military – Deloitte University Press

[9] An Introduction To Multi-sensor Data Fusion - Proceedings of the IEEE

[10] The Business Capability Map: The "Rosetta Stone" of Business/IT Alignment.

center of this business (e.g. IT) and mission (e.g. DoD) architectural strategic transformation is a shift from vertical technology, stove-piped functional process automation toward horizontal end-to-end cross-functional workflow automation. This horizontal end-to-end cross-functional workflow automation leads to the benefits and efficiencies of an iBPM platform. For a business that sells defense system sensors, weapons, radios and control systems, however, the significant features of iBPM and Value Stream modeling for horizontal integration don't apply directly to many of the company's market offerings. As such, this section will explore how iBPM and Value Stream modeling can be leveraged for horizontal integration and composability of defense battlefield products through optimizing planning and interoperability usage shown in *Figure 5. Coalition Theater Battlefield Planning - Value Stream* of these C5ISR sensors, devices, surface ships, aircrafts, weaponry, satellites, UAVs and a variety of unmanned airborne electronic warfare technology solutions.

Figure 4: Coalition Theater Battlefield Planning - Value Stream

The advent of iBPM (4th generation workflow platforms that center on value stream models) and Value Stream modeling through a strategic iBPM roadmap of some vendors in the BPM market space provides a business architecture-focused platform that is leading to a more seamless integration of existing silo stove-piped processes, applications and technology investments. Companies will outpace less agile competitors when they agree on the highest payoff Value Streams to address, build a model that includes significant automation of manual tasks and parallelization of serial queues, digitize business rules, execute vertically to new services based on a standard foundation, and change user behavior to align.

In the defense industry, these same business architecture value-stream methods can be applied to enterprise wide systems supporting the military end-to-end battle-space planning and interoperability among defense products. In fact, various academic and commercial successes around the Internet and associated Web services led to the Net-Centric Operations[11] or net-enabled workflow automation of

---

[11] http://disa.mil/news/pressreleases/2010/nces_foc_102010.html

composable operations concepts for Western defense agencies. For defense products such as planes, weapons, sensors, ships, radios, or other tactical systems that are not part of the enterprise services, the equivalent of end-to-end process integration comes from a net-ready requirement that expects an architectural definition for achieving integration with the enterprise services (core business processes following a framework standard), and then addressing certain technical standards on how to expose services and data from those net-centric devices.

To further draw the distinction from internal mission operations or the enterprise service layer, military products are generally deployed into challenging environments with interrupted communications. In this stressful environment, security must be at the level associated with the need to reduce the risk of fratricide. This leads to a unique need for policy-based management (e.g. business rules engine), in which the integration of battle-space processes from the enterprise level out to the device level can still leverage agile services but with very well–understood, predefined policy enforcement and clear ownership at every point in the process (although that ownership can change dynamically within policy limits). Finally, the flexibility and loosely-coupled architecture that are driven by net-centric services that can react to business rules (e.g. echelon security rules), complex events (e.g. radio silence) and iBPM value streams will enable next generation DoD acquisition strategies for refresh and upgrade over replacement.

The fictional coalition operations use case shown in *Figure 4: Coalition Theater Battlefield Planning - Value Stream* depicts the common end-to-end mission (e.g. the business of the military) process flow for "how coalition forces plan battlefield operations" which orchestrates and composes a number of tactical theater planning net-centric services, focusing on both the internal process and the external process triggers and subsequent messaging. With agreement, the multiple coalition force stakeholders can apply one iBPM Value Stream model on common mission processes, then iBPM tools or experienced developers can compose a set of value stages, workflow services and data system accesses that execute the same for all users. The iBPM Value Stream focuses on seamless integration of several planning applications (e.g. satellite planning, tactical-network-planning, sensor planning) built by multiple global defense companies into a single automated workflow for operations.

The current process might consist of multiple silos with some point-to-point integrations among planning systems with different methods for sharing information and no combined linkage out to the desired end effect of an integrated process, such as better allocation of the available assets across a coalition operation. Using outdated data integration methods is primarily driven by development as silo systems that don't allow the quick addition of new interoperable services and an end-to-end model of the whole mission cross battlefield process.

Notice the critical "Value Stages" and "Mission Capabilities" called out in the *Figure 4: Coalition Theater Battlefield Planning - Value Stream* supporting C5ISR high level mission capabilities defined through key scenarios (e.g. "create, simulate, re-plan and execute battlefield planning") supporting an end-to-end value stream. For the full end-to-end workflow process automation in a realistic scenario like battlefield planning, each value stage would be decomposed into vertical process models which detail a variety of task levels and activities.

To incorporate the advancements in computers and communications with the Army operational concepts, the Army has instituted what it calls "Battlefield Digitization." Battlefield Digitization is an Army modernization effort taking advantage of revolutions in electronics and information technologies to make dramatic gains in all battlefield operating systems and at every level, from crews and squads up to the National Command Authority.[12]

The common Value Stream representation shown in *Figure 4: Coalition Theater Battlefield Planning - Value Stream* provides all military forces (including the Army) with a strategic DoD viewpoint of an end-to-end battlefield planning digitization workflow shared among the coalition stakeholders and across multiple legacy military systems. The associated Value Stages can react to detailed complex events, automated workflow, mission (e.g. the business of the military) rules, service-based publish and subscribe tasks and attributes that flow down the key performance parameters to execution. An iBPM suite and a skilled business process developer can then leverage Net-Centric micro-service standards and the mission enterprise services to integrate a very cost-effective and powerful integrated solution for the DoD. With loose coupling and common end-to-end business automated workflow processes from the partnership of micro-service and iBPM, there is enhanced support for new services and technology refresh across multiple military forces domains.

DIGITAL TRANSFORMATION MATURITY AND COMPETENCY

An organization's Digital Transformation (DX) maturity and competency is not going to happen by accident. Organizations need to understand that identification and accountability for key areas must be developed. Often these are the areas that organizations simply assume are being accounted for as part of their DX programs and projects, however, most of the time they are not. This realization further strengthens the business case for creating a dedicated DX Competency Center (DX CC).

A DX CC is not free. It costs time and money in its creation and operations. It is not going to simultaneously do everything the organization requires. Organizations will need to take an iterative approach to DX CC creation and operations. Providing this type of DX CC will require changes within the DoD acquisition processes as well as the DoD contractors' adoption of iBPM and IoT transformational governance, maturity and competency processes.

Digital Transformation is a journey. The digital technologies including Social, Mobile, Analytics, Cloud, and, most importantly, the Internet of Things as powerful enablers. Digitization is also about "Workflow Automation" especially in the context of increasingly robust and intelligent dynamic cases, while leveraging these digital technologies. Automation will span software robotics by automating repeatable tasks; physical robots taking over routine work; intelligent guided and knowledge-assisted work and knowledge work itself.

In this digital era, there is a healthy tension between the fast development of applications or solutions with digital technology vs. the consistency and discipline of the Competency Center. The enablement, continuous improvement, governance, and best practices for reuse for digitization assets is within the scope of the Digital Transformation Competency Center.

The following *Figure 5 - DX Maturity Model Levels* highlights some of the dimensions of maturity[13] for IoT with iBPM and DCM.

---

[12] www.dtic.mil/cgi-bin/GetTRDoc?AD=ada377740

[13] http://cmmiinstitute.com/

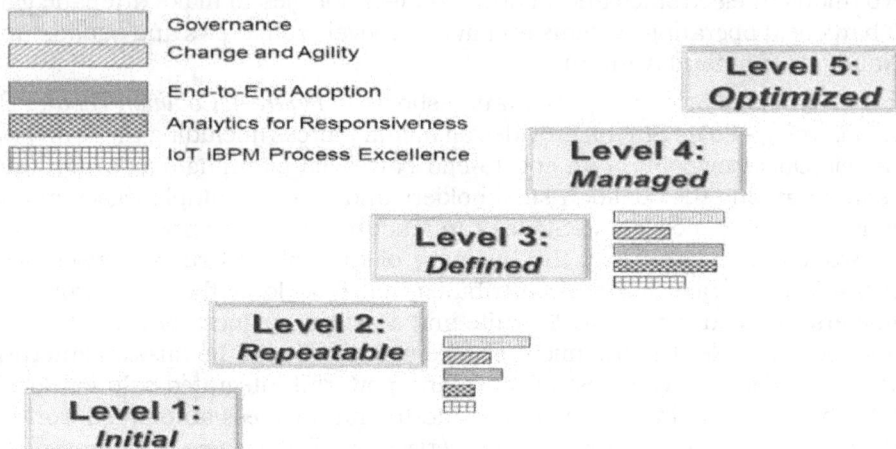

Figure 5 - DX Maturity Model Levels

At the initial levels of maturity, you typically have siloed implementations that illustrate the potential value of automation through IoT-enabled iBPM and DCM. Here, specific Battlefield units or operations demonstrate a quick win and deployment with tangible results.

- *Governance:* The operational solutions leveraging a DX Platform that was discussed earlier need to make sure implementation and automation solutions are within best practices guardrails and guidelines. A DX Platform is a powerful enabler for end-to-end automation and thus it is critical to have governance for best practices.
- *Change and Agility:* Often organizations are ossified through bureaucracy and siloed departments. In the military, this could have dire consequences. Enablement and empowerment through agile methodologies and discovering a rhythm of change are essential for Digital Transformation. Agile and iterative methodologies for the DX Platform are key.
- *End-to-End Adaption:* Digital Transformation is about digitizing value chains. These chains are as strong as the weakest link. Directly mapping the end-to-end value chain onto milestones within dynamic cases is critical for success. Each of the chains or milestones could potentially be assigned to sub-cases realized or automated through different units. The high command will thus have visibility of the performance of the overall chain and hence the ability to address and optimize the weakest links.
- *Analytics and Responsiveness:* IoT connectivity provides many opportunities for Battlefield operations to observe the behavior of assets. Big Data is becoming Thing Data. Manufacturers can also perceive the consumer or customer of the connected device; how they are used, where they are used or maintained; how often; and by whom. In other words, the dynamic interaction of the connected devices and their users is also captured through sensor data, Maturity here is climbing up the value hierarchy from data to insight shown in *Figure 6 - Raw Data, to Insight, to Action* and then action.

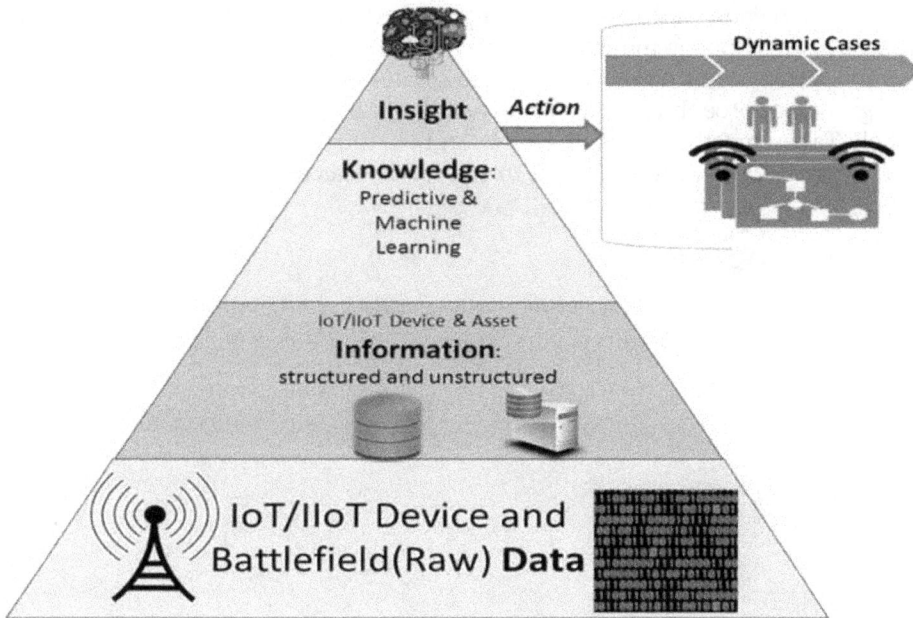

Figure 6 - Raw Data, to Insight, to Action

- *IoT iBPM Process Excellence:* Last, but not least, it is all about process optimization and process excellence practices: avoiding waste, providing end-to-end process visibility and optimization critical to time, cost, and quality measures. In other words, leading toward a maturity of *Real-Time Lean Six Sigma*[14] as applied to Battlefield operations.

To make DX CC a reality for the Battlefield, there must be DX CC adoption in the Aerospace and Defense industry contractors together with the DoD to build digital transforming solutions that leverage IoT and iBPM.

CONCLUSION

Finally, the relationship between the tiers of human-to-service and service-to-service, service architecture, and iBPM can now be drawn. If the DOD defines a mission architecture that drives common methods and standards across C5ISR domains and A&D contractor product domains, then the power of iBPM and integrated services can be threaded throughout. Horizontal integration promotes development of loosely-coupled and integrated end-to-end processes across domains using the same language for the common process itself, while maintaining the distinct practices and product focus within each domain.

On the other hand, vertical integration takes the highest priority functional processes and applies legacy methods and technologies that focuses on silo execution. A mature DOD enterprise architecture program provides the standard methods and independent review to ensure the tiers are addressed through end-to-end value streams beyond the scope of an individual projects silo process to achieve the greatest benefits.

---

14   https://www.linkedin.com/pulse/digital-transformation-iot-real-time-lean-six-sigma-setrag-khoshafian

Aspects of the defense sector, such as a greater demand for tactical communications, security and policy management than the commercial sector, along with an acquisition strategy not driven by free market efficiency, lead to a shift in vertical silo integration approach towards a horizontal end-to-end value stream integration approach. Taken together, these aspects can help the DOD achieve significant benefits in the battlefield from iBPM and micro-services as a key aspect of IoT.

BPM Farming:
Reap Benefits by Nurturing Your Existing Platforms

Kay Winkler, NSI Soluciones, Panama

BPM *everywhere* indeed! The third wave of business process management has come and receded, having left an irreversible imprint on today's technological landscape and business practices. The Internet of Things (IoT) enables business processes to extend services closer to our customers than ever before, while even more business applications sport BPM capabilities of some sort or another. Chances are that you have multiple workflow tools and BPMS set up in your organization. Thus, likely having an immense arsenal of technologies at your disposal to automate business processes, your stakes are high to harness the power of existing technologies, while avoiding the pitfalls of redundancies, information silos and misuse of applications whose main purpose is different to BPM.

The key questions a company needs to address when desiring to keep using its existing BPM while improving current and creating new process solutions, are:

- Do my current BPM and workflow tools actually support a digital transformation?
- What is the principal emphasis of my existing technology? Is it truly focused on BPM or rather something else (such as document management)?
- Is there more than a single process technology in my operation that would need combining or substituting?
- How to determine the possible delta of the costs and benefits of implementing business solutions with an existing but older BPM as opposed to acquiring a more modern technology?
- How to future proof solutions built with an existing BPM?

To achieve business transformation, all pieces of a larger and holistic strategy must fit perfectly. While such strategies allow digital transformations to take place and to be sustained long enough to allow for a digitally-mature enterprise, supporting technologies represent the propellant force for an organization to achieve that goal. Lainey Garcia, manager of brand public relations and engagement at McDonald's (interviewed regarding her insights resulting the company's digital revamping initiative in 2015) pointed out, "The biggest takeaway was the power of integration." This *power of integration* connects strategies as well as technologies.

The BPM that a company has in place may very well be the single most pivotal technology to reach disruptive organizational change and digital transformation. By its very nature, BPM eliminates communication, application and operational silos provided such a platform is truly up to the job. Important features and capabilities such as APIs, intuitive design tools and a common annotation standard must be present.

This chapter will outline some of the principal checkmarks to look out for in your current BPM in order to evaluate its future readiness. Another important aspect that we will develop is the assessment of the actual business apps that have been created on top of the BPM and how these influence your companies' current level of digital maturity.

Shortfalls within a custom-made business application that is running on a perfectly adequate BPM may be the real culprit in preventing the digital adaptation process; not the BPM itself, as often assumed. An unintended C-level decision can prove to be very costly. In that sense, we will point out suitable aspects that can be handled as part of a continued process improvement project without having to buy a new BPM technology—known as BPM Farming—thereby progressively enhancing your existing repertoire.

TAKING STOCK

Regardless of what specific digital transformation goals your company ultimately pursues, periodically updating the corporation's inventory of applications, platforms and tailor made solutions is always one of most important steps before engaging in new endeavors. You may be surprised how much ammunition you already have at your disposal, capable of furthering the organization's transformational aspirations.

The advantages of doing so are clear. Existing software and solutions often represent a company's investment in licenses, time and labor. The reason that a certain application is part of your current repertoire could be an indication that certain software and its vendor are a success story within your organization. There is also the effect of technology adaption curves, where, with time and increased maturity, the usefulness and adaptability of a given technology grows. Associated publicities and implementation the Levels of Effort (LoEs) tend to decrease in tandem with the out-phasing of given hype cycles (Fosdick, 2006).

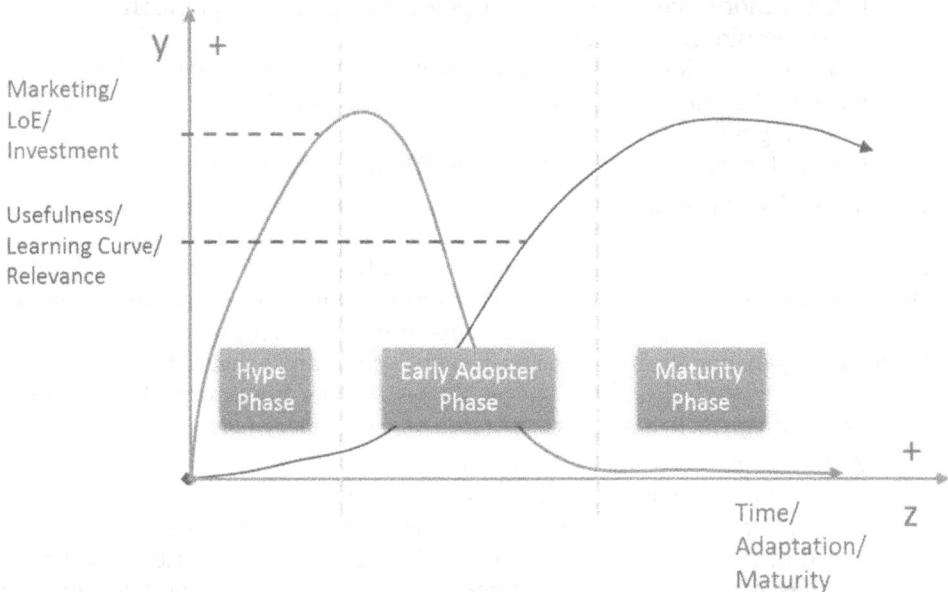

Figure 1 - Technology adaptation curves, applicable for BPM.
Based on and adapted from Fosdick et al, 2003

Industry experts, process owners and end-users generally agree that BPM has entered its maturity phase. Newer concepts and technologies such as Intelligent Business Process Management Suites (iBPMS), business rules engines (BRE)s and adaptive case management (ACM) are also on their way towards maturity. In that sense, the time is ripe for reaping the fruits of developments and lessons learned during the past couple of years in the realm of BPM.

Where to look for when it comes to existent BPM artifacts in your organization?

A good rule of thumb we have found at NSI (www.nsisoluciones.com) over the years is first to identify assets that are related to iBPMS platforms. These elements include some sort of BPM engine and simple process reporting modules to complex data cubes, process-driven ESBs, embedded content management, business rules engines, dynamic event handlers with case management capabilities and many other components. The following graphic gives a very general overview of BPM components that usually can be found around iBPMS platforms and which are worthy candidates to become part of the "application mix" that ultimately will support your transformation strategy:

Principal iBPMS features

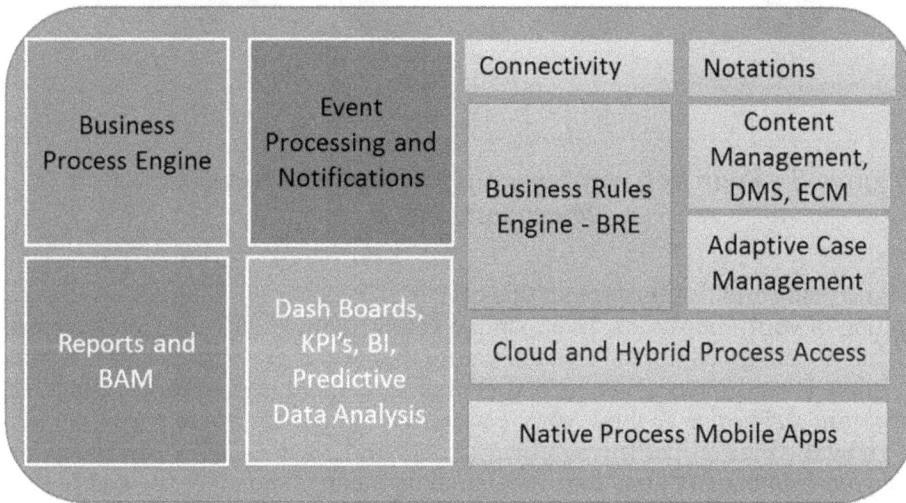

Business Process Engine	Event Processing and Notifications	Connectivity	Notations
		Business Rules Engine - BRE	Content Management, DMS, ECM
			Adaptive Case Management
Reports and BAM	Dash Boards, KPI's, BI, Predictive Data Analysis	Cloud and Hybrid Process Access	
		Native Process Mobile Apps	

Macro Architecture Components

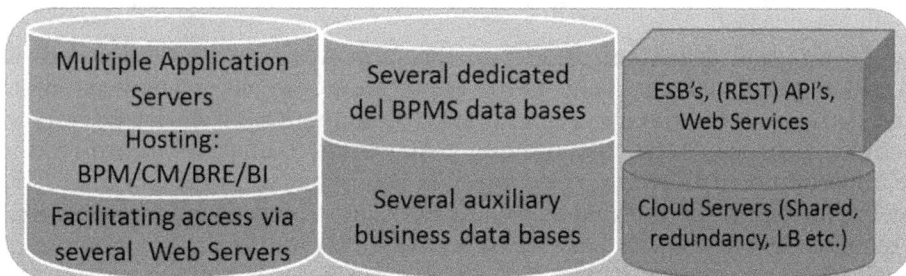

Multiple Application Servers	Several dedicated del BPMS data bases	ESB's, (REST) API's, Web Services
Hosting: BPM/CM/BRE/BI		
Facilitating access via several Web Servers	Several auxiliary business data bases	Cloud Servers (Shared, redundancy, LB etc.)

Figure 2 - Principal iBPMS components; Winkler, Kay; 2015

A Business Process Engine, at its core, will always be a crucial ingredient for any company that embarks on a journey for a digital evolution. That way, existing business processes can be enhanced to support the new strategic direction of the enterprise. New disruptive processes can be created, driving the transformation forward. Subject-matter experts such as Pedro Robledo point out that BPM is actually at the heart of the transformation lifecycle, specifically during the phases of BPA (Business Process Analysis), Process Modelling and, of course, Process Implementation. (Pedro Robledo, 2016) Counting on a robust, proven and scalable BPM engine in your IT inventory will definitively be a "big plus" on your balance sheet.

Microsoft, describing digital transformation from an end-user point of view, summarizes the points of customer engagement, employee empowerment, operational optimizations and resulting product transformations as the four key factors for success. (Chris Capossela, 2016) It is interesting to note how these components are linked by "systems of intelligence" hinting at the growing relevance of (big) data analysis, predictive and dynamic pattern recognition.

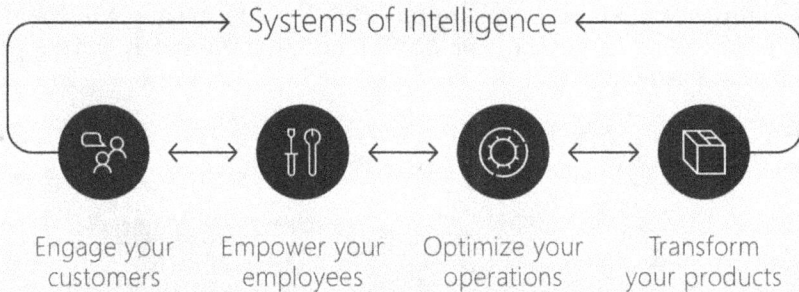

Systems of Intelligence

Engage your customers   Empower your employees   Optimize your operations   Transform your products

Figure 3 - Four key components for Digital Transformation; Microsoft; 2016

Event Processing and Notification, in this context, are naturally allies for a technical reinvention of your operations. Even simple email notifications and database registries that are triggered during specific events that occur in a process (for example after a quote for a prospect has been successfully created and sent out) will make an important difference in how your company engages its customers and ultimately, how the market perceives your products and services. More advanced features of your existing BPM environment, such as business-intelligence and predictive pattern recognition on a process level will provide your workforce with the tools to proactively engage prospects and customers alike, way ahead of your competition.

The latest evolution of modern BPMS, in the form Adaptive Case Management (ACM), places particular emphasis on the importance of intelligent data examination and dynamic event management. Additional elements such as process reporting modules, Business Activity Monitoring (BAM) and dynamic dashboards round up the important contribution an existing BPM potentially can make for improving the understanding of the internal as well as external influences on your organizations' results. BPM also continues to play a pivotal rule in the familiar continuous and cyclical improvements within disruptive strategies. Results-driven product transformations are iterative steps that can be either entirely fueled by your current process technologies or these, at the very least, can feed into extending, complementary applications in case you are missing some of the previously mentioned components in your IT inventory.

Regardless of the technological markup that your company is ultimately going to employ to accomplish its vision of enhancements and transformations, bringing your products, services and brand closer to the end customer is of absolute importance. Customer engagement through BPM has been a conceptual cornerstone for several years and can be achieved to a large degree by the design of optimized end-to-end processes with the most of the tried-and-tested technologies that are already out there. Raju Saxena from Ernst and Young goes as far as to encapsulate that process design approach into the very definition of BPM; "Business Process Management is a management discipline that integrates the strategy and goals of an organization with the expectations and needs of customers by focusing on end□ to-end processes." (Saxena, 2013)

For processes that are more complex and for "BPM-mature" companies that follow an EPM (Enterprise Process Management) approach in their organizations, it can get increasingly more difficult to identify and to keep track of the end customer as the crucial point of validation for success. Here, it is useful to establish and to embed a sound set of variables that can be measured throughout, starting from customer engagement processes (for example, sales-supporting process applications) up to supporting administrative processes (like invoicing). Such metrics typically breach departmental but also technological barriers.

Establishing and tracking these "customer-facing variables" can help you to follow a transformational strategy, even with older, existing applications. A viable alternative to establishing process metrics from scratch can be the use of existing metric frameworks and benchmarks as provided through the APQC (American Productivity and Quality Center) with its comprehensible and up-to-date PCF (Process Classification Framework) as well as benchmarking portal.

Takeaways:
- Using existing BPM technology for digital renovation and transformation initiatives can shorten the time to go-live, making use of the existing learning curve and end user adaptation.
- There can be also important additional economic benefits of extending the usage of an "already-paid-for" BPM as opposed to acquiring something new.
- Features to look for in your current BPM that can help drive a transformation strategy are around of what would be defined as an iBPMS, such as a BPM engine, a BRE, SOA capabilities, strong data management and BI elements etc.
- Any vision for technological renovation or even transformation, very much like BPM as a concept, translates into an iterative and progressive undertaking that relies on continued process improvements that are backed by "systems of intelligence".
- Establish and continuously measure viable metrics throughout existing applications and processes alike, prioritizing customer facing variables.

SORTING THE WHEAT FROM THE CHAFF

While your existing BPM applications and workflow tools are likely capable of supporting your company´s goals, there certainly is a particular risk, which not only has the potential to delay your progress, but may entirely boycott your efforts.

It certainly is not necessary to own the newest technologies with all the latest trimmings, bells and whistles. However, some very fundamental features are indispensable, without which you would be unable to sufficiently extend your processes and make a perceptual difference from the perspective of your end customer:

- A **scalable BPM engine**, able to take on mission-critical processes (high volumes at low response times).

  Only few things are as frustrating in the world of BPM, for your staff and even worse—for your customer—as slow and unstable processes that they are forced to use. Sales and customer retention may consequently suffer. An early indicator of this happening in your organization usually are end users that switch back to executing tasks manually, despite having access to a BPM. This can be typically observed during recurrent peak moments of your ongoing business cycles.

  Effective ways of determining acceptable process response times can be measuring customer facing form load times under "stress" in conjunction with gauging the customer's feedback at the same time. If your particular industry vertical is represented, taking into account existing benchmarks from organizations such as the APQC may be useful, too.

- Almost all technical shortcomings of an existing platform can be overcome by complementing current applications with other products and custom made developments provided your core engine and its extensions allow for "solid" integrations.

  You want to avoid a straitjacket approach here at all costs. If you currently find yourself with a workflow application or a BPM platform that doesn't allow integration easily through a standardized WSDL (web service definition language) 2.0 or by newer approaches (Rest API or others) to internal or external third party applications and custom developments, then it is time for you to migrate to a newer technology. Having to deal with black boxes that only allow you to interact with other technologies through very specific and usually very limited pre-made connectors, text files, database entries or not at all, will put an end to your transformation strategies and any aspirations for future-proofing your processes.

With a solid engine and robust service-oriented architecture (SOA) capabilities, you have two main pillars from which to elevate your current workflows, document processing tools and business applications to the next level. From this point on you can choose to integrate virtually to any components that may be missing for your transformation efforts such as applications that support ACM with CMMN or decision engines (that in turn may even support new notation standards such as the DMN 1.1).

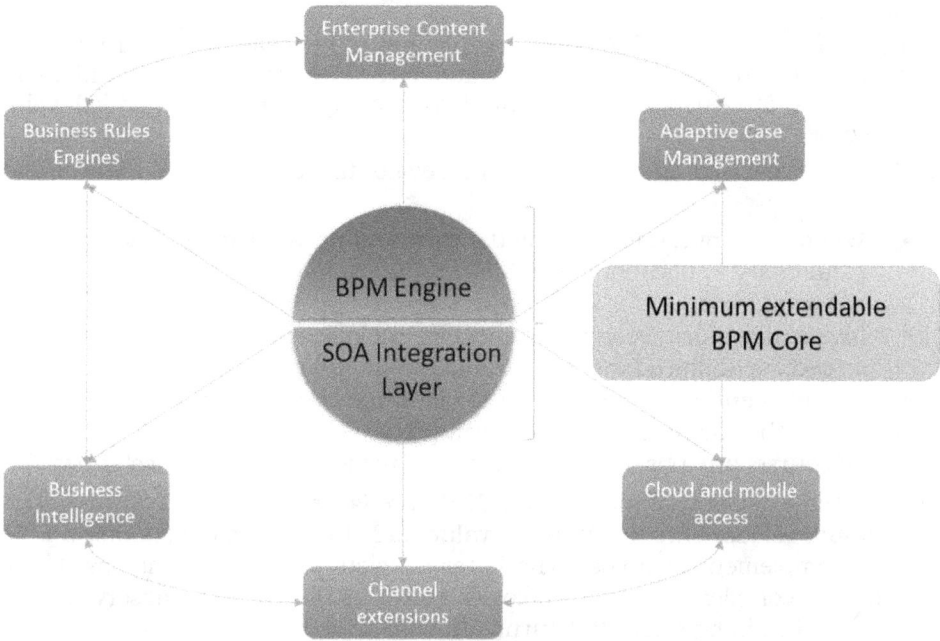

Figure 4 – Example of extending a minimal BPM Core;
Winkler, Kay; 2016

It's important to prioritize features in applications that actually make a difference to your final customer in terms of their perception concerning the quality of your services and products.

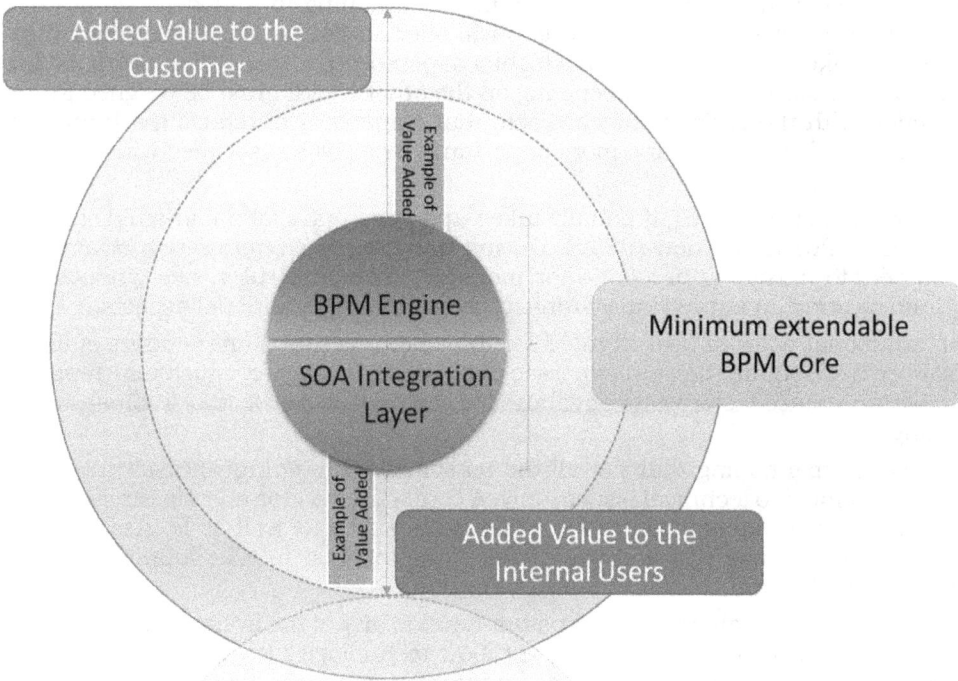

Figure 5 – Example of benefits by extending from a BPM Core;
Winkler, Kay; 2016

Extending outward from a BPM core not only has to be measured in terms of what exact added features provide the most value to the customer of your company but also in terms of cost-benefit, compared to accomplishing these added values through other means.

The decisions that management faces when evaluating existing BPM and workflow assets:

- Whether to invest, integrating the tried and proven technologies to complementary applications to achieve digital transformations as shown above (**a**),
- Invest in acquiring completely new technologies that contain all the required capabilities for such a transformation out of the box (**b**) vs.
- Complementing the existing BPM platforms by custom developments within the confines of that platform (**c**).
- Of course, any possible combination of these three points also apply.

Pursuing the extension of the existing BPM core (**a**) requires the determination of the optimum relationship between the value-added to the final customer and the associated implementation cost. The latter consists primarily of the cost for onboarding new complementary technologies as well as the professional services costs for the technical integration. If it turns out that your corporation must acquire a whole bundle of new software products which then must be implemented and integrated to achieve your goals, then, probably, one of the two other alternatives we will become more viable to you in the end.

A strict scope limitation, always with emphasis on what is most important to your client's needs, is key for success with this approach.

Alternatively, you could opt for upgrading or switching to a modern iBPMS platform, altogether (**b**). Leading providers will offer all the previously-mentioned features and likely even more. From a technical perspective, this option bears the lowest level of risk. The obtained benefits, on the other hand, must be weighed in conjunction with the typically higher costs that come with purchasing a brand-new technology of this caliber and more importantly, the costs associated with a "brand-new learning curve."

In our experience, at NSI, it usually takes up to two years for a mid-sized company to become fluent in a new iBPMS. During this time, the organization attains new skill sets to master applications for managing business rules, new annotations, administrating an entirely new architecture and many additional aspects.

An additional point to bear in mind for this choice is that some vendors of iBPMS platforms do require their customers to use specific hardware, which may represent an extra expense factor that contributes to the overall overhead of such an undertaking.

It is worth mentioning that not all the reasons for hindering your advancements must be limited to technical issues, only. A conflictive vendor-customer relationship or even unreasonable increases in maintenance fees as well as license costs, for example, can cause you and your team to be inclined to take "option b" as the choice to go forward.

Lastly, there is the alternative to custom-develop any of the eventually missing features to complement your existing workflow technologies (**c**). Of course, it applies here too that your engine as well as its integration capabilities must be up to the job. Developing specific additional features and capabilities on top of your existing BPM is often a very interesting option for many companies as it usually represents the lowest "startup costs" compared to the other choices.

The correlation that must be observed for this option is that the associated development costs have the potential to grow exponentially with increasing solution complexities, which have been developed by coding. This relationship also carries over to the related costs of maintenance for such an in-house development. There are additional complexities deriving from that approach, such as the creation of highly specialized and expensive-to-retain technical subject-matter experts, and the dependency these represent for the companies on the long run. In that sense, it is more recommendable to make only cautious use of this option for very specific features that you deemed necessary adding to your current technologies.

For all options, special significance must be given to the BPM engine itself with emphasis on its original purpose. These days, many applications come out of the box with their very own process and workflow solutions. A common combination you can find in that context are platforms such as Enterprise Content Management Suites (ECMS) that offer workflow tools to automate different document life cycles (for example contract management). While simple process automation features do go a long way for intuitively enhancing the document management experience within an ECM, those workflow tools by no means rival a BPMS and would represent too weak a BPM engine to support an operation's business transformation. Besides many technical weaknesses, the most impacting fact would be that conceptually almost all ECM-workflows are completely wrapped around the lifecycle of a document, whereas a BPMS puts the case and the individual in its center (e.g. human-centric BPM). It becomes progressively more difficult to leverage an ECM-workflow, the more complex and the more customer-focused the business process becomes. This context also applies for other combinations such as a CRM with workflow tools or CMS portals with some sort of process capabilities.

What may be enough to satisfy "in-application" short-term task automations, normally does not suffice to fulfill the requirements of a strategic transformation.

Consequently, decision-makers have to make sure that whatever technology the company plans to extend from, is in fact a BPM engine at heart and not some other tool with a few workflow features embedded, more as an afterthought than as a main purpose.

Summary for basic alternatives:

Alternative	Main opposing variables that must be balanced		Observations
a) **Extend current technologies by integrations**	Cost: • Services for integrations. • Buying new complementary applications • New learning curve for integrated apps.	Benefits: • Scaled economies for existing technologies. • Shorter time-to-go-live. • Allows leveraging existing expertise.	• Make sure the BPM engines allows for scalable integrations. • Limit complementary applications to what is important for your customer.
b) **Replace current technologies with newer ones (like iBPMS).**	Cost: • Acquisition of a completely new platform. • Development from scratch of new processes on top of new platform.	Benefits: • All required features for digital transformation. from the get-go. • Latest product features may allow for more product innovation.	• Take into account all direct and indirect costs, such as hardware (if required). • Consider strategies to confront a several years-long adaptation and

	• Complete new learning curve. • Considerable time-to-go-live (opportunity costs).		implementation phase.
c) Custom-develop on top of existing technologies.	Cost: • Low start-up costs. • High maintenance and development costs with increasing complexity.	Benefits: • Low LoE for small adaptation. • No new learning curve. • Highest level of scaled economies.	• Limit custom developments to specific needs only. • Limit developments to what is important for your customer.
d.) A combination of the options above.			

Table 1 – Basic BPM usage options for continued improvements and digital transformation; Winkler, Kay; 2016

Takeaways:
- It is essential for BPM farming that your current technologies, at their very core, are scalable and allow for standardized integration technologies.
- For building and improving upon your current BPM main emphasis must be put on the requirements and preferences of your final customers, as part of an end-to-end process framework.
- Going forward from present technologies and implementations, your company faces four basic choices:
  - Add and integrate complementary technologies.
  - Substitute your current platform completely, buying a new iBPMS.
  - Complement your current BPM with custom developments.
  - Possible combinations of above.
- For any of these choices, management must determine which option provides the best value for your company and final customers. Typical costs to be weighed against the expected benefits are:
  - Time to go-live and subsequent opportunity costs.
  - Cost of acquisition for new technologies.
  - Costs for engaging into new learning curves.
  - Development costs for new implementations, solutions and integrations.

Future-proofing your Processes

Budgets and implementation times for continued improvements and for transformation initiatives or even for simple enhancement projects can be optimized a great deal by reutilizing viable, existing components or entire technologies. Therefore, the better your current process assets are already prepared, the better the chances to "recycle" them multiple times for future projects. Having covered in the previous section the technological elements—the BPM baseline in other words—we are at this point summarizing the process elements of business applications and their role in your company's future readiness.

The ever-evolving field of business process management can sometimes seem to be excessively inflated with acronyms like iBPMS, S-BPM (Subject-oriented BPM) (Albert Fleischmann, 2013) and RW-BPMS (Real-World Objects in Business Process Management Systems). Often this causes more confusion than direction to the subject matter at hand. To filter out the relevant process components that will facilitate the preparation of your business processes for coming enhancements, it can be helpful to introduce an increased level of abstraction and simplification. The resulting overview will then ultimately help the team to identify the process components that ought to be preserved, adapted or be discarded.

Dedicated platforms enable the end users to visualize, optimize, automate, implement and to improve business processes, which thankfully causes certain core elements to recur constantly when it comes to BPM. Regardless of which technology is being used and the specific methodology that is being applied— at the very heart of things—at all times you will find flow charts, end-user forms, variables, system integrations and some sort of reports.

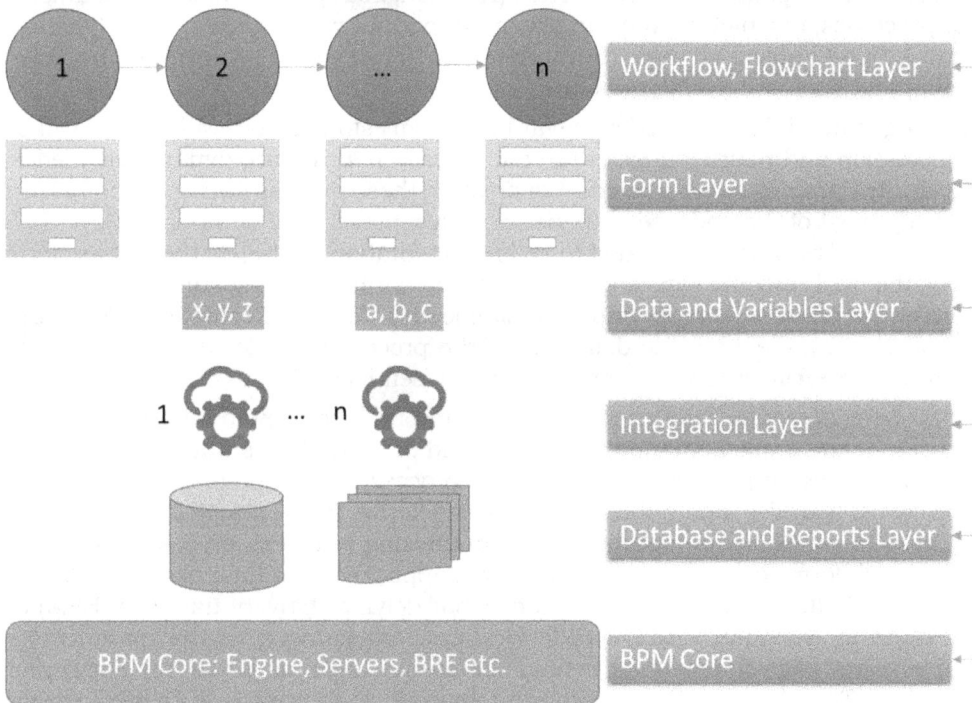

Figure 5 –Core Process Elements; Winkler, Kay; 2016

The possibility of visualizing the conditional process flow and case sequences is the most basic requirement and the very first stepping-stone into the world of business process management. Luckily, it is also one of the best-covered features in almost all respective technologies for BPM and typically requires the lowest level of effort (LoE) to accomplish. From open-source solutions to enterprise suites, all feature some sort of graphical engine that allows for a quick and non-technical visual representation of process flows. Many platforms align to various industry standards such as BPMN, BPEL, WF and others.

To ensure reusability and continuous improvements on the level of process flow diagrams, selecting a widely-used as well as well-understood nomenclature is essential. Currently, the most common annotation is the Object Management Group's BPMN 2.0. By designing all your processes in BPMN increases the likelihood that different players within and outside of your company will understand them. It is also helpful for future platform changes, upgrades and improvements. There is no guarantee however, that your diagrams will be cross-platform compatible. Despite industry agreement on what icon sets to use, vendors still do not make it easy to migrate your BPMN designs from one technology to another.

As far as current process annotations go, only a degree of the entire process workings and logics is represented in forms of diagrams. Large portions of the information are still embedded in design documents and other accompanying videos or images. These artifacts must be tailored into your future-proofing activities for any process solution. The series "The State of Business Process Management" from BPTrends pointed out that most companies still only occasionally document their processes and update such documents. (Harmon, 2016) The practice of documenting processes, in which flowcharts play an important role, and keeping artifacts in sync with all applied changes, is fundamental for successful continued improvements and business transformations.

Keeping in mind the very basics, by far biggest milestone of a BPM initiative will be the creation and maintenance of the end-user forms that are dynamically tied to the drafted process steps. The effort of creating these process forms, which in turn embody most of the end-user experience, can represent consumption of up to 80 percent of all resources dedicated to an implementation. There, on the process form level, the "real" process logic takes shape, where form fields and sub-forms react to data entry, policy validation, and both simple and complex calculations. As a sub-set of the form creation, the definition of the process variables and the resulting data universe will always be encountered in a (semi) parallel manner.

If one were to reduce BPM as a technology and methodology to a bare minimum, the design and implementation of complex and powerful forms would clearly stand out as the most important aspect of future process adaptation and success. Fast, intelligent, adaptive and robust forms are decisive for accomplishing the BPM premise of continuously improving and optimizing business processes. In some cases such forms can appear to be complete applications in their own right. These are created either entirely by code (somewhat defying the very nature of BPM) or leveraged by wizard-driven, low-code form creation frameworks that produce the active server page source code behind the scenes (such as K2 Smart Forms, for instance). This decision of creating forms by code or through a WYSIWYG wizard within the platform does also have an impact on reusability (think platform change or technology migrations) in correlation with the cost of their creation as well as maintenance.

In analyzing the role that forms play for business transformations, the importance of future-proofed process solutions in context of the IoT also becomes clear. Aspects like adaptive, zero footprint and mobile (app driven) user experiences will be furthered or hindered by the way process forms have been designed and implemented.

Taking a workflow implementation to a true end-to-end level, a third component must be present – process system integrations. No human-centric process (Khan, 2006) reaches its full potential in efficiency and effectiveness without said integrations. When considering change and innovation cycles of business software and technologies, one could argue that BPM and ERP are facing each other at the opposite ends of two extremes. While processes are meant to be adjusted periodically, within short periods, adapting to volatile market realities, ERP solutions will likely have a much slower frequency of change. From that perspective, system integrations within business processes are key tools in enhancing the end users' experiences.

There are, of course, countless system interactions that can enhance the impact of an optimized business process, such as cross-process integrations or typical interactions with systems like CRMs, BIs, ECM's, BREs and more. Some vendors have even embarked on a system consolidation effort, as seen in the previous section and what Gartner describes as iBPMS (Gartner Research, 2012), making available several of these business applications within a single framework (usually bundling together a process platform with ECM, BRE, BI and ESB), hence reducing the need for interaction with external systems.

Documenting all integrations from, to, and in-between your process solutions, as well as basing those on industry standards such as WSDL 2.0, increases the viability of their reutilization during improvement projects and especially for undertakings of digital transformations.

Reports, or rudimentary stored raw process data, could be described as the last piece of the "basic" elements of your process solutions. Now, while advanced reporting, BAM, pattern recognition and predictive analytics are certainly powerful features in process automation, they cover only the first elementary step. Far more crucial (frequently something entirely overlooked) is the next step of making sure that the whole process, as well as the business (form) data, is stored in an automated, uniform, accumulative and (most importantly) scalable fashion. When this is accomplished throughout all implemented business processes, your implementations will render real process insights and enable continued improvements. The key ingredients for viable business reports are, in some part, derivatives of the process and form-variable design efforts and, in another part, the understanding of well-defined process metrics.

There are numerous other aspects worth considering when looking at the "art of optimizing, automating and constantly improving business processes," such as identifying a fitting ontology framework. However, from our experience at NSI, it is unlikely that any of those will have as much of an influential effect on the successful re-utilization of your current technologies as it will have in readying the basic elements of your BPM for perpetual enhancements to come.

Takeaways:
- BPM Farming depends a great deal on future-proofing the most crucial process elements:
  - Workflow/Flow Chart
  - Process Forms
  - Integrations
  - Databases and Reports
- For flowcharting, select a commonly-used annotation. Keep in mind that process diagrams are only part of a holistic process documentation.
- Process forms represent the most complex and labor-intensive component for business processes. Deciding to use out-of-the-box form builders vs. the custom development of forms will not only affect your

implementation and maintenance efforts, but also your chances of re-using and improving them in the future.

- o For preparing your process form strategy, take into account the associated form and process variables.
- To future-proof your integrations, make sure they adhere to industry standards and that they can used both freely within and outside your current technologies (in case you want to migrate to something else in the future).
  - o Ensure proper documentation for all your integrations.
- For reports and business-intelligence, confirm that all the relevant processes, but more importantly, business data are being capturing in an accumulative, tabular and accessible manner.

References

Albert Fleischmann, S. R. (2013). *S-BPM Illustrated*. Springer International Publishing AG.

Chris Capossela. (2016, April 5). *Microsoft Blog*. Retrieved from Microsoft Envision: A conversation on digital transformation: http://blogs.microsoft.com/blog/2016/04/05/microsoft-envision-a-conversation-on-digital-transformation/#sm.001vkz9jg15fkej2qs72hpzkklm9q

FORBES. (2014, June 26). *Forbes/Tech*. Retrieved from Adaptive Case Management: http://www.forbes.com/sites/larryhawes/2014/06/26/adaptive-case-management-could-be-the-foundation-for-networked-business/#6fff372a5d12

Fosdick, H. (2006). The Sociology of Technology Adaptation. *Enterprise Systems Journal*.

Gartner Research. (2012). *Gartner Says Intelligent Business Operations Is the Next Step for BPM Progams*. Retrieved from Gartner: http://www.gartner.com/newsroom/id/1943514

Harmon, P. (2016). *The State of Business Process Management 2016*. BPTrends.

Khan, R. (2006). *BPM-A Global View: What makes BPM Human Centric*. Retrieved from BPTrends: http://www.bptrends.com/bpm-a-global-view-what-makes-bpm-human-centric/

Pedro Robledo. (2016, November 14). *albaTIAN*. Retrieved from Digital Transformation Life Cycle: http://www.albatian.com/en/blog-ingles/digital-transformation-life-cycle/

Saxena, R. (2013). Guide to the CBOK. In *BPM CBOK version 3.0* (p. 27). CreateSpace Independent Publishing Platform.

Figures and Tables

Creating Digital Threads, Driving Lean Startup Models

Neil Ward-Dutton, MWD Advisors, UK

INTRODUCTION

Digital transformation is a subject on every executive's lips; no matter what industry they're in. Organizations from sectors as diverse as financial services, retail, utilities and logistics see the threats posed by both new digital natives entering their marketplaces, by more traditional competitors stealing a march on them with new digitally-powered services and experiences, and even by out-of-sector players using digital channels to launch competitive products and services.

However, digital technologies also hold the promise of giving you ways to protect your company against these threats, at the same time as improving the experiences that your organization can deliver to customers; improving your operational efficiency and agility and driving more innovation into your products and services.

In this paper, we dig into several aspects of the concept of digital transformation and show the strategic role that IT has to play in delivering those aspects.

We then go on to show the extent to which modern business process application platforms fit the technology platform requirements that spring from serious digital transformation efforts.

FOUR PERSPECTIVES ON DIGITAL TRANSFORMATION

Despite widespread, cross-industry interest among senior executives in digital technology and transformation, in our own research work with leaders we've found very little real agreement within this group, even among executives in the same organization, about what 'Digital Transformation' actually means.

Understanding the core value of digital technologies

In understanding the ways in which perspectives on digital technologies differ, the first thing to understand is that despite the lack of clarity that still exists in industry, digital technologies all share one common kind of business value:

Digital technologies are important because, in combination, they can be used to co-ordinate resources (people, plant, machinery, infrastructure, market information, goods, materials, knowledge) more efficiently.

Different perspectives spring from different resource interests

We find that the common perspectives on the role and value of digital technology differ because they start from considerations of how digital technology improves the co-ordination of differing kinds of resources.

Figure 1 below lays this out: the horizontal axis segments the universe of 'business resources' into internal and external resources, while the vertical axis contrasts the resources that revolve principally around people and their knowledge with others that revolve principally around processes and 'things' (plant, machinery, infrastructure, materials, assets etc.).

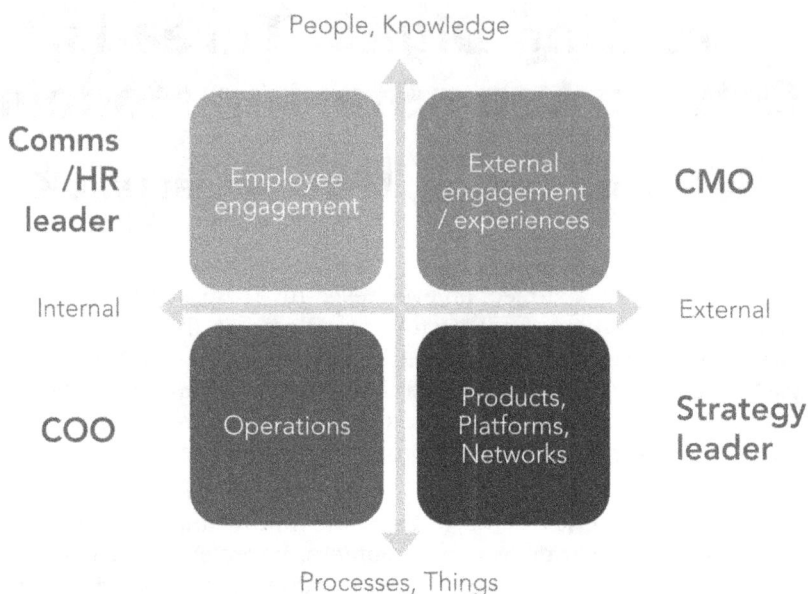

Figure 1: Four perspectives on digital technology

In our research with large organizations' CXOs over the past 18 months, we've found that leaders with particular kinds of roles tend to focus principally on the value of digital technologies in one of the four quadrants of figure 1:

- When *HR and Communications* leaders talk about 'doing digital', they're starting their exploration from the **top-left** quadrant of figure 1. They're talking about how social, mobile and cloud technologies in particular affect the workplace and the ways that employees engage with each other and with the broader organization/corporation.
- When *Marketing* leaders talk about 'doing digital', they're starting their exploration from the **top-right** quadrant of figure 1. They're talking about how social, mobile, cloud, and analytics technologies are changing how the organization needs to create experiences and engage differently with customers (other leaders may also be thinking about implications for partner and supplier engagement, too).
- When *Operational* leaders talk about 'doing digital', they're starting their exploration from the **bottom-left** quadrant of figure 1. They're thinking about how digital technologies can help the organization co-ordinate internal processes and 'things' to create 'digital operations' capabilities.
- *Strategists* tend to start their work in the **bottom-right** quadrant. They explore the realm of Uber, Airbnb, Upwork, Zopa, open innovation networks, and so on. These people are tasked with looking at digitally-powered strategies for new products and changes to business models.

THE STRATEGIC ROLE FOR IT IS TO LINK THESE PERSPECTIVES TOGETHER

Executives and others having one of these perspectives at the top of their minds are not wrong; all of these four perspectives are perfectly natural and sensible. They are all correct.

However, true digital transformation can't spring from concentration on only one of these perspectives.

Let's look at three very brief examples to illustrate why this is so:

- Imagine that a bank's marketing teams have used new digital technologies to create a leading-edge digital engagement system that delivers personalized offers to prospects across multiple channels and third-party media properties. However, no consideration has been given to how the current customer on-boarding process can be modernized, and the result is that new customers, enticed by cutting-edge marketing campaigns, immediately become frustrated and disillusioned as they encounter delays, a lack of transparency and poor service.

- Imagine that a retailer's HR department has worked with your internal communications team to create a great mobile-friendly, social intranet. However, the core applications that employees depend on to do their jobs day-to-day aren't set up to enable them to take action or make decisions on the move, or to work collaboratively with colleagues when the situation demands it.

- Imagine that a logistics company's operations teams have used digital technologies to increase its ability to respond to adverse events and fix problems – perhaps even anticipate problems before they occur – so the proactive fixes can be made. However, nobody has thought about how to provide greater transparency and insight to customers about the operations that matter to them, and how this can positively impact customer engagement and retention.

As you'll hopefully see from these examples, unless an organization is seriously exploring how to create links between the four different perspectives on digital technology outlined in figure 1 – external experiences, employee engagement, operations and products and platforms – it will fail to reap the most valuable benefits the digital transformation can bring.

In practice, an impartial and independent program to create and maintain these links can only be carried out by the part of the organization that sits separate and independent of those driving these particular perspectives. For most organizations, IT is the most obvious place for this to happen.

CREATING DIGITAL THREADS

Thus having established that a way for IT to add strategic value to today's digital transformation efforts is to have it responsible for creating and maintaining links between domains of investment – what do those links need to deliver?

A useful way to think about the kinds of links that need to be created is to think of 'digital threads' with two properties:

- They enable organizations to digitally share knowledge, co-ordinate work and make decisions effectively – linking together islands of investment and that also are focused on silos of resources, processes and systems.
- They act to facilitate sharing and co-ordination across different teams, systems, channels, media platforms and business locations, consistently, and at scale.

Digital threads: spanning complicated challenging environments with many moving parts

Creating these digital threads to weave together islands of investment in anything but the smallest and open of organizations is going to be a big challenge. For large or long-established organizations in particular, the challenge further complicated by the historical strategies that they have executed over the past 10 to 15 years.

As figure 2 illustrates, large organizations in particular have spent the last 10 to 15 years going in a direction that is in complete opposition to what we need now. They've pursued strategies to disperse their operations – creating partnerships with offshore service providers and business process outsourcing companies; creating complex supply networks; creating captive shared services centres. These things are done for ostensibly sensible reasons (principally, cost, efficiency and scalability) but they also create a challenging backdrop for any organization looking to create 'digital threads'.

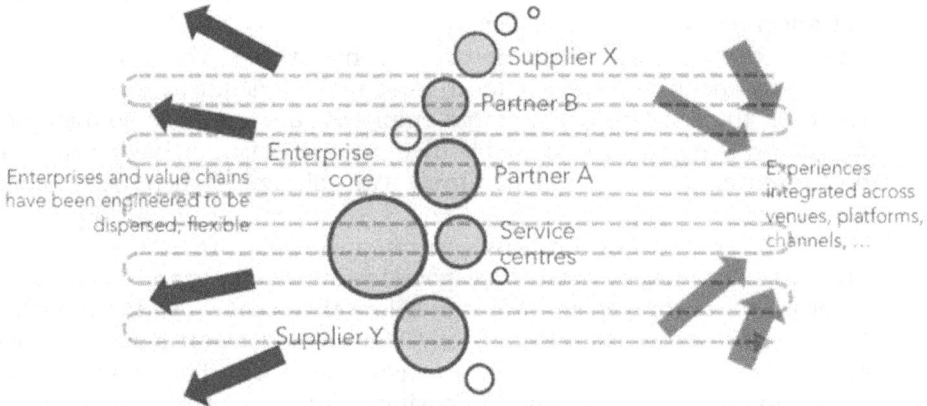

Figure 2: Digital threads enable business integration across complicated operating models

In figure 2, the dotted line snaking back and forth from right to left and back again signifies how customers' journeys play out as they find out about an organization's offers, buy, use products and services and get assistance.

For these customers' journeys to be effectively supported in line with modern expectations of immediacy and transparency, information and work has to weave in and out of operations that are controlled by multiple parties. In a distributed business operating environment spanning multiple partners, service centers and suppliers, trying to create 'digital threads' without some kind of open, consistent technology foundation will be extraordinarily difficult.

Digital threads: dealing with work fluidity in a digitally-enabled environment

Quite apart from the work co-ordination and knowledge-sharing challenges that spring from complicated business operating models, anyone considering the importance of 'digital threads' is further challenged by the ongoing digitisation of individuals' work environments.

When organizations design or evolve their business practices, they may not know it – but they're doing so based on a set of constraints and assumptions about the ways that work can be done. Specifically, organizations commonly make very particular assumptions about:

- Who needs to do the work (in terms of roles and responsibilities).
- When that work needs to be done, and in what order individual tasks need to be done.
- Where people need to be when they're doing the work.
- How tasks need to be carried out (in terms of resources, tools and so on).

Today, most established organizations' work practices, business processes and supporting information systems continue to rest on workplace assumptions that were valid in the 1980s and 1990s – but which are no longer valid.

For example: the colossal growth in mobile data network availability and device usage means data, insights and systems can be at fieldworkers' fingertips, making "admin at the local office" an anachronism. What's more, the capabilities of popular smartphones and tablets mean customers can directly participate in business processes in new ways.

In banking, it's now increasingly common for retail banks to provide mobile apps that enable customers to deposit checks by taking pictures of them with their phones; in local government settings, citizens can engage directly in reporting service issues or environmental concerns by taking geo-encoded pictures on their phones and uploading them to a local government portal.

In both these scenarios the 'who', 'when' and 'where' of work is fundamentally recast. Figure 3 highlights how these questions are ripe for revisiting not only because of mobile technology advances; but also because of the potential impacts of other digital technologies – like social platforms, cloud platforms, big data and analytics technologies, machine learning and bots.

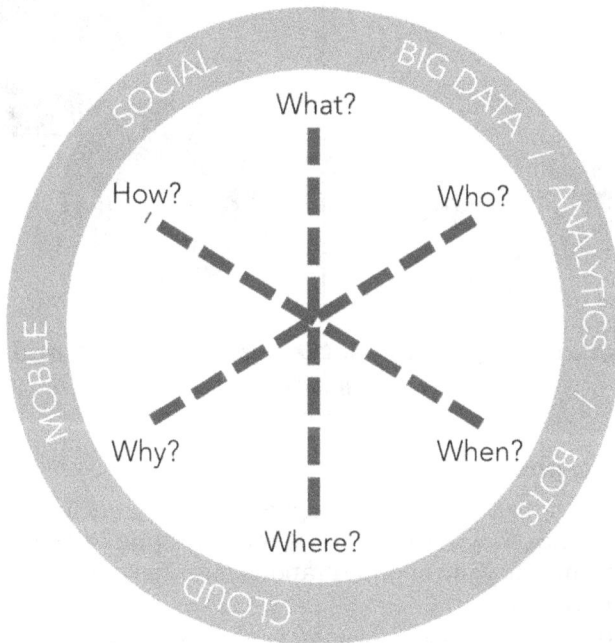

Figure 3: New answers to questions about the shape of work

Of course, not all organizations are actively investing in all these digital technologies. For some, enabling better employee connectivity and mobility may be the highest priority; for others, it'll be the scalability and flexibility that comes from leveraging cloud platforms. However all these technologies are on the table, and the digital threads we create have to be flexible in the face of technology environment changes.

Wrapping all this up: the concept of creating digital threads as a way to share knowledge and co-ordinate work across domains of digital investment has much to commend it. However, any serious effort has to build on a technology platform that enables collaboration across multiple organizational entities; and that also enables a great deal of agility in how digitally-enabled work is designed, distributed, and executed.

DIGITAL TRANSFORMATION IS NOT A DESTINATION, BUT A CONTINUOUS JOURNEY

So far in this paper we've looked at how digital transformation relies on the ability to create digital threads, and that those threads need to be created using an open technology platform.

However there's another side to the story of digital transformation, which creates more requirements for the kind of enabling technology platform that organisations need.

In summary: this other aspect of digital transformation is that digital technologies, used intelligently, actually change the nature of business and technology change itself. In other words: digital transformation is not (only) about transformation to a state where digital technologies are widely exploited; but about 'transforming digitally'. Figure 4 shows these two aspects of digital transformation.

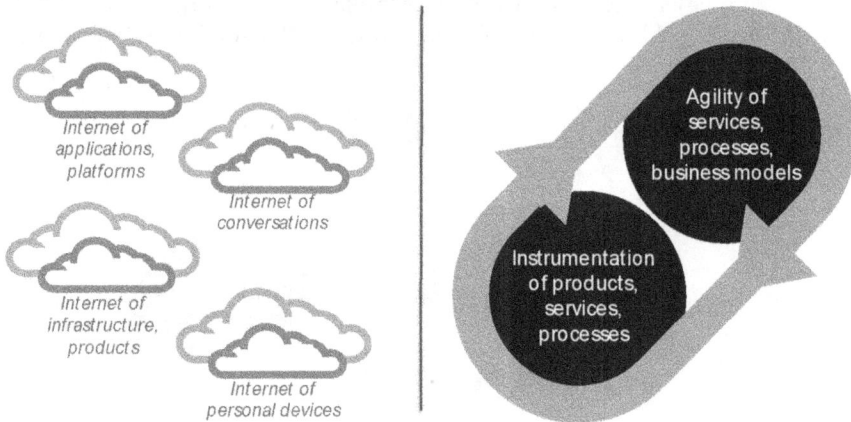

Figure 4: Digital transformation: the destination (left) and the journey (right)

Supporting a new attitude to change

When we look at organizations that are aggressively embracing digital technology platforms, we find that they have a very specific attitude to change that's fundamentally different from how most organizations have historically approached business and technology change.

This is because they understand how digital platforms enable new kinds of change techniques. Digital leaders view change as needing to be continuous, rather than episodic; and as a part of 'business as usual', rather than as being something managed separately. Change is not seen as something that's conducted by specialized teams; these organizations see change as part of everyone's responsibility. And change is not seen as something to be conducted in isolation from operations; change is driven by experimentation in real-world situations.

New platforms need to intertwine instrumentation, optimisation

Early embracers of digital technology platforms use them to do three core things in parallel, in an integrated way:
- Build new business and technology capabilities quickly.
- Measure what works and doesn't work.
- Make changes quickly, based on measurement and feedback.

In other words: digital technology platforms enable organisations to evolve their businesses quickly, based on a virtuous cycle of instrumentation and optimisation.

New platforms need to enable broad collaborative contributions

If organizations are to seriously pursue the kind of 'lean startup'[1] philosophy that promotes data-driven feature experimentation and refinement, they would be foolish to consider data gathering, measurement and analysis as activities to be carried out in organizational silos that are separate from the teams who build those features.

Effective platforms for building and maintaining digital threads therefore need to deliver feature construction, measurement and change capabilities all as part of one integrated whole. However, although these skills and capabilities need to be integrated in feature delivery, it's extraordinarily unlikely that one homogeneous group of multi-skilled individuals will be responsible for doing all the work. The platforms we need have to enable different people with different specializations to work together.

Any organization that's serious about embracing digital technologies and shifting to the new model of change that goes along with that, needs tools that enable them to manage capability delivery in an open, collaborative way – enabling change to be made at scale, with confidence.

How Process Application Platforms Fit In

To recap: we've determined that digital transformation requires platforms that enable organizations two share knowledge and coordinate work across distributed teams, departments and business entities. These platforms also need to make it easy for disparate groups of stakeholders to collaborate in order to change behavior, implement new policy and so on easily and quickly. And lastly, these platforms also need to have business instrumentation built-in – making it easy to track and manage business performance over time.

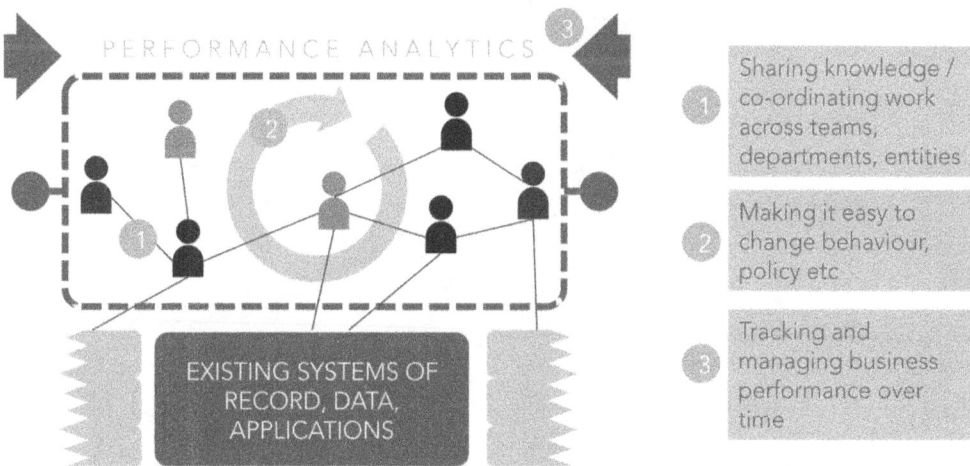

Figure 5: Modern Process Application Platforms are a perfect fit for building and maintaining digital threads

Figure 5 illustrates just how closely modern process application platforms fit this profile.

---

[1] Wikipedia / Lean Startup article, retrieved Jan 13, 2017: https://en.wikipedia.org/wiki/Lean_startup

CONCLUSIONS

If we look afresh at the underlying capabilities of business process application platforms, we see that they fit the needs of today's organizations looking to drive digital transformation very well indeed. The ability to share knowledge and co-ordinate work digitally at scale; the ability to get instrumented insights into performance and behavior; and the ability to change with confidence - these core capabilities of good process application platforms are at the very heart of what today's organizations need as they embark on digital transformation journeys.

Modern business process application platforms and approaches are no longer interesting purely because of how they can improve business efficiency; they're valuable because of how they can support the creation of digital threads, and how they can deliver digital platforms that enable a lean startup model to be operationalized.

Improve, Automate, Digitize

Frank Kowalkowski,
Knowledge Consultants, Inc., USA

A SENSIBLE METHOD OF CHANGE

Have you ever wondered why organizations spend a lot of money, get involved with large projects for improvement or transformation, get outside help, and yet, *still* don't realize the value they expected? Then, several years later, things seem to get on track or they get worse. Did the management learn anything? Every time a new technology, method or other 'hot thing' comes out, organizations try to take advantage of it before the competition. Think knowledge management in the 1990s, AI in the 1980s, Y2K, ERP packages and so on. Now we have digitization, process automation and myriad other technologies pushing their way into the business space.

Bear in mind, there are organizations that already have a staff of 1000 or more analysts doing analytics on data. Often this is not automatically captured data but is data that supports decision-making by humans. This is true especially in health care and government. The digital parts are usually not operationally integrated into processes but are linked to business needs that require support by human operators of the processes.

There are always orderly ways to proceed with integrating these new things into the organization. Such is the current case with digitization, transformation and BPM efforts. The basic idea is to start with accurate processes at the *beginning* of a transformation rather than jumping into the new technology immediately. At the same time management needs to know if the value proposition they read about is realistic for their organizations.

There are some well-known approaches to reduce risk when getting into new technologies.

Here are some typical approaches:
- Do a pilot project in a small part of the organization to minimize risk and learn about what is new. This is a good approach but may delay getting value for the new technology or methods.
- Get outside expertise to implement the technology but again start small. This trains the consultants but does not leave behind the knowledge for the organization to move forward on its own.
- Adopt a sequence of implementation that gradually transforms the organization to what you need; the incremental approach. The pace will depend on the level of experience and expertise you develop along the way. This can also limit the amount of expertise required if an internal team does the work with outside training and support.

The best approach:
- Start by focusing on a segment that needs process improvement. Apply any number of techniques, many described later in this section, that bring the process up to the functional and efficient level originally designed in the process. Add the improvements needed to make the process the most current and flexible possible.

- Apply process automation and intelligent processes to prepare for integrating not just data but the decisions the data may support. In the interim, digitization needs and data availability can be supported by existing data warehousing, data management, data governance, BI and performance management tools until ready to integrate into processes. This gives you time to learn what is involved with a large amount of data before you burden processes with that task.
- Integrate with a large amount of the digital ecosystem for better functionality. Key connection points and value will be linking into processes that have AI decision-making capabilities. Understanding what streams of digital environment are most useful to your organization will be key factors in this stage.

Following this basic approach gives you time to position the skills, software tools and other assets that lead to success in digitization. The key is to remember that the intent is to *operationalize* automation and digitization.

THE CONFUSION ABOUT IMPROVEMENT

Why do so many process projects fail? Why is process improvement sometimes very difficult and other times simple? Some studies indicate the failure rates of process projects can be as high as 75%. There are various definitions of failure such as out of budget, overdue or beyond the schedule time, incomplete functionality and others. The source of the issue may be in how organizations go about applying emerging technologies and methods. For example, identifying improvement opportunities is not always simple. In fact, identification is an interesting problem, it is a 'problem of solving problems,' in this case process improvement and business performance enhancement opportunities.

A key issue is that all of the problem may not be visible. Management may see only part of the problem and think it is the whole problem. Management then only understands what causes the portion of the problem that is visible. There are 4 reasons for this well known in problem solving:

1. A single source of a problem can manifest itself in multiple places
2. Multiple sources of a problem can combine into a single problem
3. Many sources can cause many problems
4. An external trigger can cause a problem.

Applying new technologies such as process automation, AI for intelligent processes or digitizing the relationship of processes to data can hide the real problem in the operation of a business. Simply focusing on improvement can provide enough value that management is hesitant to go the next step and therefore put the business at risk of falling behind competitors.

Resolve confusion about improvement and emerging technology. The rush to automate and digitize or digitize and automate is full of traps. There is a sequence and reasons for the sequence that improves the probability of success. History abounds with examples of what happens when you automate the wrong things.

START WITH IMPROVEMENT

The point of process improvement is to apply analytics, identify focal points for improvement and then apply various means of fixing the problem. We use the 4-point situation as a starting point for analyzing many business problems both relating to processes and those not of a process nature. *The resolution of these situations requires a set of discovery and diagnostic analytics to pinpoint the source(s) of the problem(s) and then applying one or more fixes.* Note the use of the plural option here.

These four situations are:

1. A single source of the problem causing a variety of detection points. Analytics should point back to the single source making sorting through the symptoms difficult but having a good yield because one fix takes away many symptoms.
2. A single detection (symptom for example) can be generated from multiple sources of problems making pinpointing and fixing the problem difficult. In this case a variety of analytics and solutions may be needed.
3. Many sources of problems can show up as multiple symptoms making discrimination for a fix even more difficult. In this case, multiple analytics and fixes are needed.
4. External or internal landscape/ecosystem changes can trigger symptoms such that the process is not the issue but the *trigger* is the issue. Here we need analytics that verify and make sure we can link external and internal impacts to the detection point to identify a fix.

DOCUMENT THE PROCESSES FIRST...

Current improvement approaches focus on documenting processes and then applying some degree of improvement techniques to get more from the process or at least what was expected for the process in terms of value returned to the organization. This is intrinsically valuable as a core return on investment.

The most common techniques include the following core steps:

- Using a standard and correct method of documenting a process,
- Apply observation to spot improvements or problems with the process,
- Use an additional technique such as simulation to find choke points or bottlenecks that inhibit efficient flow
- Use some basic quantitative analytics that have been around for many years to measure performance. These are still needed to maintain a level of performance from the process structure.

This approach has been around for many years and works reasonably well when done with a good cross-functional team. However, problems often return with a set of symptoms that differ from before. The best you can do is clean up a process and get it to function as originally intended. If the need is to really improve a process, then added analytics and improvement techniques are needed.

Improvement is initiated by business and environmental changes. The order in which improvement and transformation are applied depends on the purpose of the process improvement or transformation effort plus the interest of management in the change or transformation.

Typical purposes include:

- Product changes
- Business Transformation initiatives
- Mergers
- Acquisitions
- Divestitures
- Consolidations (operating units and processes)
- Federation, decentralization, centralization
- Optimize processes and other flows (to some specific goal, e.g. supply chain optimization)

- Efficiency/Effectiveness of capabilities and processes
- Lower cost/increase revenue/increase profits
- New technology in operations

APPLY A CONSISTENT CYCLE OF ANALYSIS AND IMPROVEMENT

Like other disciplines such as the TQM (Plan, Do, Check, Act), process improvement follows a successful cycle. That cycle is broken down into five basic steps:

1. Discovery – Identifying the symptoms and focusing on the improvement purpose
2. Diagnostics – Sorting through the symptoms to find the causes of the symptoms
3. Prediction – Drawing conclusions and suggesting some options for improvement
4. Prescription – Applying and deploying the fix with measures
5. Monitoring – Making sure the fix works and is returning value

A combination of analytic and improvement techniques is briefly described below that blends the four points of process problems with the five steps of improvement. Improvement includes changing the existing process suite and, at most, eliminating processes or adding new processes. The process improvement toolbox also includes things not covered here such as process strategies that encompass process automation, process execution suites, intelligent processes and some other change agents that are beyond basic *improvement.*

10 CORE TECHNIQUES OF PROCESS IMPROVEMENT

Ten techniques are identified and summarized here. In most cases analytics and related techniques are also suggested that do the discovery, diagnostics and sometimes predictive parts of the process improvement cycle. Start with the 10 most common techniques.

- *Observation:* Observation is exactly what the word implies and is the most commonly-used technique of improvement. A group, usually a cross-functional team, reviews the operation of a process and identifies any flaws or issues with the process. The key here is the identification of the process in the beginning. This is usually done by a process review team, a consulting firm, management edict due to some performance issue or a systematic performance review of the business either internally or externally performed.
- *Process Restructuring:* Often a process becomes out of date due to a number of internal organizational changes such as adding a new technology, changes in policies and procedures, adding application packages to the IT suite of software etc. These always require some process restructuring to remove some steps or whole processes, modify or add steps.
- *Quantitative performance:* Processes have quantitative attributes associated with them such as cycle time, transport time, queue time, cost, efficiency, quality and throughput. These attributes provide a measure of the performance of the process. Tracking these measures before and after a process improvement effort is critical to quantifying the benefit received from the effort. You cannot determine the degree of improvement without a before and after measurement.
- *Touch-point Analysis:* One of the more common issues today focuses on the task of deployment. Project managers report that a number of unanticipated linkages existed causing everything from a small delay in the

process deployment to a complete rethink of the deployment. A solution to this issue is to use process context to help identify all the touchpoints of the processes of concern.

- *Process Mining:* Process mining is one of the newer improvement methods gaining favor. It is used when little is known about the process, there is no documentation or the process is of the case management type with many paths. Process mining uses data logs generated by application systems and DBMSs that support the applications.
- *Enablers of the process:* Enablers are the things needed to make the process work well such as skills, technology, application systems, policies and procedures, connectivity, rule sets and even funding. Enablers are analyzed and assessed for improving process capability by using touchpoint matrices to represent the relationship between the process and the enabler.
- *Phrase Analytics:* Phrase analytics are a supporting technique used with other improvement methods especially when doing consolidation, impact analysis or rankings based on the semantic content of the process and touchpoint models. Phrase analytics work with the text instances of a model, the name of a step, a system, a technology and so on.
- *Business change assessment:* The point of business change assessment is to link the process improvement effort to the strategic and operational changes that management is directing for the next period of time usually a year or more. This is usually part of the business strategic plan and possibly by operating and staff unit tactical and operational plans. This means that the process improvement is subject to the management choices of enterprise structure, how all the components of the organization fit together.
- *Simulation:* Simulation is a supporting technique used to provide quantitative estates o process performance. The point of a simulation is to test a potential process structure for loading, bottlenecks, typical traffic flows, resources needed to handle volume and impacts of any labor or other regulations the affect the resources available.
- *Process Consolidation:* This is consolidating processes to achieve a common process. Usually this means an organization has similar processes with the same function, such as employee hire processes, invoicing, ordering etc. Usually back office processes, they may support multiple operating units. If the consolidation is more global such as consolidating operating units and their processes, then the effort involves consolidating more than processes. It may require analysis to consolidate locations, organizations technology and so on. Usually this is a major effort using professional consultants.

AT THE END OF THE DAY WHAT MATTERS WITH IMPROVEMENT?

There are a few key points to remember about improvement especially if it is to lead into automation and then digitization. Here is a summary of the points:
- A focused strategy for process improvement linked to business need
- A successful process improvement strategy that defines there results expected and the resources available to do the work

- Ranking process improvement efforts to get the most value in the shortest time. Value also includes effectiveness, service to the customer, not just efficiency and the process cost.
- Developing a trained and capable staff that understands the organization and process issues involved. Using external expertise to support the staff when needed.

AUTOMATION - ANTICIPATING THE NEXT STAGE IN PROCESS EVOLUTION

Currently one of the largest contributors to the digital enterprise is the Internet of Things (IoT). Businesses are talking about the 'digital enterprise.' Assuming that an organization has reviewed and improved the processes so the 'correct' things are being done as efficiently as possible with the current suite of processes, it is good to look at automation of the processes. It is risky to just jump to digitizing the processes. Digitizing the enterprise is not just adding new software and technology, it is about enabling processes to increase the positive impact on the organization results. That makes digitization eventually key to process automation leverage. There is considerable value currently latent in many processes. Smart processes release that value. The number one issue is when and where to apply automation through digitization to free up that value. By understanding the options and tools available to help the automation effort, an organization gains an edge in the competitive marketplace.

Existing traditional BPM approaches focus on documenting processes and then applying some degree of improvement techniques to get more from the process or at least what was expected for the process in terms of value returned to the organization. This is intrinsically valuable as it has a core return on investment. These traditional improvement techniques include correct methods of documenting a process, using observation to spot improvements or problems with the process, sometimes using simulation to find choke points or bottlenecks that inhibit efficient flow and finally the use of basic quantitative analytics that have been around for many years to measure performance. These are still needed to maintain a level of performance from the process structure.

However, truly innovative process change involves more than what we do now. For example, adding robotics to process automation in manufacturing produces large gains in productivity and reliability. In the service industries, the equivalent is to add intelligence to the process to make repeatable decisions where the alternatives are well known. Going one step further you can add artificial intelligence capability to analyze trends in decision inputs and adjust the decision-making to accommodate changes that impact the process. Finally, processes need integration among the types of automation already in the organization.

WHY IS THIS OF INTEREST NOW?

Some key questions surface when considering the BPM space today:
- How does the role of BPM change from simply documenting and improving processes to one of process innovation?
- Does available technology meet the needs of the organization with respect to process performance? Does the cost exceed the benefit?
- How do these changes impact the process risk equation? Will it be easier to remediate any risk and if so which risks, fraud, natural disasters, sabotage, process failure etc.?
- Can all this improve key areas like marketing and sales yield?

- What new skills are required especially in the user area and middle management that provide for the value yield from process automation?
- How do you adapt processes to making more decisions on their own?

Much of what we see today in process management is the result of rapid changes in technology. Such changes have been going on since the start of the industrial revolution. Changes in technology follow a pattern of entry into the business world. Technology adoption varies according to the ability of the organization to recognize the value, make changes and realize that value in terms of outcomes. Eventually change is forced upon many organizations by changes in the world around them.

At that point, organizations become interested in what can be done to deal with the change. There are three forces that impact processes:

1. *Environmental* – Either internal environment such as the context of the process or external environment working with customers or suppliers. Any of these change is an impact on the process related to that environmental connection. These changes cause triggers that impact the organization.
2. *Triggers* – These are events caused by changes in the environment that may change the nature of the processing such as the timing of input arrivals from daytime to evening. As triggers change the process must adapt. Intelligent processes can observe triggers and adapt the process to changes.
3. *Chance* – perhaps the least understood, is the one that can cause the most problems. Things which happen randomly or totally out of control and not anticipated such as a tsunami impacting the business process from a supplier or taking out communications for a bank or a sudden shift in customer preferences. Health care is very familiar with customer preferences (choosing where to go for care) and situation (emergency or elective) as it impacts staff loading and how and even which processes are executed especially in the emergency room. Intelligent processes can adapt the process to the situation and return it to a previous state when the condition goes away.

WHAT ARE THE CORE APPROACHES TO AUTOMATED AND SMART PROCESS?

What are some of the things we need to know before we innovate processes using automation?

- *Process Automation* – Removing as many manual steps as possible from a full process flow such that requests for information are automatically generated, emails are automatically sent, and responses are tallied and analyzed all without any human interaction even in many cases for exceptions.
- *Artificial Intelligence (AI)* – AI impacts the way we approach making decisions related to process execution. The decisions are documented using the Decision Modelling Notation (DMN) and fed into an intelligent BPMS that integrates the decision into the process.
- *Case Management* – Often we know the inputs to a process and the output expected such as in criminal investigation, legal proceedings, health care, hospitality and other situations, but there are many paths to get to the destination end-point. Case management and the related standard (CMMN, Case Management Modeling Notation) provides a means of organizing and taking advantage of automated capabilities to work through the various paths.

- *Robotic Automation* – This is not limited to what we see as physical robots used in manufacture. It also includes features today such as Cortana in Windows, Siri and other 'digital assistants' that improve process performance. Most of us are familiar with the GPS products that help us with driving directions. We don't think of these as robots but they are.
- *Executable Processes* – This are the result of workflow evolution. Avoid coding of processes and using diagrams such as BPMN2 diagrams to drive an execution engine that automated the process.
- *Standards* – Using the current set of standards for documenting operational process such as:
  o *BPMN2* – for documenting a process.
  o *CMMN* – for documenting case management situations
  o *DMN* – for documenting decisions that are made in a process.
- *Machine Learning* – What if machine learning is applied to a process? The AI component can schedule a machine learning run over some period (a week, month quarter etc.), train on the new results and adapt to changes in the process environment. The machine learning can also be aimed at finding new patterns that reflect more significant changes in the process ecosystem. This can make some truly autonomous processes.

KEY ISSUES IN PROVIDING AUTOMATED PROCESS CAPABILITY

All technologies that handle different types of new digital data are not yet in place or mature enough to achieve smooth integration. Organizations are still grappling with managing and governing big data, data lakes, more resources, in-memory data warehouses etc. Picture, video and audio files still require a considerable amount of development to integrate smoothly with quantitative and semantic data. With the wave of large scale and mixed data types, process integration becomes a significant challenge.

A goal of the digital enterprise is to use artificial intelligence to do automated decision making in 'intelligent processes'. AI capabilities can analyze the data in real time, suggest process changes and monitor the result, notifying a human administrator when needed. This is a gradual effort over many years that requires assessing or auditing opportunities for operationalizing digital capability.

AT THE END OF THE DAY WHAT MATTERS FOR PROCESS AUTOMATION?

There are several process-automation considerations for the digital enterprise. Ultimately you want to get value from your process efforts through effective use of innovative BPM tools, standards and methods, meaning:

- A focused strategy for process renovation, innovation and organizational change
- A successful process upgrade strategy that resolves the automation issues
- Separating the signal from the noise, know what process issues are important
- Developing a trained staff that understands the process changes

DIGITIZATION – THE HOT TOPIC TODAY

Organizations are under duress from the deluge of data. It is not clear exactly what should be done to include this influx to extract the best value. Several sources and technologies are driving this increase in data and new algorithms and types of conclusions are available from the analytics. The users of this data may be changing from management to operators of the organization processes. Once improvement and automation are complete, digitization is easier.

LARGE VOLUMES OF DATA ARE THUNDERING INTO ORGANIZATIONS

Currently, one of the largest contributors to the digital enterprise is clearly the Internet of Things (IoT). What becomes of the huge amount of digital data being generated by IoT? What part of it relates to managing a business? Several billion people are part of the IoT phenomenon. Seven out of 10 people on the planet have access to mobile devices, generating huge amounts of social data and contributing to the rapid increase in the amounts of digital information.

Traditional data management and governance approaches generate and view transaction data from internal sources as well as external. The external data input is further extended through mobile devices such as tablets in restaurants, wireless devices and monitors in warehouses and factories, tablets in healthcare services and smartphones by business users. This tremendously increased the data available for analysis and directly impacts the processes that support these parts of the business.

Digitizing the enterprise is not simply adding new software and technology, it is about the impact on the organization, the organization structure and especially the processes.

What do you do with the large amounts of data, who is going to use it, what analytics should we use and so on?

Huge amounts of data are being generated and gathered today by:

- *Companies* - as part of embedded sensors and messaging that connects the customer more directly to the business as part of customer centric and customer management efforts.
- *Governments* – as part of general governance, traffic management, air quality monitoring, temperature reporting, fire control, security, privacy and protective measures, environmental monitoring and many other uses.
- *Data Harvesters* – such as the social media API aggregation service, GNIP, and others that comb the millions of pieces of data on social and other sites
- *Social sites themselves* – as part of the data collection of the 250 plus social sites that exist today.

Considerable amounts of data also come from rapidly expanding sources such as robotics, not just in the factory but elsewhere, especially in the military, the addition of many mobile apps of different types and wearable computing. Deriving value from that data is an important goal today. The growth in these sources of data is not yet clear. Neither is the growth in unanticipated new sources. All data in its various forms is overwhelming the ability of organizations to react in a productive manner. The data needs integration between the types of data and the data already in the organization and a means of presentation and integration that enables the organization to react to changes in the business landscape and ecosystem.

WHY IS DIGITIZATION OF INTEREST?

Changes in technology follow a pattern of entry into the business world. The adoption varies according to the ability of the organization to recognize the value, make changes and then realize that value in terms of outcomes.

Impact on the organization:

- Studies show that process productivity drops when there are a variety of access points and applications that get to data. The studies show that 2/3 of workers have a problem with data access that impacts productivity. All the new sources of data complicate this access. This especially true in health care.
- The organization focus is shifting to customer service, service and product quality and reliability, shorter product cycles based on market moves etc. This has an impact on what data and data summaries are needed for management and which are the most useful in improving process performance.
- The digitization of management reporting – IoT is a big part of what is driving digitization. Digitization requires some type of 'data funnel' much like the classic marketing funnel that manages the way we see the data. Definition of what this funnel looks like is necessary and what the parameters are that control the flow through the tunnel. This has an impact on all the management reporting processes and their related decision structures.
- Operationalizing data by linking it directly into processes where needed should improve and automate some of the data access.
- New demands of integration and analytics (more complex algorithms) plus operationalizing some AI capabilities like machine learning and predictive analytics into processes sometimes automating the process response. Management and staff need to understand the significance of the analytics and what the analytics tell them.

These observations apply to all types of organizations such as product companies, service organizations, nonprofits, education, charitable and governments.

There are several articles and case studies that provide some insight into what digitization means.

A few examples of the digitization perspective:

- *Aircraft Management* - Flight data analysis encompasses a variety of functions affecting flight operations. The most prominent use is in the area of safety, where flight data is collected and analysed to reveal high-risk events and trends. This process enables operators to proactively and effectively manage risk. Flight data analysis is also widely used in support of maintenance and engineering. Finally, flight data analysis can generate some of the largest tangible returns on investment when used to improve efficiency through optimization of fuel usage, reduction of emissions and improvement of component life.
  Extracted from http://www.geaviation.com/press/services/services_20120730.html.
- *Auto Manufacturing* - To get an idea of how this might work, view the following video of the IoT and auto sensors:
  https://www.youtube.com/watch?v=QSIPNhOiMoE
- *Banking* - Banks are at a crossroads. On the one hand, they are still processing their recent history. On the other hand, we can already see the first effects of a digitalization of society, an issue that banks are struggling with. Bank branches are hardly needed any longer. Payments and money transfers can be handled by platforms and robots. These basic functions will be open and free, they do not necessarily require a bank. And soon, we will be able to pay our telephone bills using social media.

https://www.credit-suisse.com/us/en/articles/articles/news-and-exper-tise/2015/02/en/digitalization-banks-are-at-a-crossroads.html

- *Government* - The federal government's top technology official noted that "the digitization of everything" will help accelerate a new technological model that infuses cybersecurity as a core component.

  "This digitization is relentless and it won't stop and it's accelerating and it's changing everything, including government," Tony Scott, the federal chief information officer, told government employees during his keynote at the inaugural CIO Council IT Symposium in Washington, D.C. "We're going to see more change in the next three or four or five years as the technology industry responds to today's challenges and figures out new architectural models and paradigms for the future," he added.

  http://www.fiercegovernmentit.com/story/federal-cio-says-digitization-everything-will-help-enhance-cybersecurity-ac/2015-06-16

Each of the examples shows different perspective of the use of digitization in an organization. It can have several different meanings depending on the view and need of the industry.

KEY ISSUES IN PROVIDING DIGITAL CAPABILITY

Technologies for digitizing the enterprise are moving targets. Vendors are now suggesting a digital business platform may be needed to support the emerging digital execution. The current key advantage is that managers are much more tech-savvy than some years ago and find it easier to explain data and analytics issues to top management.

Many businesses are already data- and analytics-intensive, especially in government, healthcare and retail. Although you can't fix processes to react to everything in an 'intelligent' manner, the trend is toward automated responses and adaptive applications. This means limited or no human interaction.

One goal of the digital enterprise is to use artificial intelligence to do automated decision making in 'intelligent processes.' This is a gradual effort over many years that requires assessing or auditing opportunities for operationalizing digital capability.

CONCLUSIONS

At the end of the day you want to get value from your data through effective coupling with process changes and execution.

For example:

- A focused strategy for operationalizing the large amounts of data
- A successful data integration strategy that resolves the different types of data and properly makes them available and connect to the processes that need them.
- Separating the signal from the noise, know what data is important to which processes
- Developing a trained staff that understands what the analytics mean and how to link them into the process architecture for best results

These comments give you an idea of what to expect from each stage of getting to a digital enterprise through processes. The best way to transform an organization is when top management sets its mind to having the skill to transform the old environment and operate the new environment with a staff they developed.

At each stage, results should be able to fund the effort going forward. If not, then there should be serious questions as to what happened to the value proposition. The value proposition may be compromised because the situation has changed due to an external trigger of some sort or that the expectation was not realistic or better yet, that things were working pretty well and the move should be made to the next stage before value is realized. This is the situation in well performing organizations. These organizations can defer value realization in favor of longer term value since they understand the direction, goals and means related to achieving success.

A Methodology for Human BPM Processes
Keith D Swenson, Fujitsu America, USA

INTRODUCTION

We often think of digital transformation in terms of machines and data flows. As we make everything digital, what is it that we are transforming? There is little to gain from digitizing things that are already automated.

The real benefit comes from transforming things that are not automated; things that today are human processes. The goal cannot be to simply automate earlier manual processes. Many processes are done by humans today because they cannot be automated by the traditional means. Humans have a natural decision-making ability that far exceeds the capability of pre-defined rules. The important question in front of us is how to make a digital organization that works symbiotically with people. Not replacing, but *enhancing*, their work.

In this chapter, I offer a method to take a human information-worker process, and to properly implement a case process that supports the worker to get more done, to be more efficient and be more accurate.

A METHODOLOGY FOR DESIGNING HUMAN BPM PROCESSES

The way you draw a process diagram depends largely on the methodology you use to define the process, as well as the underlying technology that you are going to use to implement the process. That begs the question then; what is the methodology for *human processes*?

1.1 What Is a Human Activity?

Before we talk about a method for drawing up human processes, we need to be clear about what is a human activity. Clearly it is work that is done by a human. This is not work that is done by a computer on behalf of a user. In order to focus on the human activity, we have to ignore all of the things that are done to facilitate that work. Or rather, we need to consider those things that facilitate the work as part of the task itself.

When modeling human activity, we focus on the work to be done; wash the dishes, feed the dog, write the blog entry, and decide the menu for dinner. Naturally, for a group of people to coordinate on these tasks, there must be communications among them, but we don't model the communications. If I want my son to wash the car, clearly, I have to tell him that I want him to wash the car, but I don't think of that as a separate activity in itself. Instead, it is simply part of getting the car washed.

It should not come as a surprise that systems designed for supporting human activities allow you to model the work that is to be done at every step in a process, without worrying about *how* you will tell that person to do the work, or how the results are collected. Such systems often include customizable ways that each user can decide how they wish to be informed; some users prefer email, others like to receive a text message on their phone, and so on. As a process designer, I want to focus on the task to be done (e.g. review this document) and let the system take care of how that user is informed about the work to be done. Similarly, I know that an activity may be concluded with a decision (e.g. to either "accept" or "reject" the document), and that may affect the path that the process takes, but I do not want to be too concerned at the high level of how the system collected that response.

1.2 Identifying Human Work

There are three reasons why an activity must be performed by a human:

- There are decisions to be made that cannot be automated and must be made by a person. For example, the determination of whether an article is fit for publication is a task that depends upon recent current events, suitability of the writing style, and the editorial preferences of a particular publication. Another example; making the decision which candidate is the best fit for an open job position is a task that depends upon personalities of the candidate and the team they would join, as well as an assessment of skills and ability to perform the job. These decisions must be performed by a person because the most relevant attributes may not be able to be expressed in a quantitative way, like political correctness or personality. The rule behind what constitutes acceptable quantities of these is tacit and is not consciously known by the people who evaluate such rules. But indeed, there are people who are very good at making such decisions. This is work that will never be automated.

- The second category of tasks is those which might one day be automated, but to do so would require additional prep work which has not been done. For example, you might need someone to enter figures from a financial report which is received either on paper or in an electronic format that is not easily consumable. For the time being, it is simply less expensive to pay someone to do this than it is to pay a programmer to write the code that automatically converts the information. Eventually, these will be automated.

- The third category consists of physical tasks that must be done outside an information system. For example, driving a forklift to load goods from a truck into a place in a warehouse. Or to perform maintenance on a piece of equipment. It might be possible in the far future to automate these tasks with robots, but there are significant barriers to automation due to the physicality of the task. For the time being, we must treat these tasks as human work.

These human tasks are made explicit so that people with the right skills can be identified, or so that people can be trained to do those tasks. Everyone involved in the process needs to know what they do—not only those performing the task—so that everyone gains an understanding of how the tasks they do fit in with what the others are doing. The human tasks need to be described in a way that the people themselves will understand using the specific vocabulary that the people in that organization use. There will normally need to be additional documentation associated that contains detailed information that is useful for training or skills identification.

1.3 Meeting Human Needs

Before anyone will perform a task, they certainly must be
- informed that the task needs to be done,
- given the details of the particular case,
- able to do the work, and
- have a way to record the results of the activity.

These are part of any human activity. The human task facilitation system (Human BPM system) should provide those automatically as part of the activity node. That is to say, when a node is assigned to someone, and that node becomes active, it should send notification to the assignee, provide a way that the assignee can log in and access the details of the case, and provide a set of choices as well as ways to update the case data as appropriate for that process.

Besides the above required aspects of a human activity above, for practical reasons many human facilitation systems include the concept of a:

- deadline date for an activity, as well as
- reminders about the activity and warnings that a deadline is approaching. These are convenient built-in capabilities to help manage the work.

Thus, keep in mind that a human activity is a description of actual human work to be done, and that each activity is assumed to have (a) notification, (b) information, (d) conclusion, (e) deadline, and (f) reminders built-in. The following 9-step method can be used to create a model of a human process:

1.4 Step 1: Identify Human Work

Start by enumerating the tasks that must be done by people. List the work that is to be done by a person.

Ignore for the moment the paper form, the data on the form, or how that form is passed around. Do not think about email messages or ways that you might communicate about the work. Do not consider how web services will be accessed or updated. A common mistake is for system designers to immediately focus on the artifacts that help people coordinate their work, instead of the work itself.

Avoid including activities which do not involve humans. For example, running a query on a database is something that might be need at some point in order to support a human task. At this point in the method you simply assume that the right information is available. There is a later step that defines what information must be available, and a final step that defines how that information is retrieved, but those should be defined at the right point, which is much later in the method.

1.5 Step 2: Determine Activity Conclusions

Human tasks can be concluded in more than one way. For example, the decision of whether to "accept" or "reject" an article for publication will be concluded in two ways; "accept" or "reject." The conclusion of an activity is an explicit part of the activity itself. In many situations, there may be a third conclusion to this example activity which is something that means more or less "I am not qualified to make this decision." That is a possible way that an activity might be concluded. Some activities will have acceptable time limits, and may be concluded simply by the passing of time. Each conclusion is given a name.

Conclusions are important communication events. When you model a human process, you are modeling thing that need to be communicated to the people involved in the process. Take for example the process of writing a book where many people are involved in various roles such as writer, reviewer, editor, etc. The writer will, at some point, declare that the book (a particular draft) is ready for review. While this concludes one phase of writing, more importantly it tells others that they may start their activities of reviewing and editing the current copy. The conclusion of a human activity is most often a speech act known as a "declaration." A declaration is a statement that in the act of uttering it, changes the state of a group of people. Declarations often redefine what many people are expected to be doing. So it is with a modeled human process: the completion of one activity redefines what other people in the process are expected to do.

A conclusion should be considered a distinct conclusion only if it matters to the group. Take for example a task "Answer Question." You might think of the answer to the question as being the conclusion of the activity, and there are approximately one (or more) answers to every possible question that might be placed. Clearly it is nonsense to consider every possible answer as a possible conclusion of the activity.

Conclusions are grouped into sets which will affect the flow of the process further on. To be specific, if the flow of the process does not depend at all on whether the task is completed or not, then it is sufficient to say that there is only one conclusion: "done."

For example, the president is given the choice to "sign" or "veto" a piece of legislation, and the process continues in different directions depending upon how this task is concluded. However, there is a time limit, and if congress dismisses before the bill is signed, then this situation is called a "pocket veto." A pocket veto is considered to be completely identical to a "veto" as far as the process is concerned, so we would not need a separate conclusion for pocket veto: the timeout rule would simply be another way to conclude the activity as a normal "veto."

1.6 Step 3: Put The Tasks Into Order

The work and conclusions should be identified without getting overly involved in the sequence of activities. In many cases it is clear that a particular task needs to be done before or after another related task. There will also be branches, and certain tasks that are done only on certain conditions. This is where a diagramming tool becomes useful, but only if it can describe activities at the human level. If one activity must be completed before another, and that other activity can start as soon as the first is completed, then an arrow is drawn between them.

If an activity can be concluded in more than one way, and if each conclusion would cause the process to proceed in a different direction, then there can be an arrow coming out of that activity for each possible conclusion. Clearly, if the point of an activity is to "accept" or "reject" an article for publication, the process that continues after that point will be very different. Because this decision is the very point of the activity, the process becomes easier to read if there is a direct connection between the activity and the direction that the process goes. Some engines cannot represent this in this way, and instead save the conclusion into a variable which is then tested at a following branch gateway. This is an accepted and common practice, but because the branch is removed from the human task, it is harder to see the direct causal link.

The result is a network diagram of the human activities that must be performed properly set in a process which indicates the conditions and order of the activities.

1.7 Step 4: Determine Performers

After the tasks and order are identified, one needs to determine who should do the tasks. This is highly dependent upon a particular organization. It is also changes from case to case. In some cases, there will be a pool of people who would be qualified to do the task, and anyone from that pool might be picked. What must be determined at this point is what set of rules will be used to determine who should do a particular job. It might be that a person with a particular skill is needed, and if a directory exists that lists all the people with that skill, then the rule is to find those people and pick one. More often the requirement will be that a particular person is chosen because of their responsibility in a particular part of the organization. For example, there may be a person designated to handle requests from a particular customer. Of there may be a person who is designated as handling all the purchase requests for a particular department.

Unfortunately such a rule cannot be specified without specific consideration of the organization that will be using the process. Each organization will have unique organizing principles, some of which are based on historical accidents. Even across a single organization, the rules to determine who does a particular activity may not be consistent. Any organization that grew by mergers of other organizations will have some "special" parts of the organization that are not like other parts. There also needs to be consideration about the specific representation of the organization in an organizational directory. If skills are not tracked, then that cannot be used to determine the person to perform the activity.

There generally will need to be an expression of some sort which can be evaluated in the context of the organization structure that resolves the assignee of a particular task. This expression will usually make use of pre-existing groups and/or job titles in the organizational directory. It may require new groups or job titles. There may need to be multiple levels of groups which include groups which include groups. In some cases it may not be possible to determine a priori who will be performing a particular task. In some cases the assignee expression will narrow it down to a group of people, but immediate circumstances (e.g. who is available) may be necessary select the final assignee. It might be necessary for the users to self-select for a particular job. There may need to be case by case adjustments, since it is not possible to know everything in advance.

1.8 Step 5: Determine The Information To Be Carried.

Here you specify a schema or a set of schemas which carry the information context within which all the activities take place. If the process is for a customer to open a bank account, then there is specific information that needs to be carried for that process, such as the customer name, address, and references to other accounts or credit history. The context schema needs to be a superset of all information needed for every activity. For example, if there is an activity to assess the property value of a house, then clearly the details about the home address, prior sales information, and various reports about the locale are necessary to perform this activity. If one activity produces a result which is necessary in a later activity, such as the assessed value of a house, then there much be a variable that will hold that information between activities. By considering the information requirements of every activity in the process, you can compile a complete context schema required by the process.

The information content will be modeled differently by different implementation engines. For some there is a single schema for the context that is shared by all activities (effectively a union of all schemas required by the individual activities). Others have a collection of schemas which are transformed back and forth through the process. Either way, the idea at this point is to identify the information requirements of the entire process.

1.9 Step 6: Define Access To Information Needed At Each Activity

At some points in the process, certain parts (variables) within the shared context can be read and updated and at other points that information can be read, but not updated. There are also points in the process where information is completely hidden because it is either not yet specified at that point in the process, or not relevant to that particular activity.

1.10 Step 7: Determine Timeouts

An activity may have a requirement to be performed in a particular time period. What happens when that time period is exceeded? Does the process continue without the activity being complete, or does the process "fail" and go down a different path. There may be reminders that are additional notifications to the user that the task has not yet been completed. There may also be escalation to other people or management if the task is nearing the deadline without being completed. At this point for each activity, all time-dependent behaviors should be considered. Some tasks may have no time dependency at all, and may be allowed to remain uncompleted indefinitely.

We know that time equals money; so it is worth considering at this point the cost of every activity, as well as the cost to the organization of either delaying the activity, or not performing that activity. If you are simulating the execution of the process, these costs entered into the model can be accumulated across a simulation run in order to guide the further design of the process.

1.11 Step 8: Design The Presentation Of The Information.

This puts a face on the context information, mapping the schema to a visual presentation. This presentation might be specific to a given activity, or might be the same presentation over the entire process.

Humans don't read XML directly. Instead, the information has to be displayed in a way that is meaningful to the user. To be effective, the display should be organized for ease of use. Some of the information may be keys or links to other information, and the display should provide an easy way to access those external sources of information.

Technology to present the information is often described as "forms" in the BPM community, but you should keep in mind that any technology that can take data and generate a user interface can be used. The choice will depend on many factors outside the BPM system. Some organizations will choose Visual Basic or Java Swing because they have programmers experienced in these areas. Some might choose PHP or other web technique. They might have a powerful forms software designed specifically for this purpose. The process definition method should not get bogged down at this point in the specific requirements of the technology to be used. Instead, this step should focus on the look and feel of the displayed information.

1.12 Step 9: Integrate To Information Services

This is where the information needed in a process can be picked up from various sources and sent to various destinations. I use the term "service" in the generic sense of a "Service Oriented Architecture" (SOA). This might be through "web service" calls or any other means to access other service types. The point simply is that there is a human activity that requires a particular piece of information, and so this is where you specify how that information will be retrieved for that human user.

It is this step where you finally consider how data is sent and received between computers. Many process designers start by considering how data is transferred through the system, and it leads them to a communications centric view of the work. It can lead to activities that are optimized for computer communications, instead of being optimized for human work. Since the human costs far outweigh the compute resource costs in most business processes, it is important to start with the human tasks, and then work down to the integration tasks.

To access information from a web service, some of the process context information will need to be transformed appropriately into XML that is needed as input to a web service. The resulting XML may need to be similarly transformed to be put back into the process context. For example, if a in an account application, the process may need to access a "credit rating" service to retrieve the applicants credit rating for consideration in the application process.

Services are used not only for retrieval of information; it is also the point where you consider how the results of the human tasks will be sent out to destinations outside of the people directly involved in the process. For example, if the decision is made to approve a loan of a particular amount to a customer, then there are various parties that may need to be informed about this decision (e.g. by email) and there would also be calls to services to actually set up the account and initiate the sending of a contract to the parties involved.

1.13 Roles And Responsibility For Modeling

The business analyst and the developer take the modeling through the entire process. The modeling starts with the business side, and migrates to the technical side in the course of modeling. Different skills are needed at different phases, and these tend to be enabled or aided by people with those specialized skills. Below is a table showing who needs to be involved at each step, and how the main responsibility tends to shift from business analyst to developer right around step 5.

	Business Analyst	Users	Management	Data Architect	Security Expert	Usability Expert	SOA Expert	Developer
1. Identify Task	☑	☑						
2. Identify Outcomes	☑	☑						
3. Put in Order	☑							
4. Role Performers	☑		☑		☑			
5. Information Design	☑			☑				☑
6. Access Control			☑		☑			☑
7. Duration Deadlines			☑					☑
8. Info Presentation	☑					☑		☑
9. Service Integration							☑	☑

1.14 Summary

Nine steps lead to a model of a human process. The steps are repeated iteratively, with reviews at various points. Usually after each step there is some segment of the organization that are interested in reviewing the progress. It is also true that later steps will turn up details which were left out of earlier steps, and so there is some iteration through the method multiple times. A good system will allow simplistic execution of the process before you are complete, so that you can try out the process along the way. After step 3 you should be able to run simulations of the process in order to gain confidence on the correctness of the process. After the process is implemented and deployed, you can collect statistics on how well it is running and cycle back through this to improve things.

We call it "Business Process Management" because you are never entirely finished with designing the process. This method is repeated as long as the process can be improved, and there are always new ideas on how to improve the process or to respond to external changes.

Section 2
Execution

ARaymond, Brazil
Nominated by Lecom S/A, Brazil

1. EXECUTIVE SUMMARY / ABSTRACT

A multinational French company with extensive presence in the country, ARaymond Brazil adopted a Business Process Management suite for increasing efficiency and control of its internal processes, ensuring a sustainable growth in the country.

2. OVERVIEW

Created in 1865, French company ARaymond has, for several generations, developed, manufactured and marketed fastening and assembly solutions.

The Brazilian branch, ARaymond Brazil, started operating 19 years ago, and is currently a national reference in the auto parts sector, working with most automakers in the country, besides being an important supplier for all South America. It's based in the municipality of Vinhedo, in the state of São Paulo.

A few years ago, the company identified the need to improve its internal processes in order to support operation growth. Based on that, the company started a project to automate some of its processes with a technological suite. An agile BPM methodology was used, enabling delivery with quality in short cycles of process analysis, redesign, prototyping and validation by end users.

The deployed processes enabled improvements in:

1. Execution times: previously, for instance, the company spent on average 15 days for a product to be registered - now the process is executed in only one day and a half, with an impressive 90% time reduction;

2. Monitoring and control: for instance, about 15.000 extra hours have been tracked through the overtime authorization process, providing transparency and safety to managers to authorize and compensate employees' overtime.

The success of process automation initiatives allowed the company to move forward in the consolidation of more mature process management practices, strengthening a culture based on end-to-,,,end business processes.

3. BUSINESS CONTEXT

For the last years, ARaymond Brazil operation has been growing significantly, which required the creation of more structured processes and work practices, enabled by consistent information systems in order to facilitate operations management and results reporting to headquarters.

In addition, the company observed an increasing need to retain employees expertise, as it has a lean and multidisciplinary staff. Any dismissal involved risks and could lead to reductions in value creation, since knowledge about work routines was mainly residing in the minds of employees, not explicit. There were difficulties even to train new workers, since there were only a few documents about business process and rules.

The implementation of an ERP system was completed in 2002 and supported the integration of basic activities, but many operational problems persisted, especially the ones in work routines involving participation of several departments simultaneously.

Quoting André Silva, one of the managers for the IT department at ARaymond Brazil, "The need was urgent. The company already had an ERP system, but it did not have the proper tools for this type of process management."

Facing this initiative, the IT department began to develop several specific legacy systems in order to complement the ERP, meeting the increasing demands from business areas. This strategy, however, was not successful because IT itself was realizing that knowledge of relevant business rules was still not being adequately managed; rather than only in employees' minds, it was now embedded in software code. It was necessary to create a way to make business processes and business rules more explicit and available to end users

Therefore, the IT department began to spread internally the need to invest in BPM with the use of an adequate technology suite. The main argument was that, with this solution, business areas could gradually take over management of processes and rules, minimizing dependence from IT.

4. THE KEY INNOVATIONS

4.1 Business

Agility and autonomy for process automation were key premises of ARaymond IT department by the beginning of the project. As the subject was new and almost unknown by senior management, it was necessary to achieve results quickly so that the initiative could acquire credibility.

In this sense, the BPM suite acquisition made ARaymond change its traditional development paradigm to join an agile approach, represented by short cycles of processs analysis, redesign and automation based on prototypes built with the collaboration from business areas. The objective was not anymore to automate ideal processes at once; rather than that, a first version of processes would be quickly delivered and then feedback from execution would lead to adjustments and refinements in following versions.

The implementation of an agile BPM methodology has proved to be so successful that, after 90 days, 15 processes have already been developed and put into production. Employees were engaged throughout this work, offering improvement suggestions and participating effectively on the design of new processes.

Nowadays the BPM suite is used by approximately 130 employees and takes care of vital processes for the organization, as the registration of products, suppliers and customers, payments processing and other financial transctions, as well as routines from operations management and human resources management. The BPM suite became, therefore, one of the key management tools in ARaymond.

Below, we highlight some of the implemented processes and their results:

Tools Acquisition:

This process involves the request, approval and effective purchase of machinery and molds for new products manufacturing. It's one of the most critical processes in product lifecycle management, which directly affects the delivery time of a new project for a client and ensures business profitability. As it usually involves high amounts, traceability and control of its implementation have great importance to the administration.

Prior to automation, average time spent for a tool acquisition to be completed used to oscillate between two and six months, due to documentation involved and the complexity of the material to be purchased.

The new process runs with a delivery time of maximum one month.

Products Registration:

This process involves the adequate registration of new products. Although apparently simple, registration is critical for ARaymond since it provides information for various commercial, operational and financial processes. There are on avergage 50 product entries held monthly for the company.

Prior to automation, process execution involved 16 steps, with many manual activities and involvement of seven different departments. It took, on average, 15 days for the completion of a register.

Automation involved the formalization of numerous business rules and tacit knowledge from employees, raising the level of data consistency and greatly reducing failures and rework in other ARaymond processes. The new process involves only 8 steps, now being held at 1.5 days - a 90 % time reduction.

Payments Processing:

Process that involves paying overheads, taxes, insurance, payroll etc. with the involvement of the Financial, Accounting and Controlling departments. The automation of the process did not generate efficiency gains, however it allowed greater control for all participants. Now all documents involved in payments are available for consultation. The availability of information provides transparency and facilitates access to audits.

The increase in maturity along with first process automation initiatives allowed the company to consolidate its process management practices. Today senior management recognizes the importance of processes as a basis for definition of roles and responsibilities and also for goals establishment.

There is an initiative in progress aiming at structuring a new process architecture and repository, that will represent how ARaymond creates value for its customers and how each individual process contributes to that. Process architecture will begin to work as a key element to improvement projects prioritization for the upcoming years, to the organization of all documents associated with business processes and to competencies management, enabliing more effective knowledge management practices, as shown in figure below:

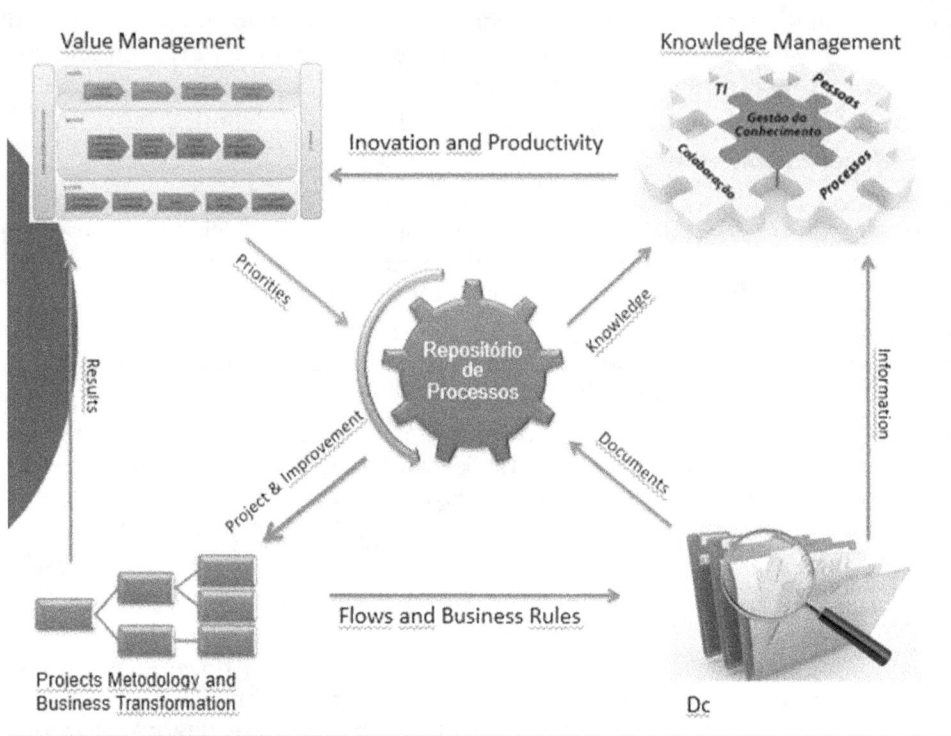

Thus, the adoption of BPM is expanding considerably at ARaymond Brazil. Previously an initiative driven solely by the IT department, it now has direct involvement from areas such as Strategic Planning and Human Resources, in addition to effective sponsorship among senior managers and acknowledgement among business areas.

4.2 Organization & Social

Within the IT department we established a BPM center of excellence (CoE) composed of two BPM experts. It was this CoE which advanced in disseminating BPM benefits and structuring process automation initiatives with the use of the BPM suite. The main idea was that it could train representatives from business areas so that, gradually, they could redesign their own processes, using the CoE as a reference for advanced integrations and for quality control.

Today, new processes are being designed and automated by business areas with the support from the BPM CoE, minimizing the dependence from IT and vendor. New processes are being implemented properly at 45 days on average.

5. HURDLES OVERCOME

5.1 Management

The first hurdle found by the team was how to convince senior management about BPM suite implementation. Although the team understood its importance, it wasn´t easy to justify budget to purchase a new tool. The concepts and benefits of BPM discipline weren´t yet spread on ARaymond Brazil.

The company had made a significant investment in the acquisition of the ERP, and leaders thought its implementation would be enough to solve most operational problems. Considering the fact BPM was a new subject in the company, it was difficult to have measures to justify an investment.

The strategy adopted was to implement small and inexpensive pilots which would be able to show benefits that would justify the BPM suite adoption.

In this sense, selected pilots sought to convince senior management that BPM, as a management discipline and with the use of a BPM suite, could bring significant productivity gains and enable a more structured growth for ARaymond Brazil.

This strategy proved successful and, gradually, following the previous plan of proving the solution to be necessary, not only senior management but also the overall company began to see it as a flexible optimization tool. Over the years, new high-level processes have been implemented with demonstrated results, turning process automation into a clear way for the achievement of operational and strategic goals.

5.2 Organization Adoption

In order to increase adoption by the organization, the strategy was to involve and train key users from different business areas for using the BPM suite by themselves, automating their own processes and gaining undertanding about its flexibility and application possibilities.

This technical training was conducted by the IT department. The plan was that key users would start automating simple processes, replacing inefficient internal forms. Preliminary goals were to demonstrate the tool, teach its use and turn it part of key users routine, and then focus on strategic possibilities through more complex processes.

Altogether, nine professionals have been trained and now conduct their own processes, under the supervision of BPM CoE from the IT department.

6. BENEFITS

6.1 Time Reductions

As shown, processes such as Tools Acquisition and Products Registration have had significant reduction in execution times, impacting critical business functions at ARaymond Brazil.

The Tools Acquisition process, for instance, was performed between two and six months on average, and now runs with a delivery time of maximum one month. Products Registration process had the most impressive reduction, from 15 days on average to only 1,5 days, a 90% reduction.

6.2 Quality Improvements

Other processes such as Payments Processing, Employee Time Register Control, Overtime Authorization and Reimbursements Control, did not have focus on achieving efficiency gains, but enabled more control, which was considered essential to support company's growth.

Payments Processing, for instance, involves amounts above millions of Brazilian Reals (BRL). The simpler and faster tracking of information and documents has facilitated audit work and has reduced noncompliance penalties.

Regarding to Employee Time Register Control and Overtime Authorization processes, traceability of historical data simplifies approvals and ensures compliance with labor laws.

Finally, operational processes such as Reimbursements Control contributed to the reduction of errors and undue payments to employees and suppliers.

7. BEST PRACTICES, LEARNING POINTS AND PITFALLS

7.1 Best Practices and Learning Points

✓ *Start simple and expand gradually;*

✓ *Conquer sponsorship and support based on evidence from real cases, not only concepts;*

✓ *Engage representatives from business areas and disseminate the idea they are the ones who need to be in charge of business processes and business rules;*

✓ *Prepare teams to redesign their own processes, in order to minimize dependence from the IT department;*

✓ *Use BPM suite adoption as a starting point for strengthening process-based management.*

7.2 Pitfalls

✗ *Avoid high initial investments that may shut the project down;*

✗ *Do not create excessive expectations with representatives from business areas: they may certainly reduce but not eliminate dependence from IT indeed.*

8. COMPETITIVE ADVANTAGES

The gradual adoption of BPM suite increased management maturity in ARaymond Brazil in a sense that the Brazilian subsidiary has become a reference to other units around the world. Currently, ARaymond Brazil is considered an internal benchmark for the execution of certain business processes.

For example, the solution adopted for product registration is considered the world's most agile and effective. As this subject is a global issue, the company is evaluating ways to replicate the adopted technology for other units worldwide.

Overall, the results achieved in the Brazilian operation have motivated the creation of similar initiatives in other bases, that will lead to the expansion of a global BPM culture at Araymond.

9. TECHNOLOGY

The adopted BPM suite favoured the rapid absorption of a process-based culture. Main characteristics include;

- Simplicity and speed of deployment;
- 100% web solution, available in all the devices (desktop, tablet, mobile)
- Developed in JAVA and database to SQL and Oracle;
- Integration with Active Directory;
- DEM: Documents Eletronic Management;
- Dashboards and Produtivity Indicators Management;
- Parameterizations / agile and independent customizations

10. THE TECHNOLOGY AND SERVICE PROVIDERS

Lecom BPM is a platform for Business Process Management (BPM), Enterprise Content Management (ECM) and Analytics. It enables the monitoring of all stages of business processes, detecting unproductive tasks and identifying trouble spots (so-called "bottlenecks"), resulting in much faster outlets and rational decision.

"Lecom BPM standardizes processes and reduces bureaucracy; this villain that makes processes inefficient and impacts productivity of most Brazilian organizations" says João Cruz, CEO of Lecom.

Die Mobiliar, Insurance Company AG, Switzerland

Nominated by ISIS Papyrus Europe AG, Austria

1. EXECUTIVE SUMMARY / ABSTRACT

The Swiss insurance company *Die Mobiliar* is the oldest private insurance organization in Switzerland. As a multiline insurer, offering a full range of insurance and pension products and services, *Die Mobiliar* needs to handle a huge quantity of documents, exchanged with approximately 1.7 million customers. Therefore, the "Mobiliar Korrespondenz System" MKS (Mobiliar Correspondence System) for ad hoc generation of well-designed and content-rich documents is vital for *Die Mobiliar*.

Each insurance document is designed and delivered in high quality by the document generation processes executed in a huge and manifold working environment. Documents are composed from building blocks following insurance regulations. Moreover, the data filled into a certain document is retrieved on the fly from diverse data sources. These complex business processes are handled in a quick and exact way by the MKS built on the Papyrus Platform and its ACM (Adaptive Case Management) and BPM (Business Process Management) capabilities. The combination of these two technologies enables flexibility from design time to run time of the document generation process.

The MKS system enables the design and content administration of documents by business staff without IT involvement. Furthermore, the system manages the whole document generation lifecycle from design over execution until delivery to customers in a highly flexible way. The capability of MKS to edit process templates any time when new business requirements demand for it, supports *Die Mobiliar* to define new documents and process templates within the boundaries imposed by predefined processes.

2. OVERVIEW

With annual mailing volumes exceeding 6.3 million envelopes, *Die Mobiliar* requires a system producing a huge amount of high quality documents in a short time. The system is production-critical as being vital for the daily customer communication of the company offering a full range of insurance and pension products and services to nearly 1.7 million customers. To satisfy such requirements, the MKS project aims to provide a centralized system that facilitates document generation processes operated by business users without IT involvement.

MKS is logically separated into document design and production stages in which the key roles of users are reasonably assigned. In the document design phase, template administrators create document templates in combination with document process templates and maintain the template collection. As a centralized system, MKS manages the template collection effectively and successfully reduces the maintenance effort. The lifecycle of a document and its related processes from design over test until production is controlled by an integrated delivery management that is flexible and adaptive for the correspondence document generation. Therefore, MKS can shortly deliver new document templates responding to new demands of the insurance market. Clerks create documents instantiated from the templates and deliver them to customers via different delivery channels. Several complex processes are operated underneath of the system to provide productive services to business users. In a few steps, business users can operate complicated tasks easily that needed a lot of time and effort in the previous system.

MKS minimizes IT involvement by adaptable processes and intuitive user interfaces allowing productive interactions of business users. Providing easy-to-use functions for the definition and editing of business processes, MKS allows business users to change processes by themselves without complex technical concerns. The compliance and consistency of the processes is ensured by the integrated delivery management. No classical program code demanding for IT skills is created during the template design stage in the production environment of MKS.

MKS supports clerks with an easy way to send documents to customers not only as print but also through different e-delivery channels like e-mail, FAX or SMS. Moreover, the transparent data exchanged between MKS and other business applications used in *Die Mobiliar* frees business users from data concerns compared to the previous system. With the support from MKS, business users can fully focus on the customer needs, thus making customer experience a key factor for business success.

3. BUSINESS CONTEXT

The initial situation at *Die Mobiliar* was only partly able to fulfill the wide range of needs. An insurance document issued by *Die Mobiliar* is not only a piece of paper; it serves as a business card, representing the company to their customers in different languages, mainly German, English and French. Moreover, *Die Mobiliar* considers well-designed and rich content documents as an opportunity to communicate and build a strong relationship with customers in different languages and different countries, especially in Europe. In the rapidly-changing insurance industry, seizing opportunities and reacting quickly is one of the key factors to have success. Therefore, *Die Mobiliar* pays special attention to the process of generating and delivering high quality documents to customers.

Document template administrators struggling with the distributed system

The insurance documents published by *Die Mobiliar* have a specific style and format representing the company. To produce such documents, *Die Mobiliar* dedicates a skilled team to create and maintain a collection of hundreds of document templates serving different insurance use cases. In the initial system, these templates are designed manually with MS Word and stored in three language versions. When a template is edited, its copies on several file servers are updated by template administrators. The data exchanged between the tools used in the MS Word based system are manually handled by business users. Although reserving high-skilled employees from the IT department for support requests, the administrator team still puts a lot of effort into the management of hundreds of templates used by more than 4000 end users, i.e. insurance clerks, creating thousands of documents during daily work.

Clerks manually executing document delivery

When customer documents are requested, clerks search on the servers for suitable document templates and copy them to their local machines. With MS Word, documents are filled in with data and might be formatted by clerks, which can lead to deviations from a corporate style. Further, clerks tend to save on local machines private versions of document templates giving rise to a nearly uncontrollable growth of template versions. Completed documents are sent to customers via e-mail, fax, or post. The delivery is accomplished manually by using independent tools, such as e-mail applications or fax machines. Since the delivery channels are not integrated, a considerable amount of time is required for sending documents to customers. Moreover, the completed documents need to be manually attached to insurance cases which are managed in other business applications used by *Die Mobiliar*.

Enhancement needed

To reduce the involved efforts for a consistent document management as well as supporting daily production with mature document processes including a document archive, the following requirements need to be considered:

- The document and related processes should be managed by a specialized system fully taking care for the document design, maintenance and production
- The time to market for documents should be reduced so that new insurance products can be released short term
- Business staff should be able to handle the document design and process definitions with minimal or no IT personnel involvement (no "coding")
- Customers should be able to receive their documents as soon as possible after the documents were created by the clerks
- Various delivery channels should be integrated and addressed from a single definition of the new system
- Data that need to be exchanged between existent business applications should be managed automatically by the new system

4. THE KEY INNOVATIONS

The implementation of the MKS has a positive impact on several aspects of the daily insurance business, which are described in the following.

4.1 BUSINESS

Quickly respond to business needs

Compared to the previous system MKS supports business users with special features of creating and delivering document templates in a facilitative way. Documents created by MKS have a consistent style and format by using building blocks, which were quality assured by the integrated delivery process. In particular, a document is composed of several building blocks that are arranged in a particular order by template administrators. All templates are stored and managed in a central repository.

MKS has an integrated delivery process in order to optimize the lifecycle of a document from design time until production. Statistics from *Die Mobiliar* show that the amount of documents produced every day increased up to 20 times. With such daily document volumes, *Die Mobiliar* can respond better to business needs and seize opportunities in the rapidly changing insurance industry.

Clerks can communicate interactively with customers

MKS supports clerks with an interactive way to communicate with customers. As shown in Figure 1, Clerks select their preferred user interface language (e.g. German) but write each document independently in the correspondence language that meets the preferences of the recipient(s) (e.g. English). The system is integrated with several delivery channels and business applications used in *Die Mobiliar*, such as CRM or claims management systems. Sending documents to customers is easily done by the process step "Select delivery channels" of the document generation process. The connection to delivery channels and the delivery processes are transparent for users. In addition, MKS provides all of the needed language variants so that a document can be consistently produced in several languages. Moreover, the generated data can be automatically transferred to the related business applications integrating with MKS. By providing such an integrated way to handle customer data, MKS assists business users to focus on customer needs and to strengthen the relationship with customers.

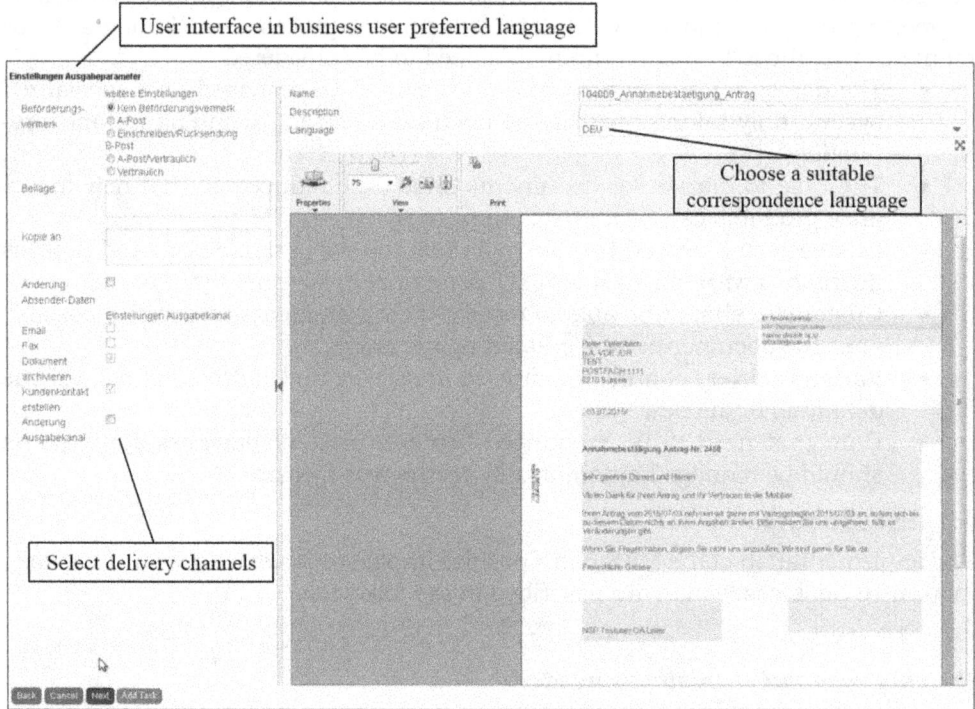

Figure 1: Select delivery channels and correspondence languages

4.2 CASE HANDLING

The overall system architecture of the initial system

The architecture of the MS Word based system is briefly described in Figure 2. Template administrators create document templates with MS Word. These templates are stored in document storages distributed over several severs. A supervisor approves templates before they are delivered to clerks. Documents are edited in MS Word and can be printed on local printers. In case the documents are triggered by other business applications, the data exchange has to be done manually by the clerks. In such a system, multiple platforms with different software tools are used by clerks to generate documents without any clearly defined business processes. The resulting complexity causes high costs and administration efforts.

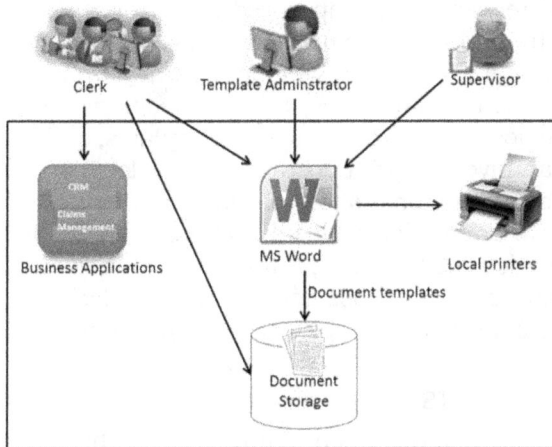

Figure 2: The initial MS Word-based document generation system

The system architecture of MKS

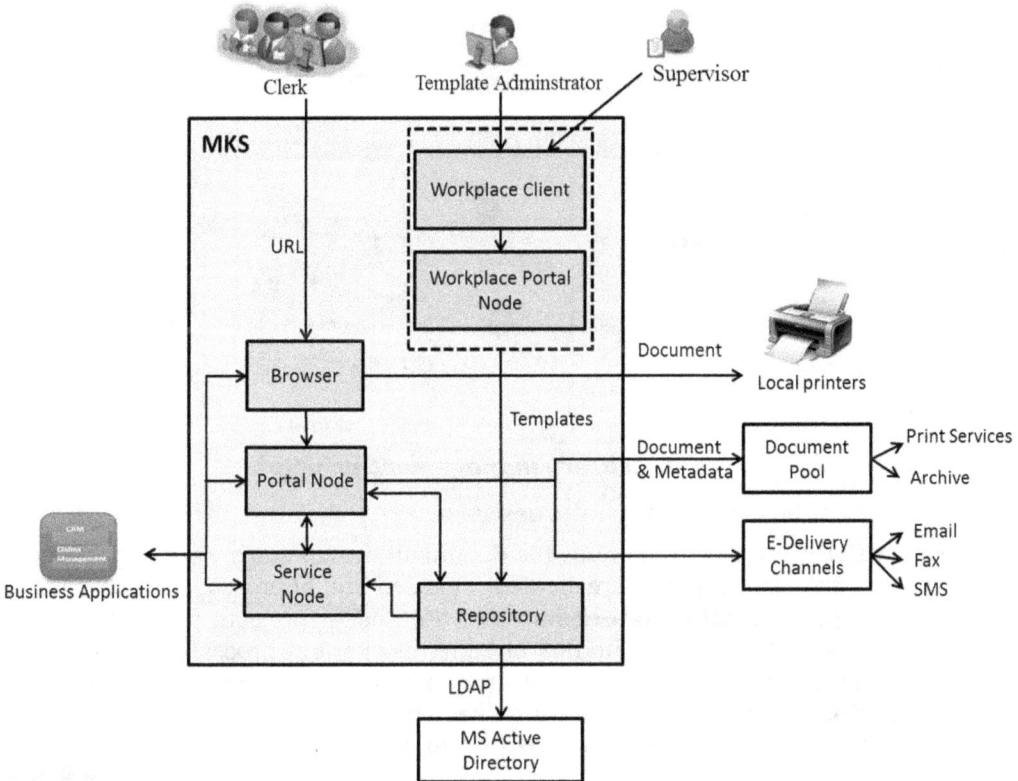

Figure 3: MKS System Architecture

To achieve greater efficiency and standardization, *Die Mobiliar* consolidates all business documents on one platform to simplify and standardize the template design (corporate identity) and its involved processes (Figure 3). Template administrators create document templates in a workplace providing a specialized user interface integrating all means for document and process design. All templates are stored in a versioned central repository and approved by supervisors before released into production for use by clerks. The solution supports a thin client browser architecture, i.e. clerks are able to access MKS independently from their office locations. The interaction between Portal Nodes, Service Nodes and the repository allows clerks to instantiate document processes from templates, exchange data with business applications, archive and print documents with local printers or by print services, and send them to customers via selectable delivery channels. MKS is supporting business goal orientation with full transparency to clerks about involved processes which are designed for an optimum balance between automation of the system operation and customer case specific manual decisions by clerks. Therefore, users of MKS can avoid the complexity of the previous distributed system and put less effort to operate their daily business work.

Assigning key roles in MKS

To improve the lifecycle of a document template, MKS has an integrated delivery management in the production environment supporting a logical separation between the document design and production stages (Figure 4).

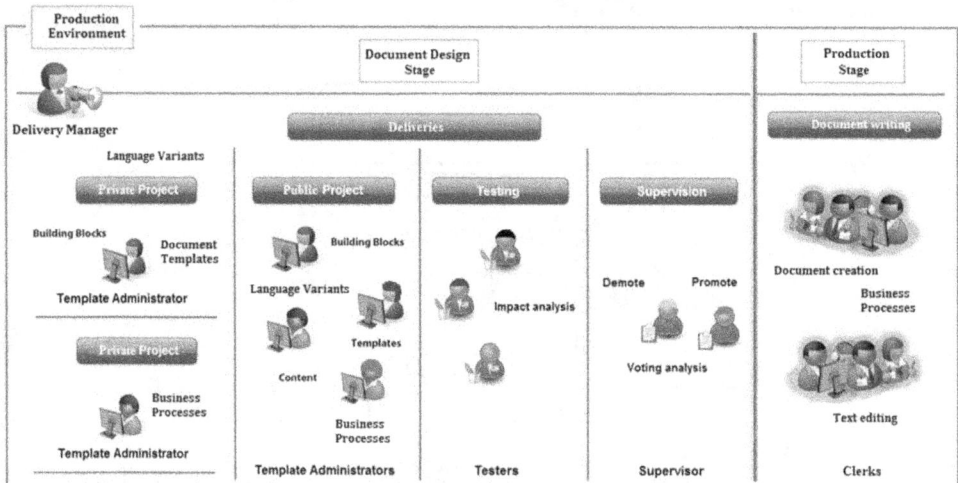

Figure 4: Delivery management principle

Each stage has the following key roles assigned:

- **Delivery managers** manage the document design stage where document and process templates are created, modified and approved.
- **Template administrators** have private design projects where the elements of documents, such as building blocks and processes are stored. Later, when individual administrators have finished their work the private projects are joined into a public delivery project where an entire document template and process is composed from elements contributed from different administrators.
- **Delivery testers** ensure the quality and compliance of documents and processes by executing tests in several iterations which at the end are approved by **supervisors**.
- The **delivery manager** coordinates the testing and fixing of reported problems until a delivery can be released into production.

In production, **clerks** create documents by using the delivered templates. Moreover, clerks can freely edit the content of building blocks where access rights are granted.

Document template creation

MKS provides an intuitive graphical user interface in the preferred language of the business user for designing document and process templates (Figure 5). A document template is composed from several building blocks in different languages defined by language variants, so that customer preferences can be seamlessly addressed. MKS supports the author in creating and editing the content and formatting the building blocks.

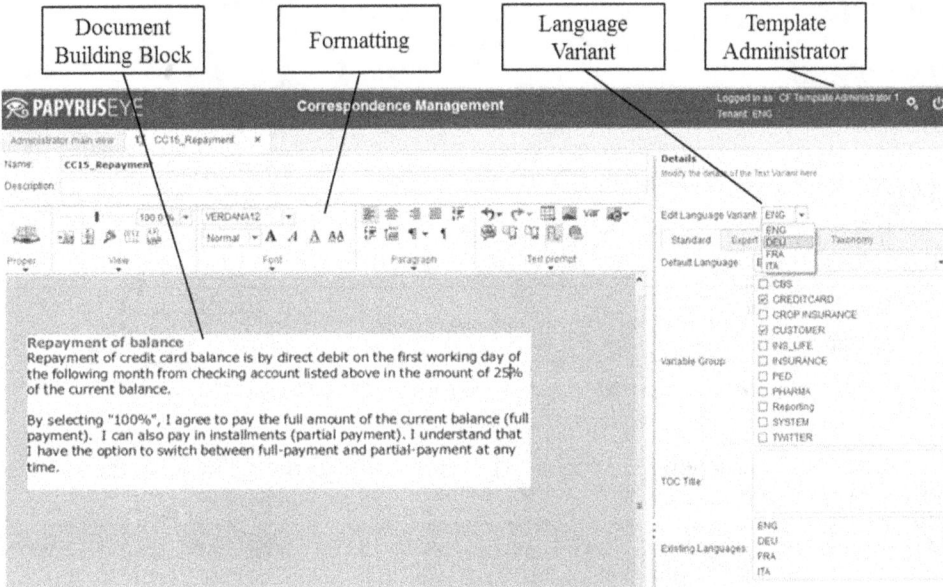

Figure 5: Template administrator creating/editing building block variants

Document instances created by clerks are driven by business processes which are also prepared by template administrators. The process assembles a document dynamically from building block templates depending on the business data for the case. Each step of a process is represented with a form allowing clerks to interact and enter case-specific data and the transitions between next process steps. In case there can be more than one step following the current step, conditions can be defined in the form of "If ... Go to ..." expressions, as shown in Figure 6 (see under "Transactions & Actions"). Moreover, each step can contain several actions defining the building blocks used in the step.

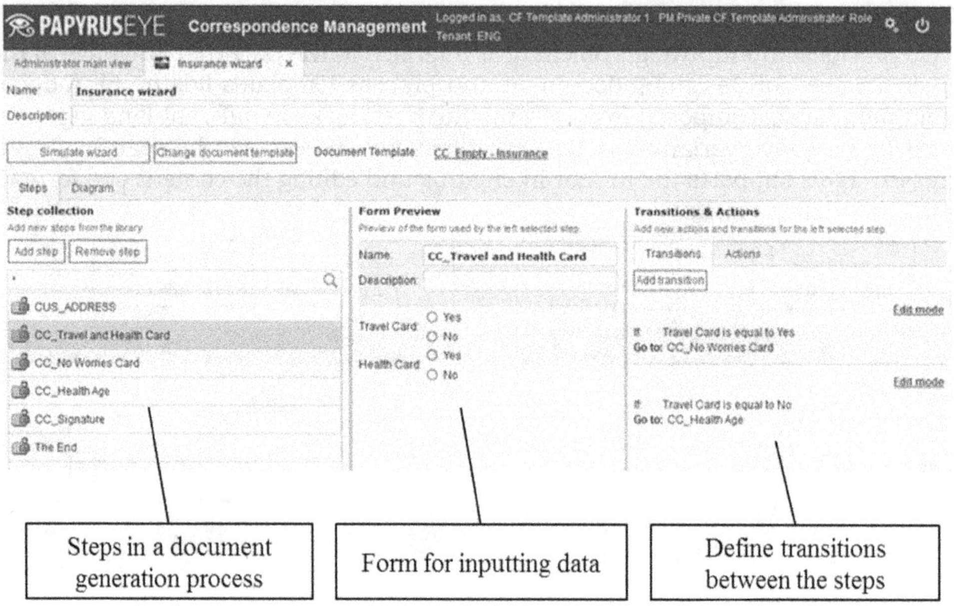

Figure 6: Template administrator creating/editing a
document business process

In a process diagram view (see Figure 7), business processes can be optionally visualized with BPM notations.

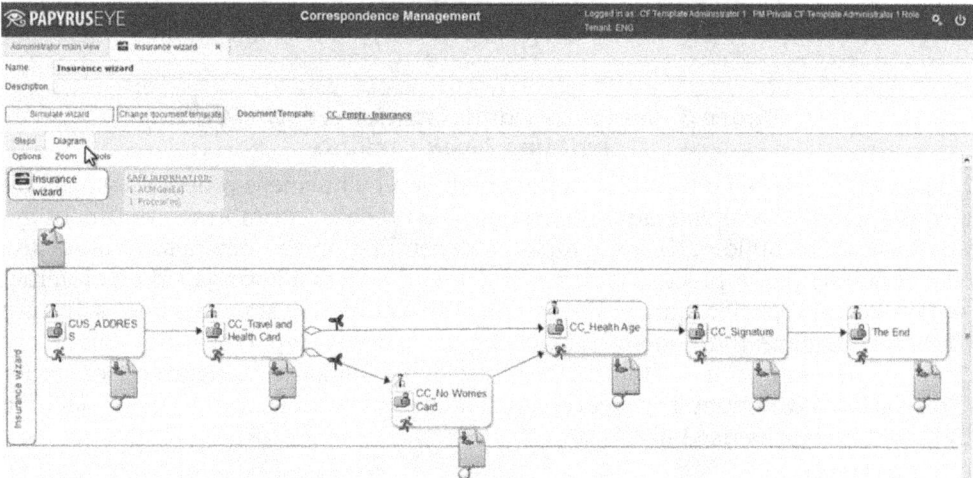

Figure 7: The defined document generation process as BPMN model

Delivery process

The template delivery is controlled by the delivery process (Figure 8). As explained in Figure 4, all templates that are created or modified by template administrators are assigned to a specific delivery which is coordinated by the delivery manager. Voting tasks are used to handle the process flexibly. Testers and supervisors issue voting results that allow the process to proceed to the next stage or return to the previous.

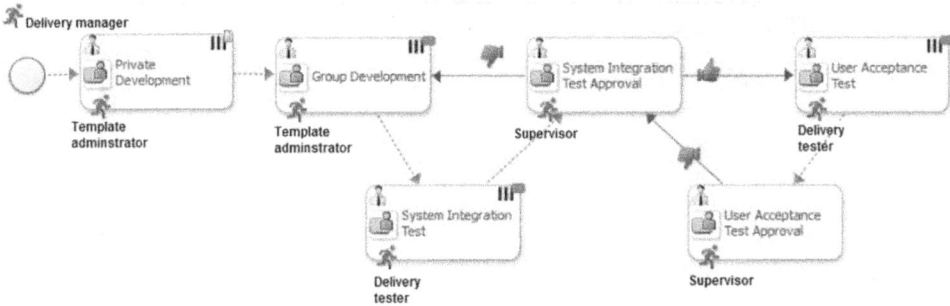

Figure 8: Document Template delivery process

Documents created by clerks

When templates are released, insurance clerks create documents based on these templates. MKS provides a set of document templates organized in a well-organized structure so that clerks can easily find a suitable template for a certain business situation (Figure 9). Each template has a preview to support clerks in choosing a suitable document.

Figure 9: Document Template selection by clerks

To generate a document, clerks follow the process defined in the template which required typically the execution of several steps to specify the key information (Figure 10). Service tasks are triggered in the background to retrieve data from business applications based on the entered information to complete the filling of the document with business data. Such backend service processes are hidden from the clerks except steps that need decisions from users.

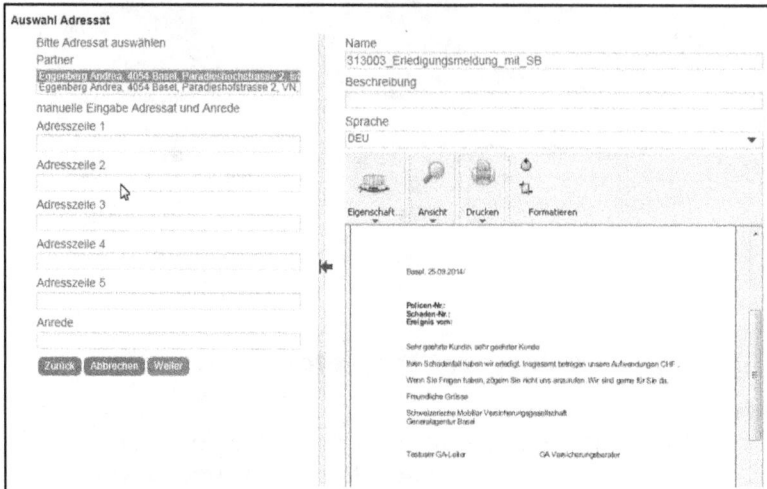

Figure 10: Execution of a process step in the document generation process

When the document process is finished, the clerk can edit building block contents where access rights allow for it (Figure 11).

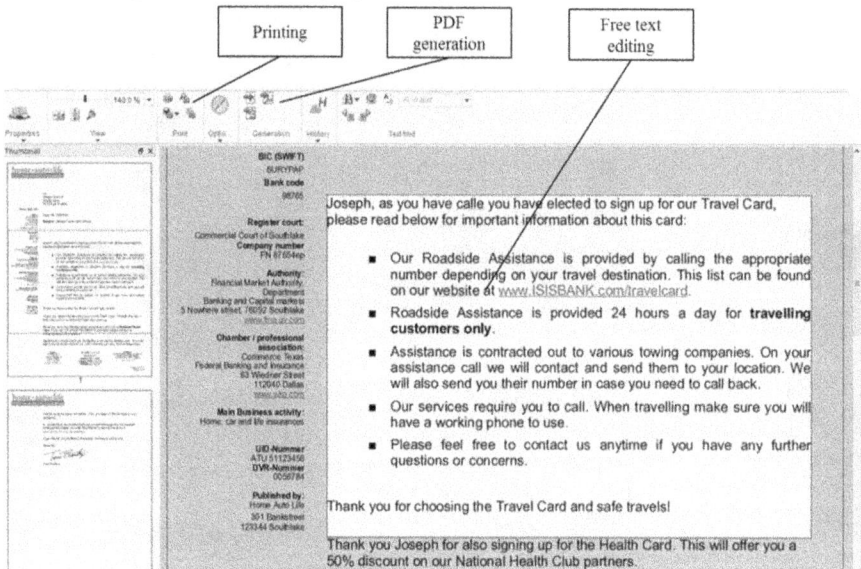

Figure 11: Content editing mode

After the document is finished, it can be locally printed, exported as PDF or sent to customers in different ways such as e-mail and fax as defined by the output channel selection step of the process.

In addition, MKS has interfaces with several business applications used in *Die Mobiliar* so that documents are automatically exchanged as needed.

4.3 ORGANIZATION & SOCIAL

Reduce the number of template administrators

MKS has a significant impact on the working life of employees in *Die Mobiliar*. The number of template administrators could be reduced four times; thus these skilled employees could be moved into other specialized business responsibilities. In the initial system, template administrators had struggled to maintain the template collection in the distributed system like copying language variants of document templates into every location with manually controlled standard file management tools. The maintenance of hundreds of templates in three languages costs a lot of time and effort, which is saved now for high value work.

Clerks can focus on customer experience

MKS changes the business operation in *Die Mobiliar* from weak process support to dynamic process enactment, from manual local work to centralized work. Steered by flexible business processes, MKS facilitates the daily work of *Die Mobiliar* with automatic and transparent business functions. Clerks do not have to waste time by manually updating different systems but utilize the centralized MKS repository to access document and process templates as needed for specific business cases. Thus, clerks do not spend time anymore on technical activities and can fully focus on the customers who are vital for the business success of *Die Mobiliar*. Any increased customer experience is the highly-appreciated consequence.

5. HURDLES OVERCOME

5.1 Management

The benefits gained from MKS are quite recognizable for *Die Mobiliar*. However, the adoption of the new system has to happen at a pace that is in alignment with the company culture. Employees were used to the former system with long-term developed habits for daily work. Changing to the new system is a paradigm change and requires the employees to accept and adapt to new activities, giving up historically grown routines. Therefore, the management of *Die Mobiliar* is much engaged in persuading team leads in the promotion of the new way of working, educating people about the benefits of MKS as accepting it as a reliable and productive system for their daily work.

5.2 Business

A huge number of templates created by MS Word in the previous system has to be migrated to MKS. Due to the historically grown number of templates and personal variants this cannot be automated. A true consolidation requires a new set of clean templates. Thus, each document template includes not only the content but an individual process for the execution by the clerks. Although essential text snippets can be migrated seamlessly into MKS, each process needs to be tested which is supported in MKS by running documents in simulation mode. Therefore, the migration from the previous system to MKS consumes one time efforts for template administrators.

5.3 Organization Adoption

Die Mobiliar provides internal trainings and tutorial videos for all employees to introduce and demonstrate MKS in a way that can be easily followed. In addition, the benefits gained from MKS are communicated to all employees. Since go-live in 2014, MKS did not have any downtime, which helps building trust into the new system for their employees.

6. BENEFITS

6.1 Cost Savings / Time Reductions

- The number of template administrators for creating and maintenance of the template collection is reduced 4 times.
- The number of documents produced per day has increased 20 times.

- MKS is integrated into several business applications used in *Die Mobiliar*. The transparent data exchanged between services and systems frees business users from the concern about data quality and synchronicity.
- MKS can be accessed both online and offline in the same platforms.

6.2 Increased Revenues

In the first phase of the project, the revenues cannot be estimated.

6.3 Quality Improvements

MKS provides a common and fully-featured platform for all business documents. Therefore, the quality of documents created by MKS has improved due to its consistent style, well-designed format and rich content. Moreover, e-delivery channels can produce documents in color for online presentation.

7. BEST PRACTICES, LEARNING POINTS AND PITFALLS

7.1 Best Practices and Learning Points

✓ *A centralized document architecture reduces efforts for maintenance of the template collection.*

✓ *Building blocks help to avoid redundancies of document templates when re-used throughout different templates.*

✓ *Language variants of building blocks make language handling seamless and worry free. Based on a flag in the customer database defining the preferred language, the system dynamically includes the appropriate language variant into each customer document and generates separate copies for each desired language.*

✓ *Daily work is better organized through the dynamically selectable process templates, supporting consistent documents and automatic services for document generation*

✓ *Integration with various business applications and services enables a single point of access through a commonly available and fully-featured document management and process platform.*

✓ *E-delivery options facilitate the delivery of documents to channels preferred by the customers*

7.2 Pitfalls

✗ *It is very important to involve business users at an early stage of the project, when the requirements of MKS are analyzed. This was not sufficiently done and caused acceptance discussions when users where exposed to not only new user interfaces but also to changed processes.*

✗ *Business users shall be responsible for the definition of user stories (Who/ What/ Why) for all document processes.*

✗ *The specification of the most important business definitions (document templates, layout, content and languages, user interface with its functions and processes) must be signed off by business user representatives. By this way, business user requirements are fully considered in first place so that involved people get familiar with the new system and accept it easily.*

8. COMPETITIVE ADVANTAGES

With MKS, a huge number of high quality documents can be produced in a short time. The business processes executed in MKS can be edited by business users without IT involvement. The centralized system containing release management can optimize the lifecycle of document templates. Thus, new templates can be released quickly to meet the business needs. MKS ensures the high-quality documents produced quickly to catch the business needs in the insurance industry. Moreover, MKS brings relief from technical operations so that business users can focus on customer experience.

9. Technology

Die Mobiliar uses the Papyrus Communication and Process Platform[1] as basis for their customized "Mobiliar Korrespondenz System" (MKS, Mobiliar Correspondence System), with full functionality for online interactive business document production and archiving. MKS is built on Papyrus WebRepository utilizing the Papyrus Adaptive Case Management (ACM) Solution and the Papyrus Business Correspondence Solution. While the correspondence solution handles the design and content of documents, the ACM solution manages the processes for the document generation with its integrated BPM capabilities.

10. The Technology and Service Providers

The MKS implementation was done solely by ISIS Papyrus Europe AG and its consultancy services handling the customization of the standard platform solution. ISIS Papyrus offers a consolidated, end-to-end solution for inbound and outbound business communication and process management, based on standard software components and solution frameworks:

- Papyrus WebRepository
- Papyrus ACM Solution
- Papyrus Business Correspondence Solution
- Papyrus Postprocessing/PrintPool
- Papyrus Server

ISIS Papyrus - Communication and Process Platform:

https://www.isis-papyrus.com/

---

[1]   http://www.isis-papyrus.com/e15/pages/software/platform-concept.html

Fujirebio Diagnostics, USA
Nominated by Wonderware, India

1. EXECUTIVE SUMMARY / ABSTRACT

Fujirebio Diagnostics, Inc. (FDI) is a premier diagnostics company and the industry leader in biomarker assays. We specialize in the clinical development, manufacturing, and commercialization of in-vitro diagnostic products for the management of human disease states with an emphasis in oncology.

FDI personnel identified a major opportunity to save time and paper by automating the acquisition of equipment data and generating electronic reports for review and approval.

With direction from FDI's executive management driving a strategic "Electronic Initiative" as a vision for future systems, a project team was assembled to define and implement a system capable of addressing a complex set of user requirements to streamline our existing paper-based GMP record system and manual data logging process with an electronic system.

A comprehensive Project Management Plan was then developed to drive the ensuing project to completion by incorporating FDI's System Development Life Cycle (SDLC) procedures to ensure that all deliverables were generated and the project completed in accordance with company requirements to comply with FDA regulations.

2. OVERVIEW

Using existing Standard Operating Procedures (SOPs) as benchmark criteria as well as current industry standards such as ANSI/ISA-95 (Enterprise - Control System Integration), and guidance from GAMP 5 and GAMP Good Practice Guidance for MES, detailed questionnaires were prepared for use during initial meetings with departmental personnel. This provided a standardized approach for documenting user requirements with the ability to easily generate a more detailed site-wide User Requirements Specification (URS).

Once the URS was completed, a request for proposal (RFP) was developed and approved for distribution to leading System Integrators (SI) experienced in delivering similar solutions for FDA-regulated companies.

Because there were several variations of system solutions as well as architectures, the vendor selection and technical analysis to identify and refine the right solution-set to meet FDI's needs was rigorous and appropriately time consuming.

After careful deliberation and analysis, a solution-set was chosen, project deliverables specified, and project activities scheduled to address the design, integration, testing, validation, and ultimate release of the system for production use.

The selection of Business Process Management (BPM) software and a supporting System Platform provided the differentiating functionality to implement the equipment monitoring system (EMS) solution chosen to ensure compliance for electronic reporting and documentation to meet regulatory agency requirements.

Using BPM software allowed us to implement an electronic production record (EPR) solution with email notification to equipment owners of warning and out of specification conditions, the documentation of comments and electronic signatures, and the routing of monthly reports for to department and QA personnel for review by exception (RBE) and electronic signature approvals. The addition of full audit trail capabilities provided us with a solution that fully complies with 21 CFR Part 11. The System Platform chosen was appropriately integrated with FDI's existing infrastructure to provide a comprehensive solution that has become a way-of-life for system users.

Measurable efficiencies and added benefits have been achieved through this system, including:

- A savings of over 1,000 man-hours per year by generating electronic records with Review By Exception (RBE) and eliminating manual data logging.
- Eliminating the need to review paper logs and charts and reducing the monthly report review cycle from over 15 hours to just minutes.
- The ability to generate, review, and store electronic record files while eliminating the need to store hundreds of paper records per month

3. BUSINESS CONTEXT

For over 20 years, Fujirebio Diagnostics, Inc. (FDI) is the trusted source of innovative solutions in clinical diagnostics. Our products form the base of a product line that has been long recognized as the *worldwide standard of excellence in cancer biomarkers*. FDI's proven manufacturing process for the production of biomarkers has made it a global partner of choice among leading diagnostics companies around the world.

Over the course of the year, FDI's 160,000- foot production facility in Malvern produces over 75 million tests that are distributed to patients throughout the world. It is an FDA-registered facility that is required to meet a variety of Title 21 Code of Federal Regulations in the USA as well as other global regulatory agency regulations. The site is both ISO 9001 and ISO 13485 certified for quality systems.

In order to meet rigorous FDI user requirements, the chosen solution needed to contain an enabling functionality to migrate our manual paper-based process to an electronic record system, address global agency regulations, manage data capture and work flows associated with the management of electronic records, and to also be scalable for the implementation of future EPR projects.

4. THE KEY INNOVATIONS

The implementation of this project has greatly impacted the entire organization and has set the stage for future innovations.

By designing a system utilizing industry standard terminology and models, the basis for design was more easily understood by vendors and suppliers. This led to adapting these models and terminology to describe FDI processes for the basis of system design.

4.1 Business

In addition to the measurable efficiencies previously described, the EMS at FDI enabled a multitude of operational changes, all of which continue to allow personnel to perform in their roles with great efficiency and flexibility, including:

- Enabling personnel to monitor equipment from their own workstations
- Being able to maintain all temperature readings in electronic records
- Notifying authorized personnel in the event of adverse temperature trends
- Generating electronic Good Manufacturing Practice (GMP) reports for review by exception
- Providing authorized personnel electronic signature capabilities to approve reports

4.2 Case Handling

Prior to the implementation of this system, all documentation comprising the monthly production record "GMP Packs" consisted of paper records with manual data logs periodically recorded by departmental personnel and paper chart recordings where instrumentation was being utilized for controlling several pieces of equipment. Every month each of 18 departments assembled these paper GMP Packs and manually reviewed all logs and charts. Comments and corrections were also made with handwritten signature approvals. Once reviewed and signed off at the departmental level, record packs from all departments were brought to Quality Assurance for final review and approval. A team of Quality Analysts provided a 100% review and approval of the data and resultant paper records.

FDI's executive team identified an electronic initiative strategy as a concept for implementing electronic records. The EPR team then identified a strong business need for this specific EMS. A project justification and ROI calculation based on implementing an infrastructure conducive to installing future applied solutions was developed for management review. The project was approved based on these justifications.

Architecture

The project team agreed on using International Society of Automation (ISA) ISA 95 and ISA 88 standards and models as guidance for system design. Personnel from the entire company were engaged to obtain their feedback and expectations from the new system. Twenty seven individuals from all departments participated in the development of the user requirements specification (URS).

Project Team

An extensive project team consisting of FDI personnel from IT, Manufacturing, Operations, Supply Chain Management, Quality Assurance, Quality Engineering, Quality Control, Product Development, and Facilities all participated in the successful implementation of this initial automated data acquisition and electronic record system.

After appointing a project manager, a comprehensive Project Management Plan was developed to provide the basis and direction for managing the System Development Life Cycle, generation of project deliverables, and management of a multitude of service providers and suppliers engaged to design, build, install, and test the system.

Business Lifecycle

The Engineering team at FDI has System Administration responsibilities as well as the overall responsibility for managing projects associated with system enhancements, added functionality, and system expansion.

IT maintains system software and infrastructure through approved SOPs. IT's System Development Life Cycle (SDLC) and Change Control SOPs provides a step-wise process for developing, implementing, and changing system in our FDA-regulated environment.

An established Project Management program provides the guidance for controlling project activities using a standardized process to ensure consistency of results and the delivery of quality solutions within budget and on schedule.

Project Success Principles

Adhering to a written project management plan driven by formal System Development Life Cycle procedures provided a basis for the successful implementation of this project to address both user requirements and regulatory compliance.

- Representatives from each department participated in the development of requirements and specifications documentation to give the project team a strong understanding of what functionality was needed for systems users.
- Weekly schedule updates with periodic project newsletters were communicated to all site personnel.
- Formal meetings with the system integrator, software supplier, and other supplier companies were conducted according to agendas with meeting minutes and notes documented.
- SDLC documentation was thoroughly reviewed and ultimately approved for each activity.
- Timely risk analysis and mitigation was managed as an integral part of the project.
- All system users and administrators were appropriately trained.
- All users and system documentation is accessible on demand.
- Processes and procedures were established to ensure that ongoing system management, administration, and maintenance are in place to ensure that the system continues to operate as required.
- Change control procedures are in place to ensure that enhancements and revisions to the system are managed to the same high standards as the original project.

4.3 Organization & Social

The impact to employees is best described in the words of a lead manufacturing document analyst at Fujirebio; "Before the EMS system went in, I was spending about 15 or more hours manually reviewing the GMP packs. After the system, I went from hours to minutes."

"The key benefits of the system are the electronic signatures with the review by exception, and not having to worry about missing papers or chart recorders. The system has just made my life a whole lot easier."

The new EMS relieved staff of the tasks related to manually logging equipment parameters and reviewing paper logs and charts on a daily basis. The amount of time saved is significant and is detailed later in this document.

5. HURDLES OVERCOME

5.1 Management

Executive management at FDI provided the strategic direction and positive environment that allowed this project to move forward and thrive. As previously stated, FDI's executive team identified an electronic initiative strategy as a concept for implementing electronic records. The project team embraced this concept to design and implemented the solution described in this document.

5.2 Business

Perhaps the key business metric of the EMS is the time saved as a result of going paperless, which is especially important in a regulated industry. With the BPM software and system Platform chosen, FDI is able to comply with 21 CFR Part 11 for electronic records and electronic signatures.

5.3 Organization Adoption

Prior to going live with the system, a comprehensive document package was completed, robust qualification testing was executed for validation, and more than 60 users were trained. After formalizing a system support team and process, the system was then operated in parallel with existing, manual SOPs for three months. In addition to system level training, we also included training on our electronic signa-ture (e-signature) and electronic record (e-record) SOP which is based on 21 CFR Part 11 requirements. Comparison of e-records to paper records was integrated in our approach to system qualification for validation.

At the end of three months, the user community was comfortable with the new system and was also eager to make the transition to e-records after seeing how much easier it is to use compared to the time previously spent in manually logging data and reviewing stacks of paper records. Migration to the electronic record sys-tem was then made official with manual activities relegated to a back-up role. Ex-isting SOPs previously used for generating manual logs and paper records are now be used only if there is an operational interruption to the automated system.

6. BENEFITS

6.1 Cost Savings / Time Reductions

The new EMS has relieved staff of the tasks related to manually logging equipment parameters and reviewing paper logs and charts on a daily basis. The amount of time saved from the initial implementation of the EMS is significant and equates to annual savings of:

Activity	Time Saved
Logging Data	439 hours
Check Recorder Charts	230 hours
Change Charts	30 hours
Prep & Review Doc Pack	89 hours
Dept. Review Doc Pack	112 hours
QA Review Doc Pack	192 hours
Total	**1,092 hours**

In total the equipment monitoring system saves about 1,100 man hours per year:

- The tasks related to manually logging equipment parameters and re-viewing paper logs and charts were eliminated and reduced data re-viewing time from 15+ hours to just minutes for both departmental and QA reviews and approvals.
- Subsequent expansion of the original EMS now produces an esti-mated time savings of over 2300 hours per year.

6.2 Increased Revenues

The Return on Investment (ROI) justification of this project is based on the cost savings associated with the reduction in time to perform prior activities. With our company in a growth mode, these time savings have allowed company personnel to do more work without increasing headcount in certain areas. This has had a positive impact directly to bottom line financials.

6.3 Quality Improvements

As an operations information infrastructure, this system is already being used to provide data input for continuous improvement. The EMS contains an often-used functionality to filter and retrieve historical data as needed for analysis and the generation of graphs and reports. This capability allows users to more easily analyze operations and fine-tune controls to increase equipment efficiencies. Current plans include extending system operations to Manufacturing for process analysis and operations improvements through a Process Analytical Technology (PAT) Framework. Data analysis of Critical Process Parameters can then be correlated to Critical Quality Attributes (CQA) to better control manufacturing processes and reduce product quality variability.

7. BEST PRACTICES, LEARNING POINTS AND PITFALLS

After completion and release of the system for production use, project team members met to identify lessons learned and establish best practices to implement future system functionality and enhancements.

The objective of this exercise was to identify ways of improving on the implementation of future EMS projects to:
- Increase overall efficiency of resources
- Decrease the number of document revisions
- Standardize activities and documentation
- Develop best practices for working among groups both internally at FDI and with our external service providers, suppliers, and vendors

7.1 Best Practices and Learning Points

✓ *Implement a structured System Development Life Cycle (SDLC) methodology to standardize the process for delivering systems to meet project quality requirements.*

✓ *Generate a detailed User Requirements Specification (URS) at the start of each project to capture feedback and system requirements from the user community.*

✓ *Scope of Work – a comprehensive scope document should be prepared for each service provider and supplier and mutually agreed upon*

✓ *Use tables, work flow diagrams, spreadsheets, and associated tools to clearly depict functional and design details.*

✓ *Perform a Risk Assessment for all system changes to ensure that any business, operations, technical, or regulatory risks are appropriately mitigated*

✓ *Ensure that sufficient time is allocated to rigorously review and approve all project documentation, especially those related to design, installation, and testing of the system.*

✓ *Conduct formal design reviews at various stages of system development and reconcile results back to user requirements to ensure the design meets agreed on requirements.*

✓ *Comprehensive testing must be performed during project design and execution to find problems as early as possible. Consider integration testing, Factory Acceptance Testing (FAT), Site Acceptance Testing (SAT) or Commissioning, Installation Qualification (IQ), Operational Qualification (OQ), and Performance Qualification (PQ) as required for your particular industry*

✓ *Properly train all system users and administrators before using system.*

✓ *Ensure all testing is properly documented, reviewed and approved before issuing a system release for use in production.*

✓ *Implement a formally documented Change Control process to properly manage future system changes and revisions.*

7.2 Pitfalls

✗ *Not including the user community at the beginning of the project and all through implementation.*

× *Jumping to conclusions to solve a problem without truly analyzing the issue at hand.*

× *Forgetting to fully document system design, installation details, configuration, revisions, and other "as-built" changes.*

× *Not verifying required licenses were properly installed before system testing begins.*

× *Not following Best Practices, Project Management Plans, and an SDLC methodology.*

8. COMPETITIVE ADVANTAGES

Justification is required for the approval of new projects. Criteria for this justification are easily achieved when the solution provides value-add benefits that provide a competitive advantage and address:

- Enhancing Product Quality
- Increasing Operational Efficiencies
- Decreasing Operational Costs
- Ensuring Regulatory Compliance

The implementation of this project established a benchmark within our company regarding the value to all operations for utilizing a workflow based BPM solution. The ability to generate e-records and route them for review and e-signature approval in a timely manner provides FDI with a value-added solution that is now being expanded to other applications in the company.

We are currently kicking off a new project to expand the EMS into our Manufacturing domain to monitor in-process parameters. This new Manufacturing Monitoring System (MMS) will operate in parallel to the EMS and provide the same benefits to manufacturing and operations going forward. User requirements are being documented and will provide the basis for design for new electronic production records with new business process workflows to address the justification criteria previously described

Every day thousands of people all over the world are living a better life because of the products we manufacture at Fujirebio. The solution provided through the EMS helps to ensure the quality of our products to all patients.

9. TECHNOLOGY

Future EMS applications were identified early into the initial planning phase of this new system. Visioning this "future state" at the start of the project allowed our team to design an architecture that is appropriate, flexible, and scalable for adding new application solutions.

The EMS implementation consists of 4 servers, 1 engineering workstation, a data collection Programmable Logic Controller (PLC), and now 20 PLC Input / Output Panels. A dedicated Ethernet network was installed in Operations by FDI to enable communications between the data collection / concentrator PLC, I/O panels, and the application server. FDI system users access the EMS via secured logon through their own workstations using web browsers.

At the start of the project, only the Business Process Network and user workstations existed. The balance of the architecture was installed with the initial EMS installation. The current system architecture is depicted in the following graphic.

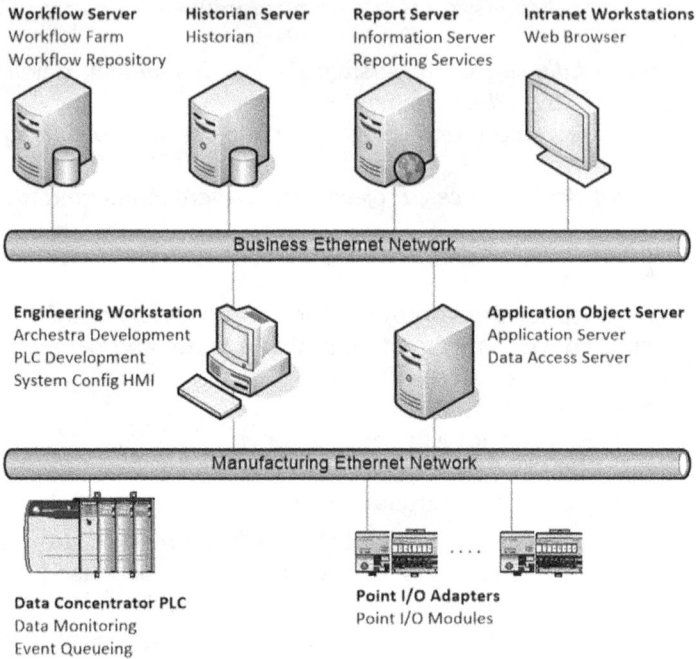

Workflow Server
Workflow Farm
Workflow Repository

Historian Server
Historian

Report Server
Information Server
Reporting Services

Intranet Workstations
Web Browser

Business Ethernet Network

Engineering Workstation
Archestra Development
PLC Development
System Config HMI

Application Object Server
Application Server
Data Access Server

Manufacturing Ethernet Network

Data Concentrator PLC
Data Monitoring
Event Queueing

Point I/O Adapters
Point I/O Modules

10. THE TECHNOLOGY AND SERVICE PROVIDERS

Wonderware Skelta BPM is at the heart of Fujirebio Diagnostics' EMS. What it does is digitize and automate FDI's manual processes that include people, equipment and systems, based on a sophisticated Business Process Management (BPM) foundation standard. This enables staff to generate electronic records and file them automatically. The combined functionality of Wonderware Skelta BPM with Wonderware System Platform enables Fujirebio to model, execute, analyze and improve work processes, enhancing collaboration, productivity, and innovation.

System integration engineering and design services were provided by EZSoft, Inc. with support from Wonderware North.

Each day, companies such as Fujirebio Diagnostics execute complex work flows involving both people and systems. Consistent execution of critical work leads directly to better operating performance. With Wonderware Skelta BPM, FDI is able to route critical reports for review and approval, ensuring that vital work flows are executed correctly every time. This drives accountability and better stewardship within the organization.

References:

Standards and Guidance:

1. ANSI/ISA-5.1-2009, Instrumentation Symbols and Identification
2. ANSI/ISA-95.00.01-2000, Enterprise-Control System Integration Part 1: Models and Terminology
3. ANSI/ISA-95.00.03-2005, Enterprise-Control System Integration, Part 3: Models of Manufacturing Operations Management
4. GAMP 5, A Risk-Based Approach to Compliant GxP Computerized Systems
5. GAMP Good Practice Guide: Manufacturing Execution Systems – A Strategic and Program Management Approach

INTA, Argentina

PECTRA Technology Inc., USA

EXECUTIVE SUMMARY / ABSTRACT

In order to optimize institutional management, INTA[1] (National Institute of Agricultural Technology) developed the "Administration Modernization" project which included implementation of a Business Process Management System (BPMS) parallel to modification of internal regulations and structure in order to reduce the complexity of processes, while maintaining legal protection and improving the information system. More than five years after the implementation of the BPMS, INTA's National Directorate for Information Systems, Communication, and Quality reports multiple benefits: greater adoption of BPMS (rising from one to 30 implemented processes); 1400% growth in number of users and the incorporation of 15 regional centers, five research sites, 50 research stations, 16 institutes, and more than 300 extension units; greater employee satisfaction (99%) due to the reduction of administrative and manual tasks—mostly tracking the status of internal procedures.

The project made it possible to integrate and digitize the information from multiple applications and manual procedures. A BPMS Center of Excellence (CoE) was created and it continues optimizing and automating processes. Reports and control panels for all processes were configured.

Today the BPMS implemented at INTA manages more than 7,500 daily automated process transactions that manage funds of up to $700 billion and involve internal and external organization users, showing improvements in time management, organizational transparency, and ease of access to the information.

OVERVIEW

Prior to the implementation of the BPMS, INTA administrative processes were long and bureaucratic, due to the complexity of the organizational structure. This caused serious difficulties in issues affecting various steps and the generation of information. INTA did not have a network infrastructure in the diverse points of operation in the country, management of the various operating units was uncoordinated, with units operating as isolated departments, and processes resulting in bureaucratic and burdensome management.

The project consisted of an Integrated Management System, through the implementation of the BPMS as a processes and systems integration solution for managing internal procedures, which also allows for integration and digitalization of the information coming from multiple applications and manual procedures.

Currently, INTA has a BPMS Center of Excellence (CoE), consisting of specialists that transform the needs of the organization and help incorporate the technology necessary to automate processes. To date, more than 25 processes have been automated and more than one process is automated every month.

---

[1] The National Institute of Agricultural Technology (INTA, by its Spanish acronym) is a dependent agency of the National Ministry of Agriculture, Livestock, and Fisheries. Its main functions are to generate, adapt, and transfer technology, knowledge, and learning processes for the agribusiness, forestry, and agricultural areas.

Through the Business Activity Monitoring (BAM) tools provided by the BPMS, reports and control panels for all processes were configured to improve activity monitoring and control. Since the BPMS architecture allows interaction from mobile devices, users can participate in processes from different access points.

With the implementation of the BPMS, INTA administrates: 9,600 internal users, more than 22,000 users outside the organization, an average of 500,000 transactions per year and up to 7,500 transactions per day, and it also reports numerous benefits, including:

- Time reduction: processes that took weeks now require hours or minutes.
- Cost reduction in management time and use of paper documents.
- Increased productivity: elimination of activities that do not add value to employee management; automatization of manual activities.
- Simplification and increased efficiency of procedures for employees.
- Transparency in management and access to information.
- Effective management processes: workflow integration to create productive, fast, and well-organized processes.
- Service quality: providing the necessary tools to become an administration focused on its core activities—projects.
- Strategic information: the automatization and transparency achieved allows access to key information to make critical decisions, enabling precise planning and control of resources and costs.
- Tracking of online transactions.
- Measurement: BAM tools make it possible to have measurable results for responsible use of budgets, and enable time measurement in order to identify areas of opportunity for improvement.
- Participation from any location through implementation of processes from mobile devices.

BUSINESS CONTEXT

The National Institute of Agricultural Technology (INTA) is a decentralized government agency, with operational and financial autonomy, dependent on the National Ministry of Agriculture, Livestock, and Fisheries. Its main functions are to generate, adapt, and transfer technology, knowledge, and learning processes for the agribusiness, forestry, and agricultural areas. INTA generates information and technologies applied to processes and products, which are then transferred to the producers.

Currently, INTA represents a key contribution to the agricultural, agrifood, and agribusiness sectors. Its efforts are focused on innovation as a driver of development and it integrates capacities to enhance inter-agency cooperation, generate knowledge and technologies, and put them at service of the sector through its extension, information, and communications systems.

INTA has more than 9.000 employees and has a presence in the five ecoregions of Argentina (Northwest, Northeast, Cuyo, Pampas, and Patagonia), through a structure that comprises a head office, 15 regional centers, 5 research sites, 50 research stations, 16 institutes, and more than 300 extension units.

"Projects are the heart of INTA. The organization exists for the projects. Any activity has a direct or indirect impact on information management for the producer," says Juan Manuel Fernandez Arocena (National Assistant Director of Information Systems, Communications, and Quality (DNA SICyC-INTA, by the Spanish acronyms). *"The mission and purpose was to work under a normalized system but one which does not involve an unnecessary workload. Because certain administrative rules*

were established, all they did was bureaucratize. The idea was that people could naturalize technology."

From the Quality and Processes Department, whose objective was to modernize the institutional management, serious problems were detected in relation to the generation of information, arising from the complexity of the organizational structure.

INTA did not have a network infrastructure in the diverse points of operation in the country, the management of the various operating units was uncoordinated, with units operating as isolated departments, and the processes resulted in bureaucratic and burdensome management.

Prior to the implementation of PECTRA BPM Savia, activities were performed manually and by means of written documents, leading to high indirect costs in monitoring, validation, and submission of information. Both administrative staff and researchers devoted hours to the managing and monitoring procedures.

It was very difficult to see the status of a process. The internal steps or procedures involved an extensive approval process. Generally, each of these procedures was handled by isolated systems and managed on paper, going through various instances of approval in various offices in the country, taking weeks to be resolved, regardless of complexity. These applications used to generate huge traffic of e-mails and follow-up calls. There were numerous administrative positions per unit dedicated to these steps, assisting the authorities in revision of the documentation.

Therefore, it was necessary to optimize processes and have tools that integrated the applications and databases from the systems and allowed them to develop an integrated management system which involved all administrative and project-related activities and systems.

THE KEY INNOVATIONS

Business

Adoption of the BPMS allowed the INTA's National Directorate for Information Systems, Communication, and Quality to have a positive impact on their mission to "develop search and technology innovation actions to enhance the competitiveness and sustainable rural development of the country." Also, the deployment of a process-based approach contributed directly to the following:

Quality management: improvement cycles applied to processes optimize management and consequently, the provision of services provided to producers (farmers) by the INTA.

- Digital management: using new information technologies and telecommunications allowed automation of management related to the inner workings of the organization.
- Lower cost management: more efficient processes by reducing activities which do not add value, lowering administrative costs, and optimizing resource allocation.
- Regulatory improvement management: eliminating excessive processes and ensuring greater agility as a key factor in boosting overall competitiveness.
- Transparent management: opening information for consultation made the management transparent for decision making.

Internally, it brought about an important transformation in the way the organization works and in its employees' attitudes.

The decentralized application of processes has allowed the INTA to overcome the barrier of geographical dispersion, allowing it spread operations out beyond the limits of the central office, connecting the headquarters and operational staff throughout the country. Everyone is simply connected by the Internet.

Thus, INTA has achieved:

- Full knowledge of all the activities carried out in each extension unit and research site.
- National standardization of activities, eliminating tasks which do not add value.
- Detailed follow-up and control of resources through a technological platform. Mainly of processes that manage large budgets and impact a large number of contributors and third parties.
- Availability of means of work—online and over the Internet—open for consultation.

Other important achievements and effects of the BPMS Project are described below in the following sections of this document.

Organization & Social

Thanks to the Administration Modernization Project, the INTA structure was aligned with its goal. Today, there are process reference models in various units and locations. At the beginning, INTA created an interdisciplinary team of professionals from different fields: Processes and Quality, General Administration Management, HR, and Systems (IT). Currently, INTA has a BPMS Center of Excellence, made up of experts who transform the needs of the organization and help incorporate technology needed for process automation. Mainly operating in the Processes and Quality area, the CoE manages the integrated management system and provides internal consulting on this tool, and in different units and locations, where experts act as points of reference for the processes applicable to each.

From 2012 to the present, the coordination of processes has shown sustained growth, currently publishing more than one computerized process monthly. Each process that has been deployed contributes to an increase in the efficiency and efficacy of the operation of our organization.

As Raúl Kremer, Manager of Processes and Quality at INTA, says, *"Each process is an invitation to transparency, going paperless, traceability, and making the most of our resources. Each process allows the areas involved to lighten their workload, as well as the opportunity to redistribute the resources and activities of their contributors in order to generate new significant contributions."*

As part of the benefits obtained, it was possible to adjust a complex institutional structure to a computerized format of profiles (previously, they did not exist), adapting the most important systems to exchange information with the workflow, being forced into keeping an updated maintenance of data of institutional interest and at one site.

"We manage using 'pillars of implementation' such as HR Assistants, Unit Managers, and IT experts. We also trained process managers, unit employees acting as a connection to the management for all development and maintenance stages that formally include, manage, and solve processes," points out Raúl Kremer.

The BPMS Project has allowed INTA's contributors to automatize operational tasks, increasing the productivity and efficiency of public employees, and fostering communication and cooperation among different areas participating in the processes involved. In other words, doing more in less time and reducing paper use and administrative expenses.

Overall, the results of user and operating staff surveys show an increase in user satisfaction, which now has reached 99% of employees satisfied.

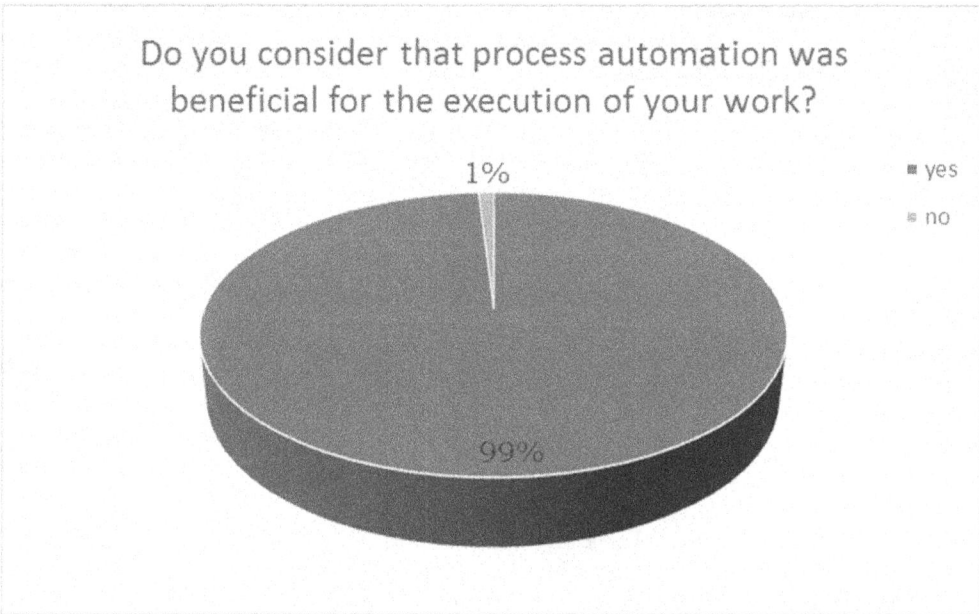

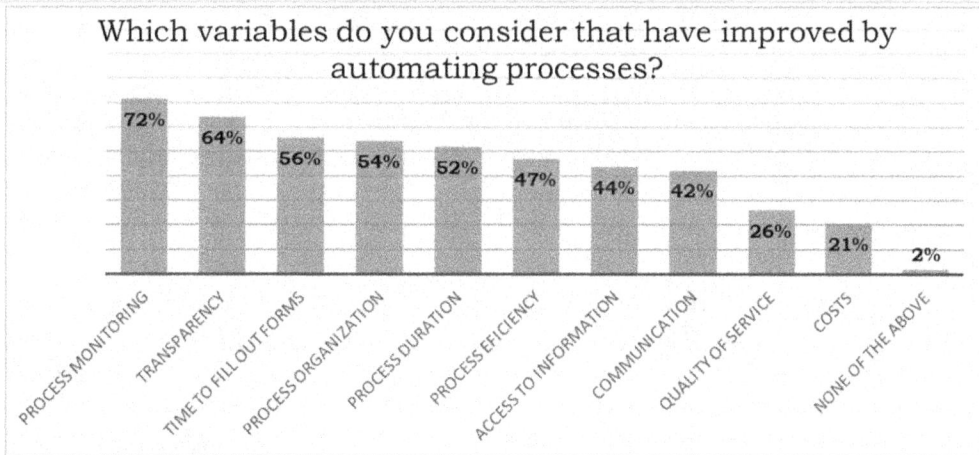

Do you consider that process automation was beneficial for the execution of your work?

1%

■ yes
■ no

99%

Which variables do you consider that have improved by automating processes?

PROCESS MONITORING	TRANSPARENCY	TIME TO FILL OUT FORMS	PROCESS ORGANIZATION	PROCESS DURATION	PROCESS EFICIENCY	ACCESS TO INFORMATION	COMMUNICATION	QUALITY OF SERVICE	COSTS	NONE OF THE ABOVE
72%	64%	56%	54%	52%	47%	44%	42%	26%	21%	2%

HURDLES OVERCOME

At the beginning, the deployment of the project was complex. It required numerous meetings in order to engage and train all people involved who did not have the time or commitment needed to participate in the data survey and automatization process.

Currently, success and results demonstrated by the automatization of processes are bringing about wider adoption and commitment by different agencies, which make change management easy. In this sense, CoE is responsible for internally spreading the results of other processes in order to reduce resistance to change. Nowadays, the whole organization is committed to and involved in the automatization of processes, from administrative employees to National Unit Directors. It has defined "pillars of implementation" or points of reference from different areas and specialties, who act as a connection to the management for all development and maintenance stages that formally include, manage, and solve processes. Every month CoE receives numerous requests for automatization.

Each process involves data survey, computerization, training, and deployment stages. After this, approximately six months of maturity are required (improvement iterations made by administrators, analysts, and programmers), which are followed by a stage of baseline maintenance.

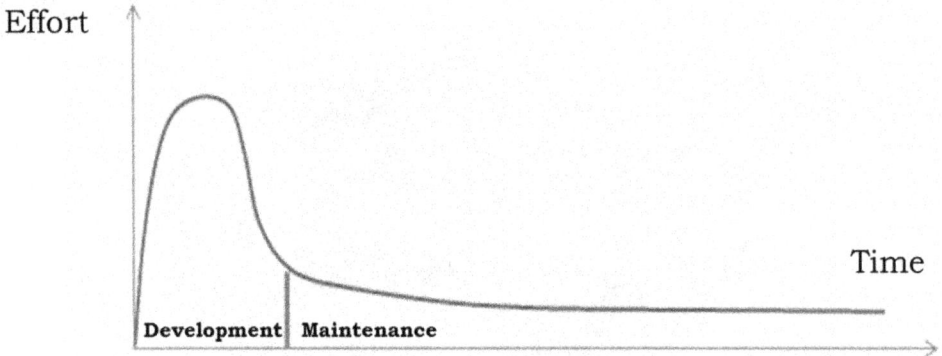

The above graphic shows the effort distribution for process development and maintenance. After an initial period of six months, approximately, in which there is a very high level of exchange between administrators and programmers, is a period of baseline maintenance. During this period, a level of response in order to provide answers to issues and queries by users should be maintained.

"Today we are reaching the limit of our capacity and we do not want to be a bottleneck for our own goals," states Raúl Kremer. That is why they are using a prioritization matrix of processes to automatize them, according to the impact on the organization (number of users and resources it affects) and their complexity.

BENEFITS

The deployment of PECTRA BPM Savia has brought INTA important benefits related to operating efficiency, allowing the organization to focus on its core activities.

Raúl Kremer, Manager of Processes and Quality (INTA), states the following: *"Clear goals towards management computerization through processes have led to the alignment of the organizational structure and the creation of specific tools, which are bearing their fruits. We are managing to systematize our work and focus on long-term quality management. PECTRA contributes to the integrated management system and provides us the foundation to define the profiles' position of a complex institutional structure, linking diverse computer systems of units through processes."*

Cost Savings / Time Reductions

Time optimization and productivity:
- 1200% reduction in administrative management time: processing that used to take weeks now requires hours or even minutes.
- 200% reduction in hours used in report generation thanks to the BAM tools.
- Integration with existing computer systems allowed a 40% acceleration of process management.

Generally, INTA has demonstrated a significant reduction of administrative activities, by 58%, eliminating those which do not add value, such as duplicate reports, filling out forms, and sending them by messenger services or mail.

Cost reduction:
- Of hours/staff invested in the task of report generation (45% of time reduction)
- Of data transmission
- Of courier service and fax (total reduction)
- Of telephone calls (by 60%)
- Of supplies needed for report generation (paper, equipment, etc.)
- Of opportunity, when substantive activities are left undone: 400 administrative employees ceased to play a role in follow up processes.

Increased Revenues

Although the INTA is a non-profit organization, its processes involve managing funds worth up to US$700,000,000 for projects that directly affect farmers and families. The "Agricultural Change" (Cambio Rural) project manages subsidies that affect 33,000 beneficiary families. The projects are regulated in real time. Thanks to the implementation of the BPM, farmers can download updates from their own homes. Thus, the Ministry of Agriculture can have access to the updated and online information on the current impact of the subsidies granted.

Quality Improvements
- Increased productivity: eliminating activities that do not add value to employee management, and automatization of manual activities.
- Simplification and increased efficiency of procedures for employees.
- Transparency in management and access to information.
- Effective management processes: it integrates workflows to create productive and fast processes which are rigorously organized.
- Service quality: providing the necessary tools to become an administration focused on its core activities— projects.
- Strategic information: the automatization and transparency achieved allows access to key information to make critical decisions, enabling precise planning and control of resources and costs.
- Online status procedure tracking.
- Measurement: BAM tools make it possible to have measurable results for responsible use of budgets, and enable time measurement in order to identify areas of opportunity for improvement.
- Regulatory approval of the local, state and regional technology.
- Efficiency of the current technological systems maximization.
- Process definition, design, and monitoring in a digital system and online documentation.

Best Practices, Learning Points And Pitfalls

A year ago, new BPMS features were implemented which allow process analysts, after basic training, to create forms that work as an interface between users and processes, automating 90% of the processes without the intervention of an IT technician, and a great part of the maintenance performed dynamically.

Since 2012, training courses have been carried out to spread "how to be an expert automating process." This year employees developed 100% of a testing process during the two days of the training course.

Because there were numerous permanent incidents, we developed a new process portal, achieving higher speed, better parameters for future needs, bringing advantages for today and tomorrow.

Recently, the first phase of the "Rural Change II" process was released. This process adds 1,870 new external users and links to external agencies.

Each major process and each demanding client push the CoE to improve its tools and develop new methods that can later be adapted to apply to all processes.

Indicator	2012	2015	Evolution (Q)	Evolution (%)
Automated processes	1	30	+29	3000%
Number of users INTA	650	9625	+8975	1481%
Number of external users	5	1869	+1864	37380%
Amount of annual transactions	4.471	501.798	+497.318	11223%

COMPETITIVE ADVANTAGES

Thanks to the BPM project, the INTA's National Directorate for Information Systems, Communication, and Quality can analyze ongoing activities in real time to make the necessary corrections to the current processes in a simple and agile way. Thanks to this flexibility, the office can adapt to the constant changes in the social, political, economic, and regulatory environments, enhancing responsiveness and its image before society.

The foregoing translates into better services rendered to the agricultural sector in with shorter response times to the demands of the context, which in turn enhances farmer competitiveness, allowing the country to reach greater potential and opportunities to gain access to regional and international markets.

TECHNOLOGY

The technology used was PECTRA BPM Savia, with the goal of simplifying the implementation of process management in organizations, facilitating analysis, data collection, design, implementation, automatization, and monitoring, and optimization of INTA processes.

The abovementioned BPM Suite allowed for:
- Integrating the BPMS with CASE tools to generate forms developed by the INTA team and with internal systems of agencies such as the ERP and HR systems.
- Integrating the BPMS with external agency systems such as the Federal Administration of Public Revenue (AFIP, by its Spanish acronym) http://www.afip.gob.ar/ws/
- Managing different types of processes on the same platform.
- Integrating process execution from mobile devices.
- Setting performance indicators for managerial monitoring of organization processes so as to detect bottlenecks and to support decision-making.
- Integrating all INTA agencies by means of remote access over the Internet and doing so under a scheme that favors transparency.
- Speeding up procedures on all operating levels of the organization because it manages online information officially, in a timely manner, and reliably for fulfilling tasks and essential operating programs.
- Having search mechanisms, report-generation possibilities, help features,

- collaboration spaces for comments and observations.
- Having centralized and systematized information to quickly obtain critical management indicators.
- Being 100% supported on web technology, working on desktop web browsers and on mobile devices.
- Having a graphic process designer, working independently of the main engine using the BPMN standard.
- Having user, role, and profile management tools that are easy-to-use and allow incorporation of pre-existing IT security in the organization.
- Having an integrated user security system with an Active Directory, which simplified IT security management.
- Using the BPMS service layer to create a customized portal adapted to the agency's specific needs.

THE TECHNOLOGY AND SERVICE PROVIDERS

The project was developed by the CoE created within INTA and the technology provider was PECTRA Technology.

PECTRA Technology Inc.: a company specializing in Process Management, with over 15 years of experience in the market and 150 successful implementations in the USA, Argentina, Mexico, Panama, Colombia, Spain, Paraguay and Chile. We have an extensive network of partners in the entire Latin American region and we provide services to more than 80,000 end users who, in turn, serve 6,000,000+ users/customers. For more information, please visit: www.pectra.com.

Ministry of Interior, Colombia

Nominated by AuraPortal, Spain

1. EXECUTIVE SUMMARY / ABSTRACT

The platform meets the needs of legal representatives from over 5000 religious entities, which according to the figures estimated by the Interior's Public Information Bureau, agglomerate over 10 million parishioners.

The Ministry's religious entity process was confusing for the general public. This situation was exploited by unscrupulous people who acted as intermediaries in managing the process and charged very high rates for their services. Furthermore, it was difficult maintaining updated information in the public record which led to circumstances of misinformation and duplication problems.

The Religious Affairs processes were analyzed, developed, tested and put into service on time; and in March 2015 the Ministry was able to offer the free online certificate of recognition of legal status to non-Catholic religious entities.

Both the Ministry and citizens are pleased with the results. Now, thanks to the automation of these processes, requested Legal Entity recognition certificates are issued within a few minutes.

The certificates are sent via e-mail free of charge. This constitutes an important alignment with the Ministry's mission of transparency, effectiveness and efficiency, hereby providing the citizens optimal services.

2. OVERVIEW

The Ministry of Interior of Colombia is responsible for the internal sector which involves other affiliated and related entities; Religious Affairs is one of its mission areas.

Juan Fernando Cristo, the Minister of the Interior, invited all the churches and religions of Colombia to unite for peace. Furthermore, for the first time in history, the country's non-Catholic churches submitted their proposals for resolving Colombia's internal conflict to the National Government through the Ministry of Interior.

Following this, in compliance with the Online Government guidelines and the requirements of the Anti-Corruption and Citizen Care Plan, the Plan for efficient Administration Act and Zero paperwork, the Ministry of Interior of Colombia's OPI (Office of Public Information) systems group and the Legal Office implemented an administrative system for Religious Affairs proceedings.

Before this implementation, the difficulty in accessing information made the Ministry's proceedings relating to religious entities confusing for the general public. This situation was exploited by unscrupulous people who acted as intermediaries to manage the process and charged very high rates for their services.

Furthermore, the intermediaries often charged up to 1000% more for the Certificate of Recognition as a Legal Entity than the usual cost of the certificate.

To address the problem, the Ministry of Interior, which already had an intelligent Business Process Management (iBPMS) platform in operation for other projects, including their process for monitoring and managing electoral complaints and denunciations known as URIEL (Immediate Reception Unit for Electoral Transparency), launched a high-impact solution for the general public which fulfilled the Ministry's missionary goals.

Religious Affairs processes were analyzed, developed, tested and put into operation in record time and without any programming (zero code); and in August 2015 the Ministry of Interior initiated the online system for issuing Recognition of Legal Status Certificates on their iBPMS platform.

The platform meets the needs of legal representatives from over **5000 religious entities,** which according to the figures estimated by the Interior's Public Information Bureau (OIPI), agglomerate over **10 million parishioners.**

3. BUSINESS CONTEXT

The problems were those common to the administrative management of paper documents that require multiple actions and involve extensive documentation with many variations and exceptions.

The geographical conditions also needed to be taken into consideration. Colombia has an area five times greater than that of Great Britain, extensive mountain ranges, tropical forests and a significant rural population posing further difficulties for administrative proceedings.

The management issues concerned the large volume of documents and information related to the religious entity procedures: their recognition as a legal entity, statutory reform logs, legal representative updates and changes of address, among many others. All these procedures require updating or the creation of a record in the Public Registry of non-Catholic religious entities protected by the Ministry of Interior.

Moreover, it was difficult to keep the records updated in the Public Registry resulting in circumstances of misinformation and a lack of data unity.

Due to this context, procedures could take longer than a month to complete and results were costly and complicated for the applicant, often requiring them to travel long distances.

4. THE KEY INNOVATIONS

The innovations that had the biggest impact for the entity, its employees and the public were:

Online Processing

- Online Processing, via the Ministry's public Web, enables church representatives to make Religious Affairs applications simply, quickly and cost free.
- This modality benefits 20% of the Colombian population that belong to a non-Roman Catholic religion or belief.

Distributed Treatments

Religious Affairs Case Management is very complex and requires the combined execution of six processes and 44 sub-processes. In unison these processes can solve any eventuality.

Using Distributed Treatment technology, these processes can flow in harmony and all actions are synchronized. The system is responsible for changing the flow from one process to another at any time in accordance with the diverse conditions that arise, combining personalized management for each individual applicant and mass management (to optimize certain proceedings), and its return and delivery of information to the original processes, ensuring work optimization by the comprehensive automation and coordination of all the actions performed.

The technology, known as Distributed Treatments, is explained later in this document.

Work Automation

In addition to all the advantages of working with a BPMS, the functionality that makes a Project most effective is the capacity to automate the majority of the activities involved in the processes.

One of the automation features that had the biggest impact on the Project was the System Tasks feature (these tasks are performed directly by the system through process motors and without any human intervention). This results in significant savings in time and money and drastically reduces the possibility of error.

System Tasks can input data (values, fields, documents, etc.) and where necessary apply business rules and process rules, automatically create documents, automatically report information to employees and external parties, run scripts, invoke web services, redirect the workflow to other processes, etc.

In this project, the approach started with the typifying of possible issues, normalizing its solution based on predetermined conditions.

Thus, of the 171 Tasks that make up the set of coordinated processes, only 21 are performed by people. Human input is required in these tasks to make decisions, take responsibility or verify and inform in the case of an error in Internet communication or if the applicant makes an incorrect application. The vast majority, i.e., the remaining 150 tasks, is performed without any human intervention, therefore the degree of automation is extremely high.

Furthermore, these automated flows enable the monitoring, control and analysis of every process and also every transaction made. This analysis of each individual procedure and the final analysis of groups of procedures are important for continuous improvement.

5. Hurdles Overcome

Adopting a Process Management approach in a public organization the size and complexity of the Ministry of Interior of Colombia requires substantial changes to the way work is managed and also to develop an understanding of the new way of working within the entity. Therefore, undertaking a BPM implementation project of this caliber is a major challenge that must allow for all technical, business and even psychological factors.

The attached comments can be used as experience for other entities hoping to implement an iBPMS.

5.1 Management
- **Incorrectly documented processes in the entity's Process Map.**
  Sometimes, in State entities, the processes are registered to comply with a regulation or control, therefore the documentation is not sufficient for modeling purposes. This means that all processes need reengineering to be suitable for iBPMS automation. In some cases, processes are automated first and documented later, which is incorrect.
- **The method for making changes**. Contractually, the person responsible for the version changes in the BPM platform and in the processes must be clearly identified. If this responsibility is unclear, it will result in various

versions of processes which could lead to reprocessing, delays or technical incompatibilities.

- **Rely on good "know how"**. This issue is very important from the very beginning of the Project. Having a good team of external consultants is vital for Project execution and then to assimilate the knowledge throughout the entity. In such projects, consultants cannot improvise; they must have a sound understanding of the creation of information families, terms, structures, etc. In our experience and thanks to the support from the software company, we learnt how to improve the modelling and automation making it more versatile, flexible and faster.

5.2 Business

Who should lead and/or coordinate the Project. For the Project to be supported on an iBPMS tool, this type of project should come from the strategic planning department or directly from senior management and supported by the technology department. If it comes from any other department, it will be considered as an initiative for that specific department and not for the entire entity.

Integration. If you have a good process map, endorsed by the planning department which is a true reflection of what the users do in their day-to-day work, the integrations with other systems are clear, their SOA development will be faster and more efficient. It is advisable to have a clear Web Services inventory of the entity from the beginning or as they are being built.

The service. We believe the most important success factor for the processes in this entity was the support we received from the iBPMS headquarters. This direct contact enabled us to do things that external consultants could not. They gave us training, support and responded quickly to any queries we had.

Regulations. At State level, all these processes should have online Government guidelines, ISO 27001, transparency and state efficiency, therefore all these parameters should be considered from the beginning.

5.3 Organization Adoption

Senior Management support. This is one of the most important factors to consider when implementing a BPM Project. If senior management is not aware of the impact, doesn't issue guidelines or get involved wholeheartedly, the Project will not be successful.

Internal changes. At State level, the changes to administration or changes of functional leaders are frequent, resulting in a high risk of the modeled processes being rejected by the new leader. This can cause delays for process implementation or even process rejection, requiring the process to be started from scratch by the new person.

The time required for legalities supporting the automation. In our experience, on the technical side we were ready 5 to 6 months before the launch but, as the supporting decree was not ready, the whole process was delayed.

Reaction to change. In our experience this is another important factor, given that the end users are the ones who will use the platform and may be reluctant to change their way of doing things. With the support of senior management, it is simply a question of following a guideline or instruction and the entity will respond to the request.

The atmosphere surrounding the change. The ultimate satisfaction and process success is to see it working correctly and being employed by the users. Specifically, in Religious Affairs, it only took one worker who "fell in love" with the tool to promote it to all other users. With the new coordinator and the confidence placed in the system group, legal issues surrounding the process flowed more easily.

6. BENEFITS

In addition to the **quantifiable benefits** presented later in this document, the implementation of the automatic system for Religious Affairs procedures, there are other benefits that, although may not be quantifiable, are just as important, such as:

Closing the gap between the Government and the citizens. With this type of service, the perception of these target groups is that the Government is helping its citizens, spending public resources wisely and making their presence more functional than political.

Bringing services to remote communities. Religious groups in particular can be found in the most remote and difficult areas of Colombia, this means that all administrative procedures incur travel expenses and time, not to mention the public order risks in certain areas.

The fight against corruption. The implementation of these online procedures on behalf of the Government clearly stops illegal intermediate companies, abuse of trust and unnecessary high costs which have a direct impact on citizens' economy.

Building trust and security in minority religious communities. Since the launch of the Project, the system group has not received any complaints or criticisms about service unavailability. Indeed, from August 25 to September 30, 2015, 1222 certifications were issued in total, without any failure or complaints from users.

Transparency. By not generating costs, it is clear that the citizens put their trust in government officials who, in turn, are barely involved in the process due to the highly-automated nature of this service.

Less Paperwork (in accordance with the Anti-paperwork Law). Citizens no longer need to physically visit a bank to pay for their certificate, or go to the Ministry in person to deliver hard copy of their documentation and then wait 15 days for their certificate. With the online service, the documents are printed only if and when required.

Document Security. Whilst the document remains in the virtual environment, it is completely safe. When printed, its authentication is guaranteed by the implemented security marks, including watermarks, URL verification, digitally signed stamp and QR code which is now recognized and used in airports.

Optimization of civil servant activities. Being an automated and mainly unattended service, civil servants can get on with other tasks and assignments that benefit the country.

Colombian Television echoed the importance of the project in a one-minute video summary:

> https://youtu.be/rhIUgpNHZkc

6.1 Cost Savings / Time Reductions

As it involves public service procedures, cost savings and time reductions must be expressed on two levels: the direct benefits for the citizens that use the service and indirect benefits for the general public thanks to the cost savings made by the Ministry's business management.

The citizens who benefit directly from this process represent 20% of the Colombian population, that belong to a non-Catholic religion or belief. Specifically, the implemented platform meets the needs of the legal representatives of over 5,000 religious entities which, according to the figures estimated by the Interior's Public Information Bureau, agglomerate over 10 million parishioners.

In particular:

- The procedure has been drastically expedited, as the average completion time for the entire process has reduced from 15 days (before the software implementation) to one minute.
- The average management costs have been reduced by 80%, this is mainly due to the increased productivity, resulting from the coordinated workflows, and the high level of automation, which has resulted in a reduced workload.
- The cost savings have enabled the Ministry to offer the process for free, whereas previously the corrupt intermediaries often charged over 10 times the previous stipulated cost.

6.2 Quality Improvements

- The work coordination and especially the automation have drastically reduced the amount of errors made in the process. On average the errors have been reduced by 98%.
- With the new implementation, as each procedure is performed, the system registers all the information throughout the flow, including all data manually input by the users and automatically generated by the system. Meanwhile, the KPI registers set values to measure performance. Thus, this information is automatically registered and organized according to the predefined structure so that the suite's intelligence tools: BAM, Dashboard, Reports, etc., also automate the monitoring, control and analysis of the facts and data, without having to wait for subsequent audits. This increased analytical capacity and decision making ability is estimated at 83%.
- As all regulations are included in the process execution, it guarantees compliance with all internal and mandatory regulations, with the consequent reduction in risk exposure.

7. TECHNOLOGY

The technological features that have proved the most beneficial to the project are the following:

7.1 Modeling without programming

The installed platform uses an innovative system known as Generatriz which enables the creation of processes (however complex they may be), thereby substituting a high level of programming with a user-friendly system of selecting in order to achieve a high-level modeling.

Zero code, in this context, refers to the ability to build a process model without having to program a single line of code, determining down to the last detail how the process should operate upon completion.

Naturally, it does not include prior process analysis in line with the strategic plan and business objectives (because this doesn't require a code) or integration with other systems (because although the BPMS includes tools that facilitate integration without programming, it always depends on the specific characteristics of the device or application).

The Automation Project for Religious Affairs' procedures, which is considered very complex, was completed without programming a single line of code, which resulted in an 80% reduction in work (time/cost). It also helped and guided the modeler to achieve a high-level of modeling.

The most important benefit of the project was undoubtedly the fact that, with technical support, the functional department was able to repeatedly modify the processes in a matter of minutes, whenever errors or possible improvements were detected. We also had the added reassurance that this capacity can be used for all modifications and optimizations throughout the entire useful life of the processes.

7.2. System Tasks

As their name suggests, system tasks are performed directly by the system without any human intervention using process motors. They substitute personal tasks, since the work previously performed by people is completed automatically at no cost, in no time and without the risk of human error, so its effectiveness is maximal. They are created simply and quickly without requiring a single line of code.

System Tasks are classified by Type, with each Type representing one or more similar Functions. Some of the most used Types in this Project are:

- **Creator**
  Tasks create and delete users, roles, accounts (for example, new churches), etc.

- **Uploader**
  Tasks input any information (documents to or from libraries, processes or any managerial element, dates, etc.) or calculated value (math, with dates, business rules, etc.). It is also capable of creating all kinds of complex documents, by merging sophisticated templates with process data (e.g. issuing Church certificates, confirmation emails and generally all internal and external documents which are created during management procedures).

- **Transferrer**
  Tasks transfer information among Groups of Fields Containers and document libraries.

- **Notifier**
  Tasks automatically create and send notifications to employees and external users. All internal and external notifications involved in the management of the procedure are automated in this way.

- **Deviator**
  Tasks change the flow to an event in other processes, hereby initiating the process or enabling it to continue, and return to each original process. They make very sophisticated flows by constantly transmitting all essential information.

7.3. Distributed Treatments

The Distributed Treatments concept was created to handle homogeneous pieces of information which, although generated by the same process or by similar processes, require different specific treatments throughout their lifecycle.

Distributed Treatments represent an important part of business activity as they are present in many procedures. In addition, Distributed Treatments are an influential feature for managing the majority of complex cases in Case Management.

Complex Distributed Treatments generally involve the intervention of more than one process. The procedure must follow the lifecycle of each Line generated within the Group of Fields, which flows through different Processes to obtain the necessary treatments and then return to its original process, hereby completing the lifecycle of the Line.

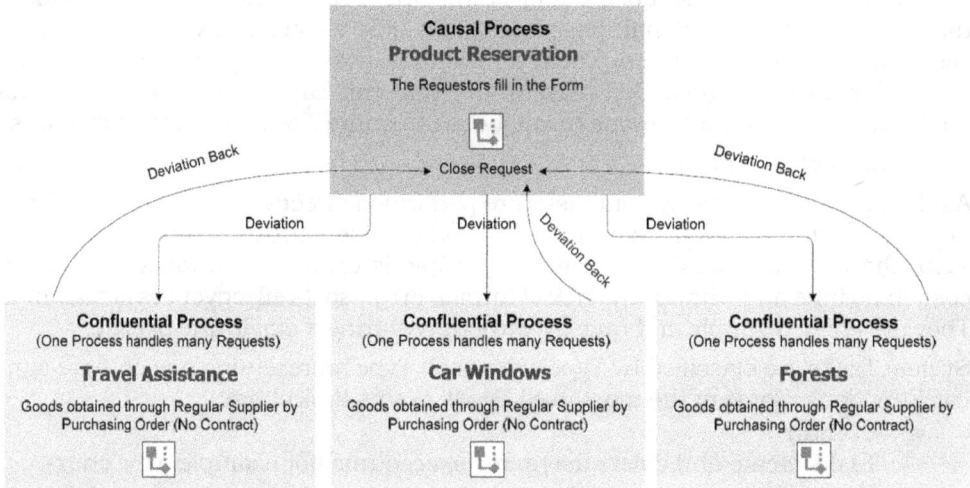

Groups of Fields are lists of fields which are structured into columns and can contain different values which are represented in rows. In this case, the individual products listed, with all their data, which are together in some stages of the process and have their own management flow in different processes.

7.4. DAD Technology (Dynamically Activated Divisions)

To perform a certain task, the forms may contain a large number of fields, documents, action buttons, instructions, etc., (to cover all eventualities) however, depending on their circumstances, the task performers need only view or act on very few of these elements.

For example, to initiate the process from the public Website, the first step is to identify which entity they wish to use for the process: Existing Entity or New Entity. Each type of entity requests the selection of the type of process they wish to start

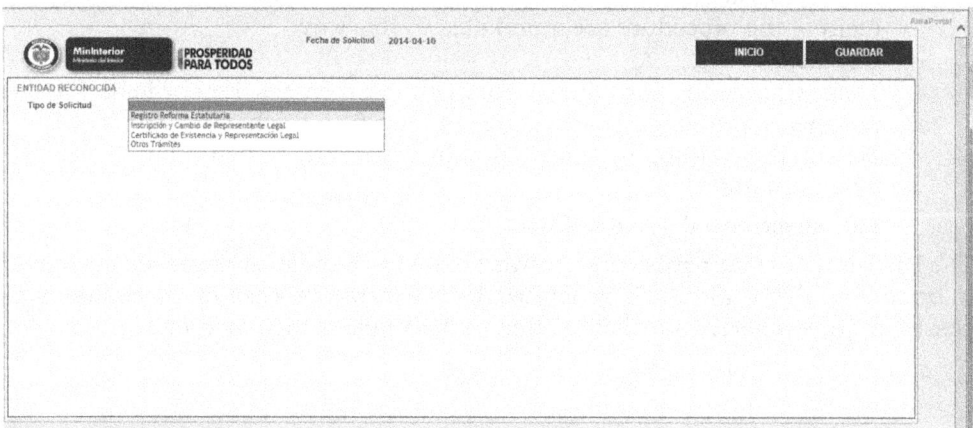

and then requests the necessary information and documents for the timely management of that process. This presents a varied casuistry which would mean that the form would have to contain hundreds of fields, although very few would be relevant to each individual case. It would be totally inoperative for a religious entity to receive a form of this nature (the IM (Initial Message) alone contains 37 internal windows). In fact, no company would use this system.

Initial page for procedure selection

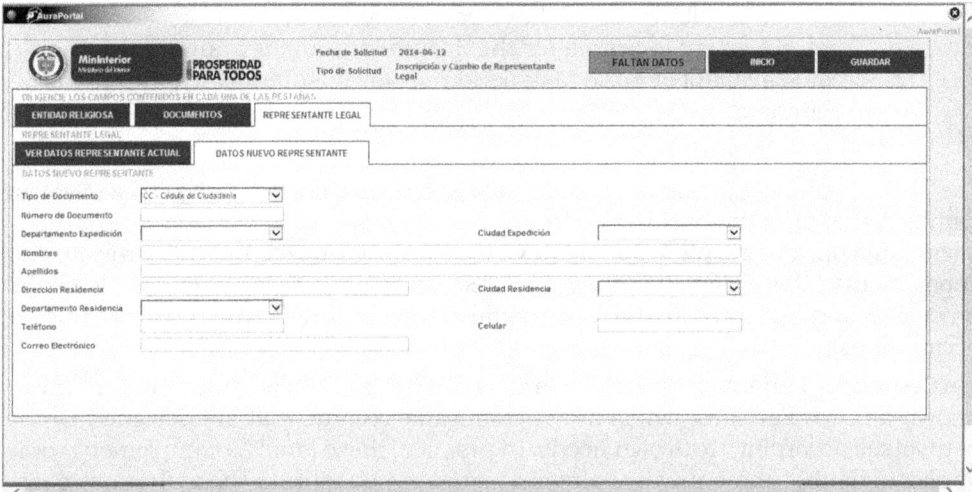

With DAD technology, as the performer carries out the task, the system makes the necessary elements, and even entire divisions, appear automatically, depending on the actions performed, the decisions made or on the automations that have been determined in the modeling phase: divisions, conditional fields and pages, calculated fields, business rules and calculation, automatic document creation (based on the information in the form), action buttons, link buttons, etc.

This system greatly simplifies work and enables the creation of a simple task execution system made up of different predefined activities.

7.5. *Document Management by Processes*

The synergy created by integrating all documents into the BPM makes it possible to manage all the corporate documentation efficiently, regardless of its complexity. This is not because Document Management has a workflow. On the contrary, as document management is dealt with in the context of an activity, when designing the entity's operational processes all actions performed with the documents are included, hereby automating the entire life cycle:

1. **External Capture**. The citizen uploads the documents requested at the start of the process (Process Request) or from an intermediary task, and they are integrated in the system with all the required metadata for this type of document and process.

2. **Creation**. All the internally-generated documents are created automatically by the system itself (using sophisticated templates and actual data from the process) and integrated in the system with all the required metadata for this type of document and process. This is the case for all documents, regardless of their complexity.

3. **Storage**. The Captured or Created documents will automatically be placed in the Processes (electronic file) and/or in the corresponding Libraries. These Libraries, which can be very complex due to the large

quantity of control and search elements provided by the iBPMS, are automatically structured in relation to the predetermined metadata and labels for the document and process class in the Capture or Creation (Virtual Intelligent Archive).

4. **Flow**, **Access and Elimination.** When designing process tasks in which some performers may wish to use documents (for queries, modifications, approvals, elimination, etc.), the necessary documents, or even entire libraries, will have been included in the tasks. Thus, it is not necessary to search for the documents, as they automatically become available for the task performer to consult, modify, approve or eliminate.

7.6. Own Families

The iBPM tool incorporates the basic management elements (known as System Families) that form the backbone of the entity: Employees, Accounts (Citizens, Suppliers, subcontractors, etc.), Items (Services, Fixed Assets, etc.), Entity Projects and departments. These elements are structured information records accessible by the processes and can be consulted or modified at any time (subject to appropriate permissions).

Furthermore, it enables the agile creation of other families (without programming) known as Own Families, which are customizable records that are designed by the entity itself according to its own needs. In practice, these families complement some applications that the entity are already using and substitute those that are obsolete.

The Own Families can support any type of Additional Management that the entity requires. They are designed by the entity itself according to its own needs and their design and creation is very simple, and doesn't require any programming. They offer great managerial power as they are totally interconnected and linked to all the other Families and elements (Processes, Documents, etc.).

Generally, the information elements that may be included in an Own Family are the following:

- **Structured Information**. With all the management and information fields that have been created for this Family.
- **Unstructured Information**. Documents and/or entire Libraries.
- **Related Information**. Through relation networks between all the Families.
- **Activity Information**. Via links with the Processes and with the Workflow Open Tasks.
- **Control and Analysis Information**. Control of Costs and Profitability and direct access to times, reports, statistics, analysis, etc.

All these Families (System and Own) constitute an intricate structure that links each of the elements and connects all other Platform elements (processes, documents, etc.), hereby enabling a new level of managerial potential hitherto unknown.

Various Own Families were created to implement and support this project, including Registration, Church, Person, Household, Administrative Act, Document and Consignment.

8. THE TECHNOLOGY AND SERVICE PROVIDERS

Although the project initially received the collaboration of a renowned consultancy company, it was executed exclusively by a team made up of business staff, internal consultants and system staff from the Ministry of Interior of Colombia, supported by the Consultancy department at AuraPortal headquarters.

The features mentioned in Section 7 'Technology' are exclusive AuraPortal innovations, some of which have been highlighted by Gartner in the 2015 Magic Quadrant report for iBPMS.

AuraPortal http://www.auraportal.com

National Bank of Kenya

Nominated by Newgen Software Technologies Ltd, India

1. EXECUTIVE SUMMARY / ABSTRACT

National Bank of Kenya was incorporated in June 1968 and officially opened in November 1968. National Bank is a leading commercial bank in Kenya, licensed by the Central Bank of Kenya. It operates as "One Bank" with common branding, standards, policies and processes to provide consistent and reliable services. The objective for which it was formed was to help Kenyans get access to credit and control their economy after independence. It has a unique network of more than 75 branches.

National Bank of Kenya is one of the largest banks in the country providing financial services to all the sectors of the economy. The bank needed a platform to include digitization tools and provide statistical data on stock, incoming and shredded documents. Earlier, manual and paper-based transaction processing/data entry was done in the branches. Customers had to wait in long queues. There was no tracking and monitoring of files.

National Bank of Kenya was facing several business challenges such as: lack of process standardization because as the processes were not centralized, all the business processes were working in silos. Manual intervention in business processes was slowing things down and there was no process visibility and audit-ability. The client wanted to manage document archival, facilitate the identification and access to documents in real time and improve upon the efficiency of the corporation's operating services. They needed a platform to include digitization tools; the turn-around-time was high and courier usage was high too. Also, there was no tracking and no workflow for approval.

To centralize and streamline the business processes, the bank decided to implement a product suite for automation of Business Process and Document Management System. The bank has automated and integrated several business processes such as account opening (personal and corporate accounts) and credit approval (loans and credit cards).

In Account Opening Process, a new/existing customer walks into the branch with a request for opening an account. A FATCA template is generated based on nationality. Based on the type of customer (i.e., Personal Individual/Joint/Minor, Corporate Limited Liability/Sole Proprietorship/Partnership/Non-Profit Organization), minimal data entry is performed and scanned documents are sent to the next level in the workflow for approval.

In Credit Approval Process, an existing customer walks into the branch with a Loan/Credit Card Request. Based on his eligibility (DBR) criteria, minimal data entry is performed and scanned documents are sent to the next level in the EDMS for approval.

Key features:
- Centralized system and ease of sharing scanned documents in workflow
- Eligibility Calculation (DBR) for Loan/Credit Card; quick data entry at branch

- Scheme/Non–scheme specific interest rates are computed in the back-end based on pre–defined formula: Interest Rate = KBRR + Margin
- Decision-making on the basis of Score Card, Rating Commission, Insurance Calculators and detailed data entry at central branch
- Delegation matrix for amount approvals at various levels
- Complete Tracking of application at various levels
- Template generation and alerts based on business rules
- Folder-based hierarchy for easy storage and retrieval of forms and scanned documents for references

A Centre of Excellence (COE) was created which takes care of continuous process improvement and allows further scaling up of new processes. The solution resulted in quick benefits. Some of these benefits are:

- Reduced Turn-Around-Time for end-to-end solution
- Increase in Customer Satisfaction
- FATCA-compliance for US Citizens/Non-Kenya Residents along with template generation
- Relieve branches from time consuming back-office operations and make them more focused on efficient delivery of customer service
- Workflow-based movement of scanned documents from one user/group to the next level maintaining complete transparency and a better tracking mechanism

2. OVERVIEW

National Bank of Kenya had their business spanning 75 branches and multiple lines of business (LOBs).

In the existing system, manual and paper-based transaction processing/detailed data entry was done in the branches. CSRs in branches used to have less time available to interact with customers regarding National Bank's various products and services. FATCA information which is mandatory for compliance was not captured. In the Account Opening Process, the option to open the account for blacklisted customers was at the discretion of head office. In Credit Approval Process, the option to provide loan/credit card for non–eligible/blacklisted customers was at the discretion of Head Office. Compliance was not involved in decision-making. A lot of paper flow used to happen in batches from branches to head office and used to be assigned to different user/group(s) after physical sorting.

After evaluating a host of solutions, National Bank of Kenya decided to go with a solution comprising a proven Business Process Management (BPM) platform, Enterprise Content Management (ECM) platform and Scanning and Digitization engine for an end-to-end automation of its Account Opening and Retail Loan/-Credit Card Approval processes. The solution offered enhanced business flexibility, better credit risk management and rules-based processing, resulting in an improved business performance for the bank.

Below is a brief overview of the processes that were automated:

Account Opening Process:

In the Account Opening process, a new/existing customer walks into the branch with a request for opening an account. A FATCA template is generated based on nationality. Based on the type of customer, minimal data entry is performed and scanned documents are sent to the next level in the workflow for approval. The CSR Authorizer reviews and approves the electronic form for back-office processing.

Corp Mailing performs verification for the list of corporate cases generated through the template in the EDMS for external agency/lawyers. QA and Screening are performed as a single step. Report is generated through third party systems and is uploaded in the EDMS. Requests such as Mobile Banking, Cheque book, Internet Banking and Mobee-on-Board are processed through a click of a button in the EDMS. If required, a case can be referred to escalation matrix (i.e. Segment Head/Compliance) for required approvals/advisory. If the Escalation Matrix (i.e., Segment Head/Compliance) refers back any case in the EDMS for additional approval, the CPC Maker performs detailed data entry and fetches additional details from CORE. The case is then sent to the CPC Authorizer who reviews and approves the electronic form and it is archived. Reporting tool (Business Activity Monitoring) for management level dashboards and reports.

Credit Approval Process:

In the Credit Approval process, an existing customer walks into the branch with a request for Loan/Credit Card. Based on his eligibility (DBR) criteria, minimal data entry is performed and scanned documents are sent to the next level in the EDMS for approval.

The CSR Authorizer reviews and approves the electronic form for back-office processing. Workplace banking performs employer verification for confirmed cases. The CPC Maker performs detailed data entry, with automatic score card calculations done based on minimum inputs. The form is then sent to the next level. The CPC Authorizer reviews and approves the electronic form and sends it to the next level. The Credit Risk Authorizer performs risk operations based on score and rating. If required, he can refer a case to the escalation matrix (i.e. Credit Risk Head/Chief Risk Officer/Managing Director) in the EDMS for required approval/advisory. The Escalation Matrix refers back any case in the EDMS for additional approval. The Disbursement Maker uses commission and insurance calculators to perform calculations. The Disbursement Authorizer reviews and approves the electronic form and it is archived.

Direct and Indirect Benefits accrued to the bank include:
- Branches relieved from time-consuming back-office operations and made more focused towards an efficient delivery of customer service
- Electronic application form movement has been based on customer eligibility and business rules defined by the bank. System alerts have also been based on business rules and eligibility
- Eligibility check (DBR) provisioned for Loan–Scheme/Non-Scheme and Credit Card
- A higher customer satisfaction achieved as customers no longer need to wait in queues
- Reduced TAT for processing an application end to end
- Credit Risk Department will have the authority to either approve or reject the loan credit card for non-eligible/blacklisted customers
- Various Reporting Templates such as TAT, Pending items in queue etc. can be configured as per need

3. BUSINESS CONTEXT

National Bank of Kenya had been aggressively looking at expanding its business. To facilitate its growth agenda the bank wanted to automate key retail processes and decrease the process cycle times, while enhancing operational efficiencies.

In the existing system, manual and paper-based transaction processing/detailed data entry was done in branch. Customers had to wait in long queues which had led to a lack in customer satisfaction. The CSR in branches used to have less time to interact with the customers regarding National Bank's various products and services. FATCA information which is mandatory for compliance was not captured. In Account Opening Process, the option to open the account for blacklisted customers was at the discretion of head office. In Credit Approval Process, the option to provide loan/credit card for non–eligible/blacklisted customers was at the discretion of Credit Risk Department in Head Office. Compliance was not involved in decision making. There was a lot of paper flow in batches from branches to head office and the same could be assigned to different user/group(s) only after physical sorting

The bank realized that to address all these challenges they needed a BPM platform to underpin their operations, which would not only bring complete automation and process visibility but also ensure adherence to regulatory compliance. It would enable continuous process improvement and help improve the quality of customer service. The bank decided to start with the automation of two key processes: Account Opening and Credit Approval.

Before the implementation, all the physical documents used to be processed manually. Every work-step including filling of the details, processing of the request for approval and opening of accounts was manual. Even eligibility for loan was checked manually.

Key issues that the Bank was looking to resolve through implementation include:
- Centralized system and ease of sharing scanned documents in workflow
- Eligibility Calculation (DBR) for Loan/Credit Card, Quick data entry at Branch
- Computation of specific Interest Rate (KBRR + Margin) in the back-end Scheme/Non–Scheme
- Decision making on the basis of Score Card, Rating Commission, Insurance Calculators, detailed data entry at central branch
- Delegation matrix for amount approvals at various levels
- Complete Tracking of application at any level
- Template generation and alerts based on business rules
- Folder based hierarchy for easy storage and retrieval of forms and scanned documents for references
- Providing visibility to employees for all work items pertaining to them, to help in streamlining their activities in an efficient way
- Providing easy access from desktops to all the documents and processing status of cases
- Establishing best–in-class operations and productivity standards through analysis of time and motion data coming out of the workflow database, rather than using traditional averages that could be skewed by idle time, low skilled staff and poor practices
- Skill-based dynamic work allocation and tracking
- Faster exception resolution
- Higher process efficiency
- Tracking the status of applications
- All the documents were physically managed
- Reducing turn-around-time
- The bank did not have a comprehensive audit trailing facility

- Manual hand-offs of documents made it difficult to track and manage the right versions of documents
- Escalation and exception management process was manual and error-prone
- Manual processing of all customer requests, received via multiple channels

4. KEY INNOVATIONS

4.1 Business

Newgen's solution offered some innovative features and capabilities that helped the bank achieve operational efficiencies. Some of the innovative tools are detailed below.

- Eligibility Calculator – The Eligibility Calculator is an application within the Loan Eligibility process to perform loan calculation based on a customer's credit history, income and other details. A prospective customer submits a request for Credit Approval through National Bank of Kenya. The bank officer logs into the Eligibility Process and enters the necessary customer details (Salary, DOB etc) in the relevant fields. He/She then clicks the "Calculate DBR" button to perform necessary calculation. The system carries out the calculations as per National Bank of Kenya policies and the results are displayed to the Bank Officer.
- Blacklist Check – Blacklist check is performed to check if a customer is blacklisted. To perform Blacklist check, the user clicks on the Blacklist (IPRS) button on the form and the report (Yes/No) is successfully downloaded and uploaded in the BPM system.
- Fetch Customer Details – This operation is used to fetch the customer's details from Core Banking System. For fetching the customer's details, user needs to press an action button – "Fetch Customer Details". At this work-step, the system automatically checks existing customer database and update CIF (Customer Information).
- MIS – Below mentioned custom reports are made available in the Personal Loan process apart from the inbuilt product reports.
- Branch Initiation Report: It will be generated on daily basis at EOD and will provide the details about the total number of cases initiated by any branch. It will also provide details such as customer ID and account number associated with customers
- Daily Account Opening by Branches: It will provide details about the account numbers created by branches on a daily basis
- Summary Report for Approved Applications: It will provide details about the Account Opening applications approved by the branches on a daily basis
- Summary Report for rejected Applications: It will provide details about the Account Opening applications rejected by the branches on a daily basis, such as rejection code and reason for rejection
- Daily Summary Report for Pending Applications: It will provide details about the pending applications such as at which stage the application is pending and for how many hours
- Turn-Around-Time: It will provide details about the average time taken at particular user(s)/ group(s) to process an application

Case Handling

The design of the Credit Card System process is based on the Pro-Agile Approach. It is a blend of both prototyping and agile methodology. It makes early visibility of functionality in less number of iterations without any scope creep. It is very simple to understand and use. The Pro-Agile approach uses the following workflow:

Project·Implementation·Approach·—·Pro-Agile

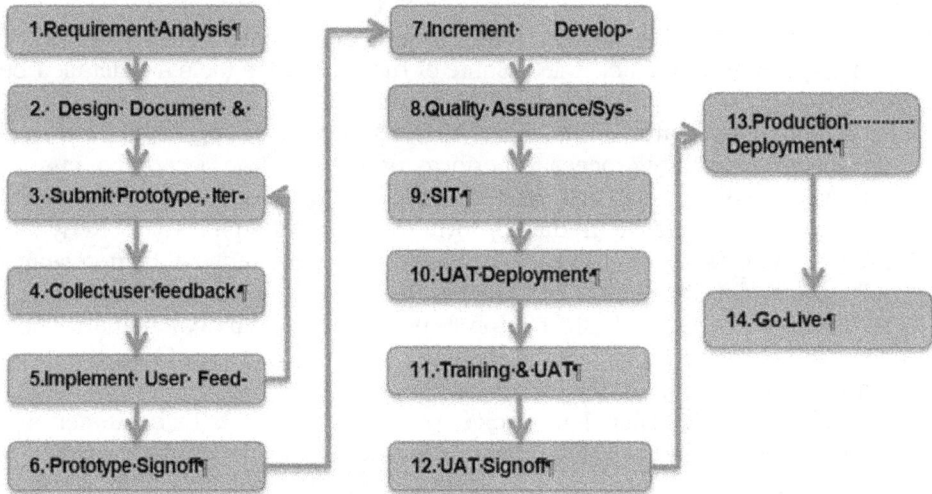

1. Requirement Analysis	7. Increment Develop-	
2. Design Document &	8. Quality Assurance/Sys-	
3. Submit Prototype, Iter-	9. SIT	13. Production Deployment
4. Collect user feedback	10. UAT Deployment	14. Go Live
5. Implement User Feed-	11. Training & UAT	
6. Prototype Signoff	12. UAT Signoff	

Architectural Diagram

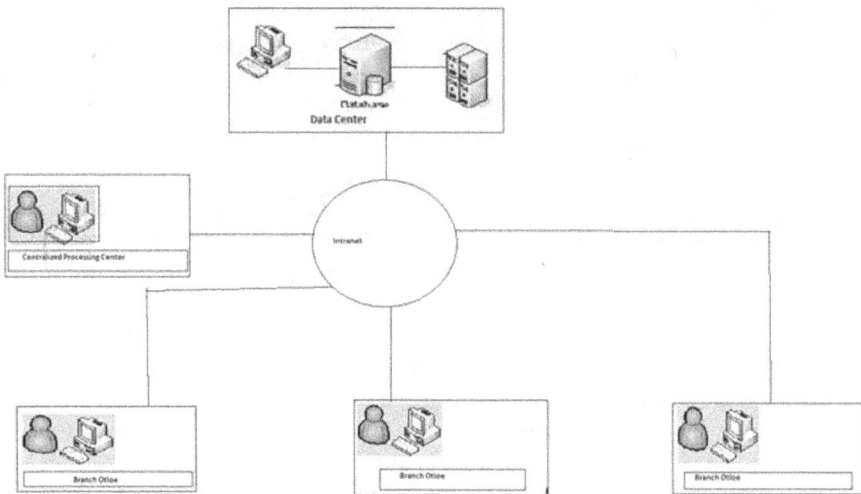

Components Used:

- OmniFlow™ - Business Process Management Tool
- OmniDocs™ - Enterprise Document Management System
- OmniScan™ - Digitization and Automatic Data Capturing Tool
- Business Activity Monitor- a graphics based process analysis tool for business processes

National Bank of Kenya implemented solution to automate two key processes i.e. Account Opening and Credit Approval Process.

- Account Opening Process – The main objective of this process is to automate the approval of the CASA and Corporate process. By means of the solution, various documents will be scanned and processed electronically, making the departments involved paperless and hence reducing cost and TAT. It will also help the bank in monitoring and controlling the various operations involved in the approval cycle. System will also generate MIS and reporting solution thus bringing the clarity and visibility in bank's operation.
- In the Account Opening Process, a new/existing customer walks into the branch with a request for opening an account. FATCA template is generated based on nationality. Based on the type of customer minimum data entry is performed and scanned documents are sent to next level in the workflow for approval. The CSR authorizer reviews and approves the electronic form for back office processing. Corp Mailing performs verification for list of corporate cases generated through the template in the EDMS for external agency/lawyers.
- QA and Screening is performed as a single step. Report is generated through third party systems and uploaded in the EDMS. Requests such as Mobile banking, Cheque book, Internet Banking, Mobee on Board are processed through a click of a button in the EDMS. If required, the case can be referred to escalation matrix (i.e. Segment Head/Compliance). The case may be referred back in the EDMS for additional approval. The CPC Maker performs detailed data entry and fetches additional details from CORE to be further sent to next level. The CPC Authorizer reviews and approves the electronic form and it is archived.

Brief Description
- Work introduction begins from OmniFlow™ by performing min. data entry and where the completed Application Form and relevant documents of the customer are scanned and the work-item/application is introduced into the workflow
- Once the work-item has been initiated in the workflow, the user starts with the processing of the work-item/application by referring to the scanned/attached documents
- The CSR Authorizer reviews the form and the scanned docs. The authorizer can raise an exception for a re-scan or missing information. Approves the form and then sends the work-item ahead to QA and Screening. It then sends the work-item to Corp Mailing.
- The Corp Mail reviews the form and the scanned documents. Sends the corporate cases for legal search and receives signed acknowledgement and scans them.
- In Quality Analysis and Screening – They verify the AML/Blacklist Check in ASD System. It raises an exception for a re-scan or missing information. Sends the work-items to Segment Head.
- CPC Maker verifies the documents and input details for long account opening from CORE systems. It sends the form to Branch–Co-ordinator for missing information/minor corrections.
- Branch Co-ordinator (Central) provides the missing information/minor correction and sends it back to the QA/Screening/CPC Maker/CPC Authorizer. Sends the exception to branch and follows up.

- CPC Authorizer (Central) reviews the document and data. It authorizes Customer Details and Account number. It sends the work-item back to CPC Maker for corrective/missing information.

Process Flow Diagram

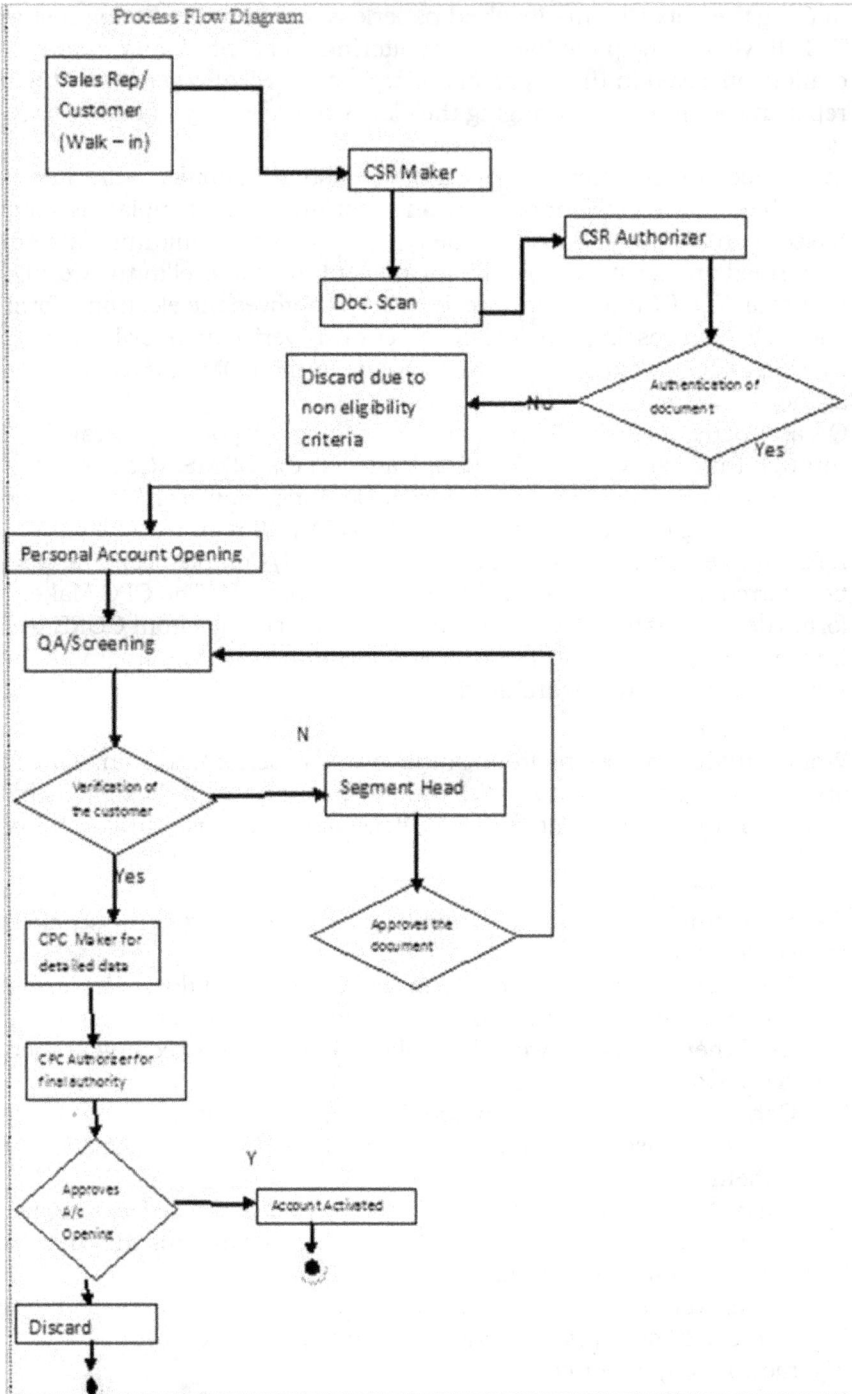

Credit Approval Process

The main objective of this process is to automate the approval of the consumer loan and credit card process. By means of this solution, various documents will be scanned and processed electronically, making the departments involved paperless and hence reducing costs and TAT. It will also help the bank in monitoring and controlling various operations involved in the approval cycle. The system will also generate MIS and reporting solution, thus bringing clarity and visibility in bank's operation.

In the Credit Approval Process, an existing customer walks into the branch with a request for Loan/Credit Card. Based on his eligibility (DBR) criteria, minimal data entry is performed and scanned documents are sent to the next level in the EDMS for approval. CSR authorizer reviews and approves the electronic form for back-office processing. Workplace banking performs employer verification for confirmed cases. CPC Maker performs a detailed data entry and an automatic score card is calculated based on minimal inputs and sent to the next level. CPC Authorizer reviews and approves the electronic form and sends it to next level.

Credit Risk Authorizer performs risk operations based on score and rating. If required, he can refer any case to escalation matrix in EDMS for required approval/advisory.

Escalation Matrix (i.e. Credit Risk Head/Chief Risk Officer) refers any case in EDMS for additional approval. Disbursement Maker uses commission and insurance calculators to perform calculations. Disbursement Authorizer reviews and approves the electronic form and further activities.

Brief Description
- Work introduction begins from OmniScan™ where the completed Application Form and relevant documents of the customer are scanned and the work-item/application is introduced into the workflow
- Once the work-item has been initiated in the workflow, the user starts with the processing of the work-item/application by referring to the scanned/attached documents
- Once the Customer ID has been provided, User can now proceed with New Loan Account Number for the Customer. A Loan Eligibility Calculator will be provided in the BPM system to calculate Debit Burden Ratio (DBR) and Annual Percentage Rate (APR) to check customer's eligibility for the type of loan.
- CSR Maker verifies the documents. They fill the Customer ID, Account Number, Loan Account Number for Existing Customers in OmniFlow from CORE systems.
- CSR Authorizer reviews the forms and scanned documents. They approve the form OR raise an exception. It sends the work-item ahead to the next level.
- CPC Maker (Central) verifies the documents. Inputs all the details for detailed data entry from CORE System.
- CPC Authorizer (Central) – It reviews the data entry on the form and scanned documents. It can approve/reject the form due to discrepancy
- Credit Risk Authorizer (Central) – It reviews the data entry on the form and scanned docs. It can send the form back to CPC_Authorizer for missing information. It approves/rejects the form due to discrepancy and sends the work-items ahead to the next level. User can escalate/refer the case for sanction to Credit Risk Head or Chief Risk Officer or Managing Director based on a higher loan amount. User will send the offer letter to the branch (through exception handling) for Customer Acceptance/Signature on the Offer letter. Credit Risk Head (Central) reviews the form and

the scanned documents. They can send them back for missing information. They can approve/reject the form due to discrepancy. They send the work-item ahead to next level. They refer the cases to the next higher/lower level.

- Managing Director – They review the form and scanned documents. They can Approve/Reject the form due to discrepancy. They send the work-item ahead to the next level. They refer the cases back to lower level.
- Disbursement Maker – They review the form and the scanned documents. They send them back for missing information. They send the work-item ahead to the next level.

Process Flow Diagram

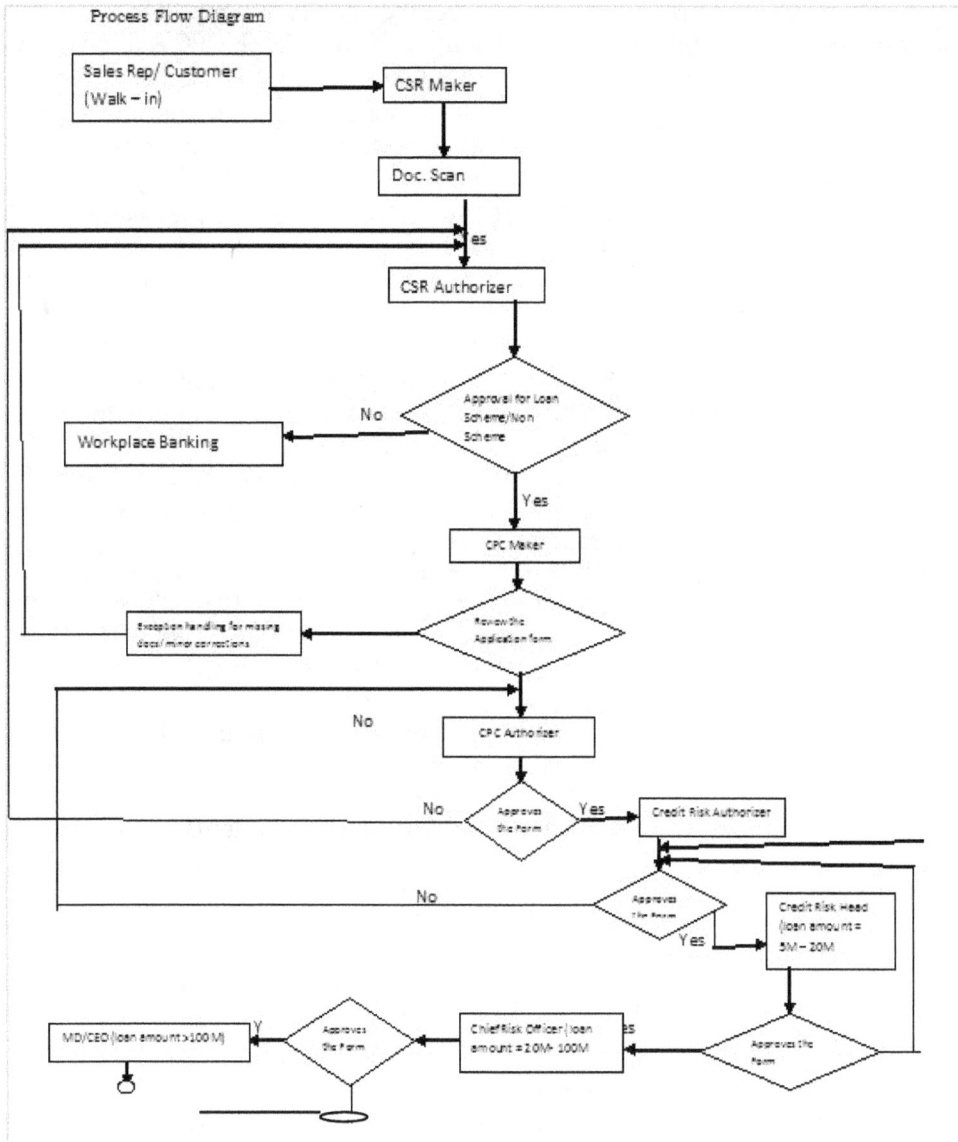

4.2 Organization and Social
- The end-to-end automation of the previously manual process resulted in an improved employee productivity and satisfaction

- Elimination of manual hand-offs resulted in a drastic reduction in calculation and other processing errors
- Centralized processing of applications at the back office resulted in freeing the branch staff to engage in business development and other customer-facing activities
- Anytime–anywhere access rights based access to relevant information helped in a better and faster decision making
- In the post-implementation scenario, the branch offices were responsible for the processing of A/O requests or any customer servicing requests and hence were heavy-loaded with various day-to-day activities. As a result, they were not able to put good amount of customer facing time.
- The centralization of the banking processes made the branch offices leaner as they no longer had to process the jobs. They were required only to capture the customer documents and some key information about the customers.
- The Turn- Around-Time (TAT) for customer interaction got drastically reduced as they had to capture only some basic information about the customers. So, this resulted into an improved productivity and efficiency of employees with a reduction in non–core activities, allowing branch executives to cross-sell other products. The implementation resulted in an improved customer satisfaction through a quicker and better servicing, a reduction in the requirement of physical forms and a reduced customer response time.

5. HURDLES OVERCOME

Following are the hurdles we faced during the project:
- Employees' resistance towards the change: change in any organization is always difficult to manage.
- On-time business/bank resource availability
- Integration calls not on time
- Change information not percolated to the lowest level
- Lack of affiliate support
- Local management was not serious
- Users were not so motivated to use the system
- Many users feared the loss of jobs

Management

Ever-changing requirements of the bank as the implementation progressed.

Business

For the success of this project an in-depth knowledge of Account Opening/Credit Approval Process and patience was the key. Understanding the requirement from the Business User's perspective and delivering a solution in such a short span was the key to success in this project.

Organization Adoption

Acceptance of the new system by the bank staff required a few training and information sessions to explain the need and benefits of the new system.

6. BENEFITS

The project was a landmark decision for National Bank of Kenya, which featured its aggressive growth plans. The solution solved the business concerns of the bank and became a game changer for them as it brought about complete Business Transformation for the Bank.

Some of the key benefits accrued to National Bank of Kenya include:

Account Opening Process

- Branches relieved from time consuming back office operations and made more focused on an efficient delivery of customer service
- Detailed data entry is being done at back-office (CPC)
- More customer satisfaction since customers don't need to wait any longer in queues
- Workflow based movement of scanned documents from one user/group(s) to the next level, maintaining complete transparency and a better tracking mechanism
- Reduced TAT for processing an application end-to-end
- Compliance Department will have the authority to either approve or reject the accounts opened for blacklisted customers
- Each customer will be assigned a risk rating helpful to National Bank down the line when offered loans by QA (Compliance) department
- FATCA Compliance for US Citizens/Non-Kenya Residents, along with template generation
- Integration with Third Party systems (QA) for cheque-book ordering, Internet Banking, Mobee On Board, IPRS
- Various Reporting Templates such as TAT, pending items in queues etc. can be configured as per need

Credit Approval Process

- Branches relieved from time-consuming back office operations and made more focused on an efficient delivery of customer service.
- Electronic application form movement based on Customer eligibility and Business rules, defined by the bank. System alerts based on business rules and eligibility.
- Eligibility check (DBR) for Loan–Scheme/Non-Scheme and Credit card–Salaried
- Credit Scoring is computed at the back-end based on input on the form (STP ready)
- Detailed data entry is being done at the back-office (CPC)
- More customer satisfaction since customers don't need to wait any longer in queues
- Workflow based movement of scanned documents from one users/group(s) to the next level, maintaining complete transparency and a better tracking mechanism
- TAT will be reduced for processing an application end-to-end
- Credit Risk Department will have the authority to either approve or reject the loan/credit card for non-eligible/blacklisted customers
- Various Reporting Templates such as TAT, pending items in queue etc. can be configured as per need

The performance improvement of the bank was observed in the following areas:

- Improved Process Cycle Time – The BPM platform significantly reduced the number of steps (almost 50% reduction) involved in both the processes. Digitization made sure that there was no physical document movement across departments and locations. This contributed to achieving faster process cycle times and lower operational costs as there was no extra expense in courier or transportation. Since all the documents were digitized there was no chance of documents being misplaced or getting damaged in any process area.

- Higher Process Efficiency – All the external processes were seamlessly integrated and run automatically with the existing banking processes. Now, the entire process requires minimal manual intervention. The system performs an automatic data entry by using a unique automatic data fill technique. The system automatically checks for duplicate customer entries and prevents the user from doing so. The double data entry method also reduces data entry errors. All the physical documents are converted into digitized documents which transverse across departments and locations. The system also generates electronic data captured forms for the Loan Process and Credit Card Process, which includes the KYC Process.

- Skill–based Dynamic Work Allocation and Tracking – Work allocation and tracking of tasks had been a major challenge for the bank. The BPM solution provided a work distribution console that eliminated bottlenecks in the job allocation process and ensured an equal distribution of tasks. Work is distributed as per the employee's skill-set and the solution supports a complete audit trail of all the tasks and activities for monitoring purposes.

- Faster Exception Resolution – The bank had an exception management process which was manual, time-consuming and error-prone. The BPM solution provided an exception-management mechanism which requires minimal manual intervention. Whenever and wherever an exception occurs, an alert message is sent to the employee as well as the concerned business manager. Different activities such as document validation, KYC verification, document re-scan, loan eligibility check, credit card limit etc. are triggered automatically when an exception is raised. Parallel triggering of necessary activities helps resolve the exception and results in a faster exception resolution.

- Improved Customer Experience – The mandated cropping is performed using the scanning tool. All customer signatures are cropped and archived separately with other necessary documents. The customer requests for credit card/home loan/personal loan are now processed automatically and the system ensures that the SLAs are maintained by giving automatic alerts or message to the users. The system automatically generates proposals for credit limit based on the rules and regulations of the bank. It sends automatic alert messages to the users once the credit limit or loan is approved, or rejected. The BPM platform supports auto-processing of e-Alerts, SMS alerts, customer queries, and other banking requests.

- Secure Banking Process to Prevent Fraudulent Activities – The BPM solution automatically performs a blacklist check at the time of data entry and prompts the user if the customer is blacklisted. The solution is seamlessly integrated with the credit scoring and KYC process to prevent forgery and fraudulent activities. Customer signatures are cropped and archived separately for future reference and online signature verification.

6.1 Cost Savings / Time Reductions

Area	Benefits	Measure
Process Cycle Times Customer Satisfaction	• Faster Customer On-boarding • Quick Customer Service Delivery	• Reduction of process TATs by 80% • Improved Customer Satisfaction
Agility and Responsiveness	• Faster change management adaptability • Lower time for new process roll-out • Taking errors to a 99.9% accuracy due to elimination of human intervention • Transparency due to simplified reporting and Management Information System (MIS) • Fraud Management via system in-built controls and checks.	• Reduction from months to weeks / weeks to days
Compliance and Quality	• SLA Adherence within departments • Customers audit-ability and adherence to regulations and compliance	• Increased to 99% • Increased to 100%
Service Excellence	• Simplified and standardized processing • Fast and Easy process roll out to market • Continuous improvement within the process and service quality management • Customer at the heart of the processes • Reduced process turn-around-time • Reduced error rates	
Operational Efficiencies	• Productivity • First Time Right • Process TAT	• Increase by 80% • Increase by 90% • Increase by 80%
Business Focus	• Focus on generating businesses i.e. revenue generation • Taking advantage of the back-office engine and processing expertise	• Increase by 90%
Costs	• Resource Reduction; • Reduced operational expenses	• Reduced by 50%

6.2 Increased Revenues

The implementation resulted in faster loan disbursals, allowing the bank to grow lending revenues and sustain profitability.

6.3 Quality Improvements

- Better process monitoring and tracking
- Better and more informed credit decisions
- Improved customer service levels
- Elimination of errors due to manual processing of applications
- 100% process visibility

7. BEST PRACTICES, LEARNING POINTS AND PITFALLS
- ✓ Ensure representation from all relevant departments during process study and planning, including the bank's IT department
- ✓ Integration requirements should be kept in mind during initial planning phase
- ✓ Use prototype approach to finalize specifications
- ✓ Involve business users in the process design phase and not just management
- ✓ Follow a methodology to keep track of interim process change requests

Pitfalls

- ✗ Attempt to establish perfect specification of a process without prototyping

8. COMPETITIVE ADVANTAGES

By implementing the solution, the bank provided a competitive advantage to its sales force, allowing them to focus on customer-facing revenue generating activities:
- Ability to scale-up operations facilitated the bank's horizontal as well as vertical growth plans
- Enhanced process visibility, monitoring and real-time tracking of applications ensured improved "First time Right" rates

9. TECHNOLOGY

The solution was built on Newgen's Business Process Management platform: OmniFlow™, Enterprise Content Management platform- OmniDocs™, and distributed scanning engine, OmniScan™.
The following solutions were proposed to cater to the client requirements:
- Document Management
- Records Management System
- Business Process Management system
- Business Activity Monitoring

10. THE TECHNOLOGY AND SERVICE PROVIDERS

Primary Vendor: Newgen Software Technologies Limited

Trademarked Products from Newgen's Portfolio:

OmniDocs, OmniFlow, OmniScan

Santos City Hall, Brazil
Nominated by Lecom S/A, Brazil

1. EXECUTIVE SUMMARY / ABSTRACT

Santos is a municipality in São Paulo, the richest state of Brazil. In 2014, the City Hall began a program called "Digital Processes" aiming at improving its internal processes. One year after implementation, the program already presents significant numbers, with countless operational and financial benefits. The initiative of Santos City Hall has been widely spread in Brazil and has become a significant benchmark for Brazilian federal, state and municipal government entities.

2. OVERVIEW

With a population of 433,200 inhabitants in 2015, Santos is currently ranked sixth place in Human Development Index (HDI) among the municipalities of Brazil, which evidences its quality of life and economic development higher than the national standard. Its GDP per capita is double that of São Paulo state.

Santos City Hall managed a 2,5 billion Brazilian Reais (BRL) budget in 2015. Its main source of income comes from the Port of Santos, the largest port of Latin America. The movement of the port traffic represents 25,8% of the Brazilian commercial balance, which puts it as the main revenue receiver for the country's seaborne imports and exports.

Public municipal administration, seeking to modernize the institution, created in 2014 a program called Digital Processes in order to replace the usage of physical documents, both in internal administrative routines and in the relationship with citizens, and thus improve quality of services. Its slogan is "Efficiency to enhance, innovation to make progress".

We can cite four main reasons for the beginning of the program:

(1) Reducing deadlines and providing agility in the conduct of organizational internal processes, as well as in the relationship with public servants and citizens;
(2) Eliminating paper usage, printing, transportation and storage;
(3) Enabling performance indicators extraction and monitoring;
(4) Providing safety and transparency for routines, with the maintenance of security copies that could be easily recovered and visualized.

Digital Processes program was based on the application of an Agile BPM methodology, with short cycles (sprints) of process redesign, prototyping and delivery. One year from initial implementation, there are already 39 processes in place and 53 under construction. Development in sprints helped to minimize users' resistance and showed great results in a short period of time. It gave power to the program team and motivated Santos City Hall to move forward with its implementation.

Regarding documents management, City Hall has already achieved an economy of over 500,000.00 BRL per year only with the reduction of paper usage. Additionally, it has achieved impressive time reductions in processes that directly impact the public servants' routine.

3. BUSINESS CONTEXT

There is a serious problem in many parts of the Brazilian public administration regarding efficiency. Bureaucracy normally exceeds limits of offices, imposing restrictions to the proper execution of labor routines and the delivery of high quality public services for citizens and society.

In Santos City Hall it wasn't different. With the lack of recent investments from previous administrations in modernization, many labor routines have been executed the same way for decades. The execution of business processes depended on several disintegrated parts that couldn't provide complete answers to citizens' demands within proper deadlines.

Lack of investments in modernization also led to another problem; huge paper consumption in manual activities. A simple observation of workstations would show a huge quantity of folders with documents in process. Execution of business processes demanded the analysis of many physical documents that were always taken in manually among the various City Hall departments.

Municipal administration knew that, over time, current work standards would become unsustainable due to physical space limitations and growing costs with documents printing, transportation and storage. Reduction of paper usage was seen as a priority to the administration because it would contribute to an efficiency increase, saving resources that could be redirected to priority activities.

Other challenges taken on by current administration were to make easier the daily working lives of public servants, who were usually overloaded and unable to meet all demands satisfactorily. Many civil servants felt unmotivated by this situation and didn't believe it could change.

Finally, there was a need for improving management control, as it was impossible to extract and monitor performance indicators for most business processes. This way, managers were not able to visualize bottlenecks and adjust resource allocation.

It was urgent to invest in modernization in order to give credibility to the municipal administration and demonstrate an adequate use of public resources.

4. THE KEY INNOVATIONS

4.1 Business

Digital Process program included the introduction of Business Process Management (BPM) concepts for life cycle management of the various processes of Santos City Hall, enabled by the implementation of a technological suite that integrates management of business information, documents and processes, and also by the introduction of a digital authentication tool. With such solutions, business processes and documents are now created, signed and conducted exclusively by digital means.

The program started in September 2014 and foresees, within in a 24-month horizon, the digitization of 158 business processes classified as priorities for municipal administration.

Currently, 53 business processes are under construction and 39 have been put into production. This totals 92 business processes, with more than 30,000 instances opened per year. The remaining 66 processes were built by end of 2016.

Many of these processes are related to improvements on the public servants' routines, as there was a strategy of initially focusing on changes that would lead to higher satisfaction and quality of life for this audience. City employees serve its citizens, therefore motivated and engaged employees will inevitably provide better services. Despite this internal focus, we can also observe some preliminary results that directly impact citizens.

In order to better illustrate the results achieved, we will describe improvements in two relevant business processes, the ones executed with higher frequency and which show benefits to both servants and citizens.

Granting of Premium Leaves

Premium Leave is a legal benefit for public servants with more than five years of effective and uninterrupted services, who may request one to three months leave. This process has been prioritized due to the high frequency of requests, and also to reinforce the importance that municipal administration has given to issues inherent to public servants' daily lives.

With the process improvement, servers can now request a Premium Leave online (via mobile or desktop) and no longer have to leave their workplaces and wait in queues at HR Service Stations. Similarly, department heads can analyze and approve leaves from anywhere outside of City Hall.

In 2014, the granting of Premium Leaves took on average 94 days. After the deployment of the new process in 2015, such claims are usually resolved within15 days, with an impressive 84% time reduction.

Debt Installments

This is a process triggered by the citizen (taxpayer) to negotiate installments of a debt with the City Hall. Depending on the amount to be paid and conditions requested by the citizen, numerous documents are required and the analysis can go through multiple instances of approval to the installment be granted.

The process was originally executed on a legacy system developed by the City Hall, but the physical processing of documents and the lack of visibility on promised deadlines caused a lot of inefficiency and complaints.

With the improvements, taxpayers can now interact online with the City Hall to request and track debt installments. All documents can be submitted and processed in digital format, and alerts provide information on status and deadlines. The average time to complete the negotiation of an installment, which was previously 22 days, is now just three days, with an 86% reduction.

4.2 Organization & Social

Throughout the program, more than 500 employees of the City Hall have already been trained to perform work routines more efficiently. A series of BPM workshops have been provided to managerial and operational employees in order to raise awareness about the subject. Workshops started in May 2015 and were completed by March 2016. Besides that, specific hands-on training sessions have been conducted for each process put into production.

Training and dissemination of BPM culture in City Hall has been of great value because it's changing public servants' values and beliefs. Now, many of them are already aware of their responsibility within end-to-end business processes. This greater responsibility has also generated a greater sense of delivery, and consequent satisfaction with the work performed.

5. HURDLES OVERCOME

5.1 Management

The hiring of services by national government entities is preceded by open tender competition to the market in which the contracting party must clearly specify in a terms of reference the requested service, with description of activities to be conducted and expected deliverables. That aims to provide transparency and equality to the tender process, as well as guaranteee the efficient use of public resources. The terms of reference originally developed for the Digital Processes program stipulated that the vendor hired by the City Hall should conduct a traditional development contract following some pre-specified steps:

(1) documentation of current situation (As Is processes), with validation involving public servants;
(2) analysis and redesign of future processes (To Be), considering the possibilities of digitization;
(3) construction and implementation of automated processes.

Deadlines for performing each step were provided on the same terms of reference and led to the original program schedule, which specified that a batch of processes should be documented, then redesigned and automated by the vendor.

Thus, the initial approach to the program has put great emphasis on generating documentation about the processes, with most activities performed solely by the vendor.

At early stages of the program, however, it became clear that this strategy would not be successful. As the effective involvement of public servants in process documentation activities was low, deliverables generated by the vendor team were poor and unreliable. As reality did not match exactly what was being documented, civil servants did not recognize process documentation as a trustworthy source of information.

Overall, only 20% of documented processes in the first batch were approved without problems. It was clear that following activities would also be challenging: understanding divergences between public servants and vendors could generate errors and rework in process automation. Therefore, the team agreed to change the way the program was being conducted.

The new strategy would no longer document, redesign and then automate processes in batches. On the contrary, a few processes would be prioritized and transformed on projects with short cycles of documentation, redesign and automation. Likewise, documentation would not be an exclusive vendor; its construction should be carried out in meetings with strong participation of public servants, who would be considered key team members for each project.

The team then moved to an agile approach for conducting small projects within the program. With Scrum elements, documentation lost relevance and prototypes became more frequent. Thus, in a short period of time, each project team conducted meetings for analyzing, improving and automating a specific process. With less information on physical media, discussions and validations were based on the prototypes, that were constantly updated based on team members feedback.

This changed one very relevant original assumption for the development: the team objective was not anymore to automate an ideal process at once; rather than that, a first version of this process would be quickly delivered and then feedback from execution would lead to adjusments and refinements in following versions.

This real 'test-and-learn' environmment provided better understanding about issues to be addressed with the automation. Also, it enabled greater involvement of public servants in the projects, allowing them to effectively participate in the construction of solutions.

5.2 Organization Adoption

Rethinking processes within the Brazilian public sector, thus changing the work routine of public servants, is a major challenge. That's because the culture of this niche is quite entrenched and inflexible to change. Public servants have stable jobs guaranteed by law, and many get used to performing work routines always within the same patterns. So enabling them understand the culture change brought about by the implementation of a BPM logic was also very challenging.

Prior to the implementation of first digital processes, there was some suspicion about the program, and some employees even doubted its benefits. A key point was to engage them effectively in the construction of new processes. The initial suspicion was broken gradually, to the extent that employees realized that:

>   (1) they could bring their own suggestions for improvement during sessions;

>   (2) their views would be considered and analyzed in an open environment for contributions; and

>   (3) their participation could bring benefits to themselves.

After several benefits were observed, we had an organizational setting much more favorable to BPM adoption. Many public servants even recognized the empowerment they have gained, as they're now less dependent on other people and bureaucratic issues to perform their tasks.

Getting to simplify routines creates welfare to servants. All this contributes to a better service for citizens.

6. BENEFITS

6.1 Cost Savings

In less than one year, the Digital Processes program showed relevant cost savings.

Measurable cost reductions to date are related to paper economy. Table below indicates savings of over 500,000.00 BRL per year:

Unit	Quantity/Year	Unit Cost (BRL)	Total Cost / Year (BRL)
Paper Sheet	9.8 millions	0.018	176,400.00
A4 Printing		0.028	274,400.00
Folders and Accessories	196,000	0.24	47,040.00
Archive Box	4,900	2.14	10,486.00
TOTAL - YEAR			508,326.00 BRL

It should be noted that this rationale does not include savings related to the rent of physical spaces for documents archiving. It is estimated that those savings represent an additional amount of 170,000.00 BRL per year.

6.2 Time Reductions

Regarding time reduction, numbers are even more impressive. Some digital processes achieved 70% to 90% reductions, as table below indicates, demonstrating greater agility and indicating agreed service levels:

Process Name	Previous Cycle Time (Days)	Current Cycle Time (Days)	Reduction
Cost Center Update	100	4	96%
Small Value Payments	201	27	87%
Debt Installment	22	3	86%
Granting of Premium Leaves	96	15	84%
Suppliers Registration	119	26	78%
Provision of Period of Contribution Certificate	90	21	77%
Rescission of Contract	48	13	73%
Closure of Leaves	14	4	71%

6.3 Quality Improvements

Business processes have become structured, thus service levels began to fall significantly in a short time of use, and will continue to fall in line with refinement of new work routines. For this reason, it is possible to see positive impacts on the quality of services.

Considering that most of initial projects focus on improving public servants' routines, the first impact is on an increased satisfaction of that audience as, with digitization, information is now organized effectively, daily work is simplified, and demands are tracked in a controlled and safe manner.

7. BEST PRACTICES, LEARNING POINTS AND PITFALLS

7.1 Best Practices and Learning Points

- ✓ Agile BPM methodology: short cycles of process analysis, redesign and automation;
- ✓ Utilization of Scrum techniques: less documentation, plus prototypes;
- ✓ Test-and-learn environment: feedback from execution allows adjustments and refinements;
- ✓ Initial focus on improvements to public servants: more motivated servants will deliver better services to citizens;

7.2 Pitfalls

- ✗ Avoid an excessive focus on documentation;
- ✗ Eliminate cultural resistances that are typical in the public sector by engaging public servants in the project;

8. COMPETITIVE ADVANTAGES

One year after the start of implementation of Digital Processes program, the case of Santos City Hall became widespread and recognized by other public organizations in the federal, state and municipal levels of Brazil. The mayor himself conducted several public presentations in order to highlight the benefits already achieved.

The case of Santos was also a finalist for the 'Governarte' Award, granted by the Inter-American Development Bank (IDB), which aims to identify, reward and document digital tools that will promote people's access to public services, carried out by the government, in collaboration with civil society or private sector.

All these factors contribute positively to reinforce the idea that the municipal administration is adequately investing efforts in modernization in order to optimize the use of public resources and improve quality of services provided to citizens.

9. TECHNOLOGY

Technological suite integrates management of business information, documents and processes. Main characteristics include;

- Simplicity and speed of development;
- 100% Web solution, available on all devices (desktop, tablet, mobile);
- Integration with existing legacy systems at City Hall, providing single interface for process execution;
- Enterprise Content Management (ECM) features, ensuring the management of documents life cycle;
- Integrated Digital certification, providing legal value to documents
- Centralized repository of information for analysis;
- Ability to generate management reports on process performance and follow-up action plans for continuous improvement.

10. THE TECHNOLOGY AND SERVICE PROVIDERS

Lecom BPM is a platform for Business Process Management (BPM), Enterprise Content Management (ECM) and Analytics. It enables the monitoring of all stages of business processes, detecting unproductive tasks and identifying trouble spots (so-called "bottlenecks"), resulting in much faster outlets and rational decision.

"Lecom BPM standardizes processes and reduces bureaucracy; the villain that makes processes inefficient and impacts productivity of most Brazilian organizations" says João Cruz, CEO of Lecom.

Seguros Universal, Dominican Republic

Nominated by Bizagi, UK

1. EXECUTIVE SUMMARY / ABSTRACT

Founded in 1964, Seguros Universal ("Universal") is an insurance company based in the Dominican Republic. Part of Grupo Universal, the organization offers a wide range of products from personal cover for fire, health and accident, through to company pension and liability plans. Universal also supports the insurance needs of retail companies and banks.

In 2013-14, Universal embarked on a BPM initiative to automate its Vehicle Insurance Claims process. Utilized by three subsidiaries (Seguros Universal, Propartes y Asistencia Universal) of the Group and nearly 500 end users, this is considered the most complex of all processes within the organization. Today, "BPM Auto" underpins the end-to-end process, complete with comprehensive and robust case management and analytics.

A key aim of the BPM system was to reduce the amount of parts returned in the claims process: which it has achieved by 30%. Additionally, BPM has given every participant in the process access to timely and accurate information related to claims, delivering a faster, more productive and error-free process that continues Universal´s reputation for service excellence. The BPM initiative is the first of its kind in the Dominican Republic, testifying to Universal´s commitment not only to innovation, but giving the 50-year old company a significant competitive edge.

2. OVERVIEW

The Dominican Republic is the ninth largest economy in Latin America. A recent boom in advanced telecommunications technologies has seen the country leave its traditional agricultural/mining roots behind and make way for the service industry.

It is against this shifting and fast-changing backdrop that Universal has grown into a large and well-respected six-subsidiary business within the Dominican Republic. The company prides itself on leading the way for continuous improvement and in 2013-14, the Universal´s dedicated Director of Processes, Florangel Suero, took the decision to automate its most complex, customer-facing process: Vehicle Insurance Claims ("BPM Auto").

To do this, the BPM platform needed to link 66 different data sources, gain organization-wide acceptance of BPM and to overcome internal resistance to change. As a result, Universal´s customers now enjoy many benefits including a consistency of service, instant feedback on the claims process, faster return of their cars following any damages, quality and competitive pricing and faster resolution of queries.

Internally, the bottom-line benefits range from cost savings (the ability to receive/process claims without a corresponding increase in headcount) time savings (30% decrease in number of parts returned post-claim) and increase in productivity, achieved through more accurate and faster validation within the process.

3. BUSINESS CONTEXT

The BPM Auto process comprises 15 sub-processes that together connect clients, intermediaries and agents. These include its Call Center, Contact Center, office staff and approved auto repair shops. The process touches many systems and entry points, including its ERP and ECM systems.

Before BPM Auto, the claims were processed through applications; but, because these were not integrated, the claim information was in different systems, not giving a global review of the process. This led to the increase of returned auto parts.

Without integration, it was not easy for the customer service staff to update clients on the progress of their claim. Simply checking the status of any enquiry could involve several conversations or emails between the customer service and claim staff.

The end result was a lot of extra time and effort, an increase in errors and ultimately the number of parts returned was too high. The bottom line objective of BPM Auto was therefore to reduce returns by 30%; a goal that has been achieved through the BPM case management system.

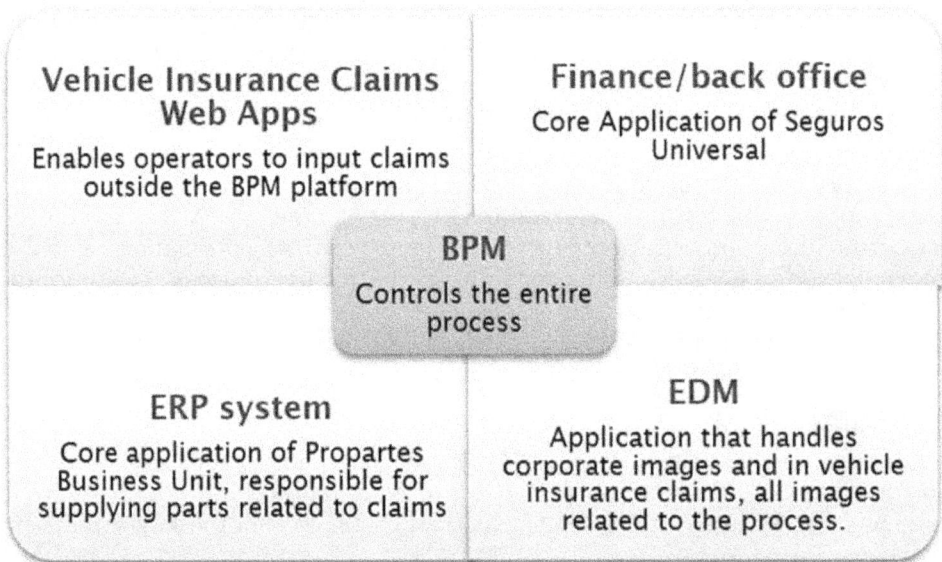

Vehicle Insurance Claims Web Apps

Enables operators to input claims outside the BPM platform

Finance/back office

Core Application of Seguros Universal

BPM

Controls the entire process

ERP system

Core application of Propartes Business Unit, responsible for supplying parts related to claims

EDM

Application that handles corporate images and in vehicle insurance claims, all images related to the process.

Fig 1: Core elements of the BPM Auto process

A general review of the process is as follows:

- The claim **opening** may generate a case either for property (vehicle) or person injured and could processed by Universal's Customer Service staff or at the repair shop.
- The **inspection** is performed by identifying and selecting the damaged parts.
- Direct link to **Propartes** (parts inventory) for quotation process and parts clearance.
- Vehicle goes to repair shop for **repairs**.
- **Payment** is made to Propartes and/or repair shop, in some cases is directly to the customer.
- Any civil liability situations that arise are automatically created and forwarded to the relevant person in Universal´s **legal** department for fast and accurate handling.

Fig 2: Automated process flow

4. THE KEY INNOVATIONS

4.1 Business

Customers: BPM has changed the way customers engage with Universal. Now, customers have 360-degree visibility of their claim and its stage within the process; they receive notifications regarding the status of their claim, keeping them up-to-date at all times (previously, only 30% of customers were privy to the communications).

Submitting a vehicle insurance claim is not a pleasant thing to do following a car accident. Therefore it is imperative to the customer that their claim is not passed between many call center operatives. With the 66-point integration within the new BPM platform, customers can expect to deal with a well-informed Call Center agent at every step. This applies equally to intermediaries e.g. staff working at the car repair shops. The platform gives them the information they need to work productively without repeat data entry or email enquiries.

Key stakeholders: BPM Auto is the first process of its kind to be automated in the Dominican insurance industry. This not only provides a distinct competitive advantage but simultaneously strengthens the internal thirst for innovation and culture for continuous improvement. This is evidenced by the strong internal sponsorship for the project which gained C-level support from the early stages and resulted in a new development scheme for Universal (see 'Organization').

At the tactical level, BPM controls and underpins the entire process, measuring both its performance and levels of traceability. Reports are available on-demand, meaning stakeholders can easily spot opportunities for improvement, validate delays in the process, make decisions regarding headcount, suppliers, etc. (see 'Benefits').

4.2 Organization & Social

Universal´s employees have fully assumed the new process into their day-to-day working. They find the new system fast and easy to use. The new dashboard is a huge improvement on the siloed systems they had previously as it brings everything they need to monitor claims into one place. Standardization of the process provides operators with consistent information no matter what stage of the process, meaning it is easier to provide quality customer service at the many different points of contact. All of this avoids mistakes, speeds productivity and builds confidence and professionalism.

Involving end-users in the system development has built knowledge and understanding of the BPM discipline and embedded the KPIs into their mindset. Thus they understand why there was a change from the old to the new, and can fully get behind its goals.

Alexander Saul Ureña's experience:

*"My experience with BPM Auto can be summarized as **a forward move**. This came to make the customer's claim process easy from beginning to end.*

*Having this new platform adds value, first to our customers, since we keep them updated every step of the process, and to our company, because **customer satisfaction** is our ultimate goal.*

*These are some of the reasons why I consider this platform **a forward move**:*

1. *Automatic notification system: keeps both the customer and broker updated of every stage of the claim, including third party damages cases (before, it was required to fill in an "Accident report form").*
2. *BPM Auto alerts if there is an open case with the same specifications, avoiding the duplicity of claims.*
3. *It allows to work more cases in less time.*
4. *All areas involved receive an automatic notification so they can intervene if needed. For example: Asistencia Universal if a vehicle needs to be towed.*
5. *The customer does not need to fill in the "Accident report form" because as the information is being entered in the system, it generates and completes the report so our client only has to sign it."*

To maintain momentum for BPM, Universal has developed a dedicated consulting group to oversee and implement this, and future generations of processes. This ensures that the business needs are closely tied to automation projects and outcomes.

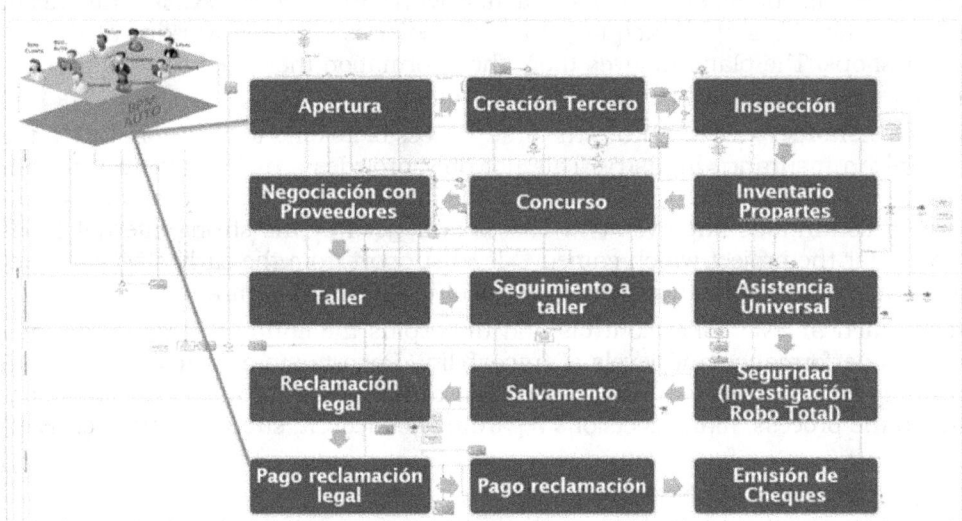

Fig. 3: Automated processes

The above diagram shows the 15 processes that were automated with the implementation of BPM Auto.

5. HURDLES OVERCOME

The implementation of BPM Auto has not been without challenges. In fact, resistance to change, incorporating new actions and defining their scope are some of the topics being handled right now. However, this has to be balanced against the larger challenge which is to constantly monitor the process and ensure that it is still meeting the needs of Universal internal and external stakeholders. This requires an agile approach which is being handled in the following way:

5.1 Management

Providing stakeholders with timely, accurate and relevant information regarding the BPM Auto process will continue to be a key driver; this information has already started to be delivered. Universal's plan is to enhance their system through the creation of management indicators, which combined with BPM native indicators will allow the organization to measure their performance and provide critical information for decision making.

5.2 Business

From the business perspective, Grupo Universal, the holding company, will continue its strategy of implementing process management, aiming to strengthen its culture of innovation and operational efficiency which has been an important factor in organizational performance.

5.3 Organization Adoption

Overall, take-up has been very positive. The input of the process owners and their involvement since the conceptualization, design, development, implementation and execution, as well as the involvement of the end users has embedded the importance of BPM to the organization. All involved now recognize BPM as the tool to manage vehicle insurance claims.

Other hurdles
- Integration of Propartes parts inventory with the vehicle insurance claim.
- Integration of the 15 sub processes to trace customer´s vehicle claim and measure it in real time.
- To keep or improve parts delivery times.
- Reduce the parts returns in 30 %.

6. BENEFITS

The benefits of BPM Auto are many. We list the most significant below:

6.1 Cost Savings
- **Headcount**: integration enables Universal to process increasing claim volumes and resolve a corresponding number of complaints without increasing personnel.
- **30% reduction in parts returns:** direct link to Propartes inventory allows parts to be more accurately identified and selected by staff within the car repair shops, generating better management of the costs associated with the claim.
- **Reduction in recovery costs:** auto-notification of total theft claims to business partner, LoJack, allows agile recovery and significant savings in the overall cost of the claim (non-recovery is declared as a total loss)

6.1 Time Savings
- **Parts delivered more quickly:** integration with Propartes catalogue allows more accurate identification and fewer returns
- **Faster escalation of legal claims:** automatic notifications instantly provide the Legal Department with information of cases requiring their attention
- **Reduction in response time to clients:** automated tracking provides greater control over intermediaries e.g. preferred car repair shops, parts suppliers and rental cars.

- **Less time spent liaising with third parties**: automatic notifications alert the external business company when stolen vehicles enter the claims process

Automatic Validations, including;
- Document validation of documents required by type of claim
- Overdue balances to date of occurrence
- Declaration of total loss of the value of the of parts that exceed 65% of the insured value

6.2 Increased Revenues

Propartes experienced increase in their sales revenues, specifically the ones related to inventory. The image below, shows the comparison of the sales for 2014 and 2015.

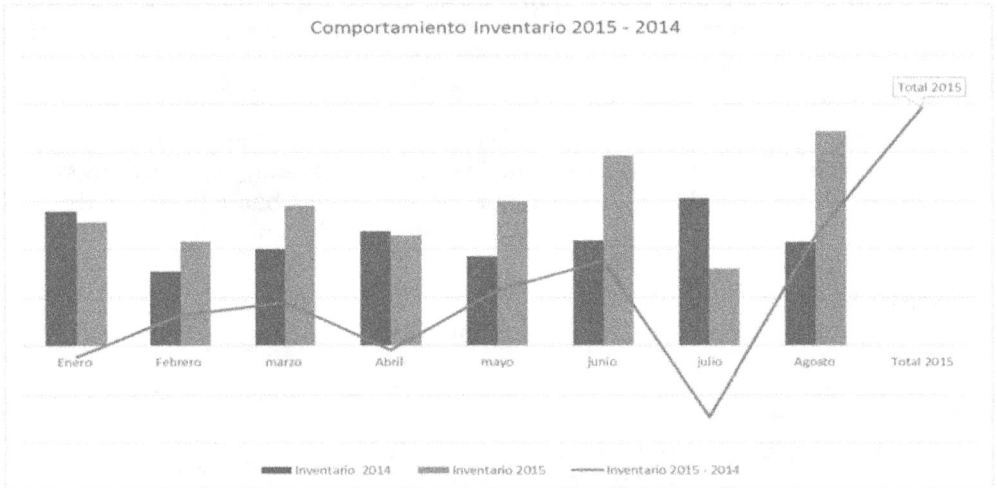

Comportamiento Inventario 2015 - 2014

Fig. 4: Propartes Sales

Period: 2014-2015. The substantial reduction in July and the important increase in August, was due to an issue in collections. In August, there was a collection process for the pending auto parts from July, which reflects in that month's behavior, as shown in fig. 4.

6.3 Quality Improvements

- **Standardized customer service**: tight integration means consistent information given at any point of contact, whether by client, agent or intermediary
- **Faster query resolution:** as a result of the above, Call Center agents are able to provide quality feedback on any area within the claims process
- **Less rework in the parts inventory**: customization of the parts quotation system creates a formal nomenclature for spare parts, reducing errors and guesswork
- **Reduction in errors and better decisions:** using BPM has resulted in a consistent process and delivered all the necessary information for decision-making.
- **Fewer duplicate cases**: BPM system automatically checks for similar cases with the same policy and date of occurrence
- **Swifter resolution of delays**: tool enables Universal to see where delays are occurring within the process and to take corrective action

7. BEST PRACTICES, LEARNING POINTS AND PITFALLS

7.1 Best Practices and Learning Points

✓ Gain the commitment of the top management team to ensure momentum during the development and production stages

✓ Create a consulting group to translate business needs to automation projects

✓ Involve internal staff in the development process to ensure the appropriate knowledge transfer post-production

✓ Recognize that you may need to move up a version between the start of the project and Go Live, and build time in for validation and testing

✓ Involve users and process owners in the testing period to gain a better understanding of process flows and to uncover errors. This guarantees their commitment to the test process.

✓ Understanding where BPM adds value and where it does not.

Learning lesson experience

During the first months of BPM implementation stage, the delivery time of auto parts increased 160% above the goal, this was due to execution issues of the users, new definitions and technological adjustments.

After in-house monitoring along with development and implementation of minor technological adjustments associated to the delivery, this time was reduced in 50% from the starting goal. This improvement was achieved without changing the application.

Details:

✓ Original delivery goal: 5 days
✓ During implementation: 13 days
✓ After adjustments: 2.5 days

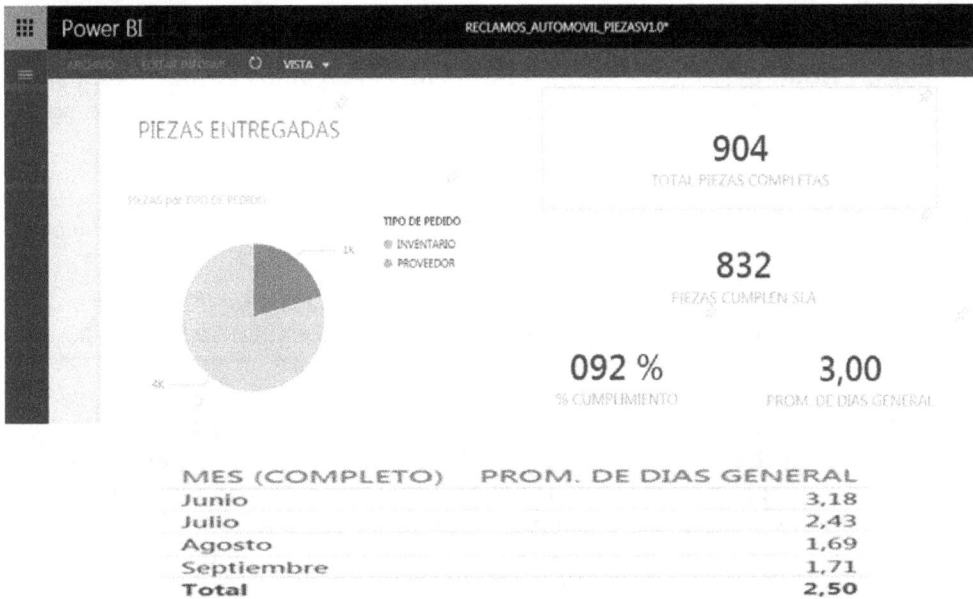

MES (COMPLETO)	PROM. DE DIAS GENERAL
Junio	3,18
Julio	2,43
Agosto	1,69
Septiembre	1,71
Total	2,50

Fig. 5: Vehicle insurance claim. Parts delivery time.
Period: Jun-Sept 2015

7.2 Pitfalls

*   ✗ *Don't let your key users fall by the wayside once development takes place. Keep them actively involved to retain their commitment and avoid delays at the testing stage.*
*   ✗ *Don't be tempted to deliver a 'BPM Big Bang.' Develop projects step-by-step to gain short-term results.*
*   ✗ *Overcome any version issues by reviewing the viability of the BPM version available at development with the one available at the start of production.*

8. COMPETITIVE ADVANTAGES

BPM Auto is the first of its kind in the Dominican insurance industry, which provides competitive advantage as it gives Universal greater control and stronger customer relationships through service excellence.

*   The automation allows the organization to increase its ability to define, deliver and adapt to processes quickly, which results in greater satisfaction for both customers and partners.
*   BPM was included in the organization´s strategic plan as an operational efficiency indicator.
*   The company revised all the processes in order to establish the prioritization of those to be automated. We now have a long-term plan for this implementation.

9. TECHNOLOGY

Technology implemented for BPM Auto include:

*   **Web applications:** enabling data input outside the BPM
*   **Integration of applications**: Seguros Universal and Propartes core applications, both subsidiaries of Grupo Universal.
*   **BPM as flow manager:** manages the whole process, indistinctly of the applications involved.
*   **EDM:** to store and manage all documents relating to Universal´s organizational processes and documents supporting claims made using BPM Auto.

10. THE TECHNOLOGY AND SERVICE PROVIDERS

BPM Auto was delivered using several technologies and suppliers, achieving an effective synchronization for automation:

*   **Bizagi BPMS**: developed in conjunction with internal staff and consulting team. The internal team was composed of functional and technical personnel. www.bizagi.com
*   **Intergrupo Dominicana**: provider who handled the development of web applications for vehicle insurance claims.
*   **Grupo Universal IT team**: for the development of web services connecting the core application of Seguros Universal with BPM, and web applications for the vehicle insurance claims with its technical counterpart, Bizagi.
*   **PKM**: provider of the images, tools and application development for the safeguard and consultation of the images relating to vehicle insurance claims.

Section 3
Appendix

WfMC Structure and Membership Information

WHAT IS THE WORKFLOW MANAGEMENT COALITION?

The Workflow Management Coalition (WfMC), founded in August 1993, is a non-profit, international organization of BPM and workflow vendors, users, analysts and university/research groups.

The Coalition's mission is to promote and develop the use of collaborative technologies such as workflow, BPM and case management through the establishment of standards for software terminology, interoperability and connectivity among products and to publicize successful use cases.

WORKFLOW STANDARDS FRAMEWORK

The Coalition has developed a framework for the establishment of workflow standards. This framework includes five categories of interoperability and communication standards that will allow multiple collaboration products to coexist and interoperate within a user's environment. Technical details are included in the white paper entitled, "The Work of the Coalition," available at www.wfmc.org.

ACHIEVEMENTS

The initial work of the Coalition focused on publishing the Reference Model and Glossary, defining a common architecture and terminology for the industry. A major milestone was achieved with the publication of the first versions of the Workflow API (WAPI) specification, covering the Workflow Client Application Interface, and the Workflow Interoperability specification.

In addition to a series of successful tutorials industry wide, the WfMC invested many person-years over the past 20 years helping to drive awareness, understanding and adoption of XPDL, now the standard means for business process definition in over 80 BPM products. As a result, it has been cited as the most deployed BPM standard by a number of industry analysts, and continues to receive a growing amount of media attention.

Workflow Reference Model

The Workflow Reference Model was published first in 1995 and still forms the basis of most BPM and workflow software systems in use today. It was developed from the generic workflow application structure by identifying the interfaces which enable products to interoperate at a variety of levels.

All workflow systems contain a number of generic components which interact in a defined set of ways; different products will typically exhibit different levels of capability within each of these generic components. To achieve interoperability between workflow products a standardized set of interfaces and data interchange formats between such components is necessary.

A number of distinct interoperability scenarios can then be constructed by reference to such interfaces, identifying different levels of functional conformance as appropriate to the range of products in the market.

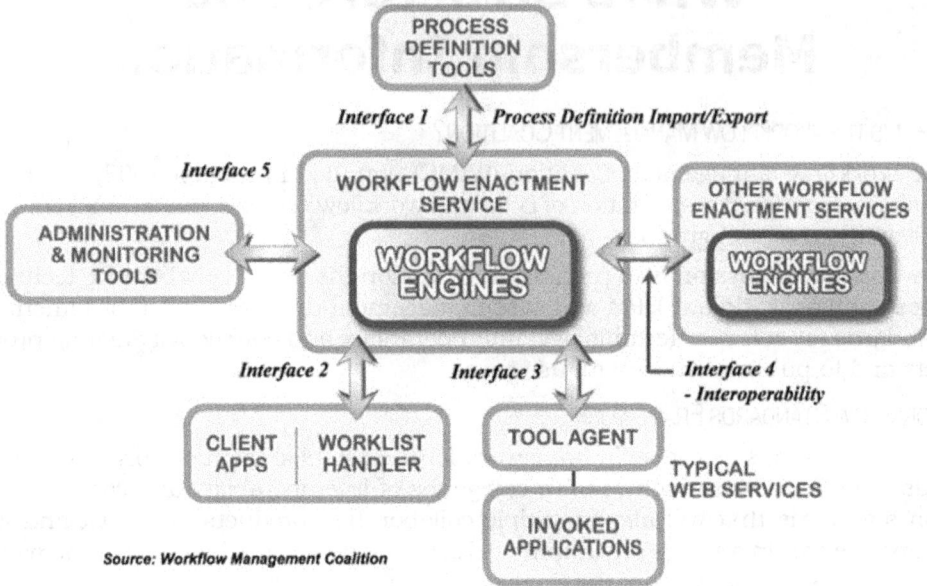

WORKFLOW REFERENCE MODEL DIAGRAM

XPDL (XML Process Definition Language)

An XML based language for describing a process definition, developed by the WfMC. Version 1.0 was released in 2002. Version 2.0 was released in Oct 2005. The goal of XPDL is to store and exchange the process diagram, to allow one tool to model a process diagram, and another to read the diagram and edit, another to "run" the process model on an XPDL-compliant BPM engine, and so on.

For this reason, XPDL is not an executable programming language like BPEL, but specifically a process design format that literally represents the "drawing" of the process definition. Thus it has 'XY' or vector coordinates, including lines and points that define process flows. This allows an XPDL to store a one-to-one representation of a BPMN process diagram.

For this reason, XPDL is effectively the file format or "serialization" of BPMN, as well as any non-BPMN design method or process model which use in their underlying definition the XPDL meta-model (there are presently about 60 tools which use XPDL for storing process models.)

In spring 2012, the WfMC completed XPDL 2.2 as the *fifth* revision of this specification. XPDL 2.2 builds on version 2.1 by introducing support for the process modeling extensions added to BPMN 2.0.

BPSim

The Business Process Simulation (BPSim) framework is a standardized specification that allows business process models captured in either BPMN or XPDL to be augmented with information in support of rigorous methods of analysis. It defines the parameterization and interchange of process analysis data allowing structural and capacity analysis of process models.

BPSim is meant to support both pre-execution and post-execution optimization of said process models. The BPSim specification consists of an underlying computer-interpretable representation (meta-model) and an accompanying electronic file format to ease the safeguard and transfer of this data between different tools (interchange format).

Wf-XML

Wf-XML is designed and implemented as an extension to the OASIS Asynchronous Service Access Protocol (ASAP). ASAP provides a standardized way that a program can start and monitor a program that might take a long time to complete. It provides the capability to monitor the running service, and be informed of changes in its status.

Wf-XML extends this by providing additional standard web service operations that allow sending and retrieving the "program" or definition of the service which is provided. A process engine has this behavior of providing a service that lasts a long time, and also being programmable by being able to install process definitions.

AWARDS

The Workflow Management Coalition sponsors three annual award programs.

1. The **Global Awards for Excellence in BPM & Workflow**[1] recognizes organizations that have implemented particularly innovative workflow solutions. Every year between 10 and 15 BPM and workflow solutions are recognized in this manner.
   WfMC publishes the case studies in the annual Excellence in Practice [2] series.

2. WfMC inaugurated a Global Awards program in 2011 for **Excellence in Case Management**[3] case studies to recognize and focus upon successful use cases for coordinating unpredictable work patterns. Awards are given in the category of Production Case Management and in Adaptive Case Management which are both new technological approaches to supporting knowledge work in today's leading edge organizations. These awards are designed to highlight the best examples of technology to support knowledge workers.
   Several books[4] have been published recognizing the winning teams. In 2013, WfMC updated the program to "WfMC Awards for Excellence in Case Management" to recognize the growing deployment of Production Case Management.

3. The **Marvin L. Manheim Award For Significant Contributions** in the Field of Workflow is given to one person every year in recognition of individual contributions to workflow and BPM standards. This award commemorates Marvin Manheim who played a key motivational role in the founding of the WfMC.

---

[1] BPM Awards: www.BPMF.org

[2] *Delivering BPM Excellence:* Published 2013 by Future Strategies Inc. http://futstrat.com/books/Delivering_BPM.php

[3] Case Management Awards: www.adaptivecasemanagement.org

[4] *Empowering Knowledge Workers:* Published 2013 by Future Strategies Inc. http://futstrat.com/books/EmpoweringKnowledgeWorkers.php

How Knowledge Workers Get Things Done. Published 2012 by Future Strategies Inc. http://www.futstrat.com/books/HowKnowledgeWorkers.php

Taming the Unpredictable: Published 2011 by Future Strategies Inc http://futstrat.com/books/eip11.php

The Workflow Management Coalition gives you the unique opportunity to participate in the creation of standards for the workflow industry as they are developing.

Your contributions to our community ensure that progress continues in the adoption of royalty-free workflow and process standards.

THE SECRETARIAT

Workflow Management Coalition (WfMC)

www.WfMC.org

Author Appendix

KERRY FINN

Enterprise Architect Fellow, Raytheon, USA

Kerry M Finn is an IT Fellow and Senior Enterprise Architect at Raytheon Corporation, where he leads the business and enterprise architecture discipline that provides oversight, alignment and architecture assurance to enterprise IT portfolio investments and projects. He is a 25-year experienced technologist focused on providing thought-leadership, best practices, and architecture guidance around intelligent business process management, digital transformation, business capability framework, enterprise architecture, service-oriented architecture and cloud computing.

He has extensive expertise in leading large-scale on-time/on-budget project, enterprise architecture initiatives, deliver customer facing web based initiatives that scale to support massive number of users, agile program and product development initiatives through the software development life cycle with DoD Engineering Product Development firms (General Dynamics, Raytheon), Global IT firms (Raytheon, Pearson Education, Arbella Insurance) and Global Commercial Engineering Product Development firms (Sun Microsystems, EMC Corporation, Progress Software and Kronos Corporation). He has received Innovation Recognition Awards at Sun Microsystem as a key architect to the Java micro-edition platform as well as Excellence Awards at Pearson Education and EMC Corporation. He has been an active member of numerous industry, technology and business standard consortiums like SNIA, IMS-GLC, JCP (Java) and ACORD. Kerry holds a MS in Computer Science.

LAYNA FISCHER

Publisher, Future Strategies Inc., USA

Ms Fischer is Editor-in-Chief and Publisher at Future Strategies Inc., the official publishers to WfMC.org. She was also Executive Director of WfMC and BPMI (now merged with OMG) and continues to work closely with these organizations to promote industry awareness of emerging technologies explaining the how and why they will impact enterprises of all sizes.

Future Strategies Inc. (www.FutStrat.com) publishes unique books and papers on business process management, business architecture and more. As such, the company contracts, and works closely, with individual authors and corporations worldwide and also directs the renowned annual awards for *Excellence in BPM and Workflow* and the *Adaptive Case Management.*

Ms. Fischer was a senior editor of a leading international computer publication for four years and has been involved in international computer journalism and publishing for over 20 years.

SETRAG KHOSHAFIAN

Chief Evangelist and VP of BPM Technology, Pegasystems Inc., USA

Dr. Setrag Khoshafian is one of the industry's pioneers and recognized experts in Digital Enterprises, especially Digital Transformation through IoT, Evolved CRM and intelligent BPM. He has been a senior executive in the software industry for the past 25 years, where he has invented, architected, and steered the production of several enterprise software products and solutions. Currently, he is Pega's Chief

Evangelist and strategic IoT & BPM technology thought leader involved in numerous technology, thought leadership, marketing, alliance, and customer initiatives. The majority of his time is spent with Fortune 500 companies, specifically on their transformational journeys leveraging digital technologies (especially digital transformation, IoT, agility & process improvement through Pega). Previously he was the Senior VP of Technology at Savvion where he invented and led the development of the world's first web centric BPM platform. He was a senior architect at Ashton-Tate where he invented Intelligent SQL, and previously an OODBMS researcher at MCC, where he invented several object databases technologies. Dr. Khoshafian is a frequent speaker and presenter at international workshops and conferences. He is the lead author of more than 10 books and more than 50 publications in various industry and academic journals.

Dr. Khoshafian holds a PhD in Computer Science from the University of Wisconsin-Madison. He also holds an MSc in Mathematics.

FRANK KOWALKOWSKI

President, Knowledge Consultants, Inc., USA

Frank Kowalkowski is President of Knowledge Consultants, Inc., a firm focusing on business performance, business/IT architecture and business analytical techniques. He has over 30 years of management and consulting experience in a wide variety of industries. He has been involved with many projects including business analysis, process management, business performance measurement, business and competitive intelligence and knowledge management. In addition to being a keynote speaker at international conferences as well as a conference chair, he has written numerous papers and spoken at conferences on a variety of subjects. He is the author of a 1996 book on Enterprise Analysis (Prentice – Hall, ISBN 0-13-282-3365) and numerous papers. Frank is currently working on a both a BPM book for managers and a new edition of the enterprise analysis book. He conducts frequent seminars nationally and internationally on a variety of business management and information technology topics. He is co-author of a quarterly column on architecture for the website TDAN.

CONNIE MOORE

Senior Vice President of Research, Digital Clarity Group, USA

As Senior Vice President of Research at Digital Clarity Group, Connie has unparalleled experience working with senior executives in business technology, marketing, and government throughout the globe. She has managed international teams in developing ground-breaking thought leadership in topics such as customer experience management challenges and trends, the changing world of business process transformation, the evolving role of digital content and omnichannel, and the ubiquity of business analytics. Her leading-edge research topics encompass the future of work in an IoT world; best practices in organizational change management; the emerging relationship of cybersecurity to customer experience management; and the impact of location marketing on trust, privacy and marketing. Connie is highly sought-after as a keynote speaker and conference chair on five continents.

In 2014, she was honored by her peer group for thought-leadership in adaptive case management and BPM software when she received the highly-coveted *Marvin L. Manheim Award For Significant Contributions in the Field of Workflow*, an industry recognition created by the Workflow Management Coalition (WfMC.org).

Prior to DCG, Connie was a Vice President, Research Director and Principal Analyst at Forrester Research for more than 20 years. She came to Forrester through the acquisition of Giga Information Group and BIS Strategic Decisions. Prior to that, she was Vice President, Product Marketing at BancTec (formerly TDC), a manufacturer of document capture systems. Connie started her career at Accenture (formerly Arthur Andersen) as a manager in the consulting division, and at Wang Labs. Connie holds an MBA in Information Systems from George Washington and a BA from East Carolina University. She is a former director of AIIM International, the leading professional association for information management.

NATHANIEL PALMER

Executive Director, WfMC, USA

Rated as the #1 Most Influential Thought Leader in Business Process Management (BPM) by independent research, Nathaniel is recognized as one of the early originators of BPM, and has the led the design for some of the industry's largest-scale and most complex projects involving investments of $200 Million or more. Today he is the Editor-in-Chief of BPM.com, as well as the Executive Director of the Workflow Management Coalition.

Previously he had been the BPM Practice Director of SRA International, and prior to that Director, Business Consulting for Perot Systems Corp, as well as spent over a decade with Delphi Group serving as VP and CTO. He frequently tops the lists of the most recognized names in his field, and was the first individual named as Laureate in Workflow. Nathaniel has authored or co-authored a dozen books on process innovation and business transformation, including "Thriving on Adaptibility" (2016) "BPM Everywhere" (2015) "Intelligent BPM" (2013), "How Knowledge Workers Get Things Done" (2012), "Social BPM" (2011), "Mastering the Unpredictable" (2008) which reached #2 on the Amazon.com Best Seller's List, "Excellence in Practice" (2007), "Encyclopedia of Database Systems" (2007) and "The X-Economy" (2001).

He has been featured in numerous media ranging from Fortune to The New York Times to National Public Radio. Nathaniel holds a DISCO Secret Clearance as well as a Position of Trust with in the U.S. federal government.

KEITH SWENSON

Vice President of R&D, Fujitsu America Inc.

Keith Swenson is Vice President of Research and Development at Fujitsu North America and also the Chairman of the Workflow Management Coalition. As a speaker, author, and contributor to many workflow and BPM standards, he is known for having been a pioneer in collaboration software and web services. He has led agile software development teams at MS2, Netscape, Ashton Tate & Fujitsu. He won the 2004 Marvin L. Manheim Award for outstanding contributions in the field of workflow. Co-author on more than 10 books, his latest book, "When Thinking Matters in the Workplace," explains how to avoid stifling creativity and enhance innovation through the appropriate use of process technology. His 2010 book "Mastering the Unpredictable" introduced and defined the field of adaptive case management and established him as a Top Influencer in the field of case management. He blogs at https://social-biz.org/.

NEIL WARD-DUTTON

Research Director, MWD Advisors, United Kingdom

Neil Ward-Dutton is MWD Advisors' co-founder and Research Director, and is one of Europe's most experienced and high-profile strategic business-technology advisors and industry analysts. His areas of expertise include digital transformation, business process management (BPM), enterprise architecture (EA) and IT strategy. Neil acts as an advisor to large European organisations across industries and sectors as diverse as financial services, retail, utilities and government, as well as providing advice to a number of leading technology vendors.

KAY WINKLER

Director and Partner at NSI Soluciones; Founder & President of the ABPMP Panama Chapter, NSI Soluciones, Panama

Kay Winkler earned his PhD in economics and business administration at the Universidad Latina de Panama. His investigation focused on establishing measurement frameworks for BPM benefit determination with "time" as a main variable. At NSI he is responsible for the distribution and implementation of BPM and ECM solutions in Latin America. Having been responsible for the automation and optimization of mission-critical processes for hundreds of international companies, he had the opportunity of accumulating proven and applied practices related to BPM and IT business solutions. He is sharing this knowledge together with insights from other recognized experts in his role of president at the local ABPMP chapter.

He can be reached through LinkedIn at: https://pa.linkedin.com/in/kaywinkler

Case Studies

NOMINEE ORGANIZATION:

Company: ARaymond Brazil, Brazil

NOMINATED BY:

Company: Lecom SA

Website: http://www.lecom.com.br

NOMINEE ORGANIZATION:

Company: Die Mobiliar, Switzerland

NOMINATED BY:

Company: ISIS Papyrus Europe AG

Website: http://isis-papyrus.com

NOMINEE ORGANIZATION:

Company: Fujirebio Diagnostics, Inc., USA

NOMINATED BY:

Company: Wonderware

Website: https://www.wonderware.com

NOMINEE ORGANIZATION:

Company: INTA, Argentina, Argentina

NOMINATED BY:

Company: Pectra Technology

Website: www.pectra.com

NOMINEE ORGANIZATION:

Company: Ministry of Interior Colombia, Colombia

NOMINATED BY:

Company: AuraPortal

Website: http://auraportal.com

NOMINEE ORGANIZATION:

Company: National Bank of Kenya, Kenya

NOMINATED BY:

Company: Newgen Software Technologies Limited

Website: http://www.newgensoft.com

NOMINEE ORGANIZATION:

Company: Santos City Hall, Brazil

NOMINATED BY:

Company: Lecom SA

Website: http://www.lecom.com.br

NOMINEE ORGANIZATION:

Company: Seguros Universal, Dominican Republic

NOMINATED BY:

Company: Bizagi

Website: http://www.bizagi.com

Index

More Reading and Resources

Introduction to BPM and Workflow
http://bpm-books.com/products/ebook-series-introduction-to-bpm-and-workflow

Financial Services
http://bpm-books.com/products/ebook-series-financial-services

BPM in Healthcare Second Edition
http://bpm-books.com/products/bpm-in-healthcare-2nd-edition

Utilities and Telecommunications
http://bpm-books.com/products/ebook-series-utilities-and-telecommunications

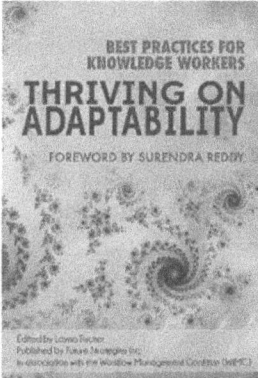

THRIVING ON ADAPTABILITY:

Best practices for knowledge workers

http://futstrat.com/books/ThrivingOnAdaptability.php

ACM helps organizations focus on improving or optimizing the line of interaction where our people and systems come into direct contact with customers. It's a whole different thing; a new way of doing business that enables organizations to literally become one living-breathing entity via collaboration and adaptive data-driven biological-like operating systems. ACM is not just another acronym or business fad. ACM is the process, strategy, framework, and set of tools that enables this evolution and maturity--*Surendra Reddy.*

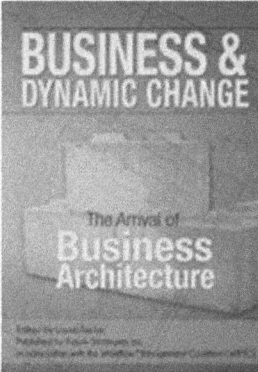

BUSINESS AND DYNAMIC CHANGE
The Arrival of Business Architecture
http://bpm-books.com/products/business-and-dynamic-change

These visionaries see the need for *business* leaders to define their organizations to be agile and robust in the face of external changes.

This book will stimulate thinking about a more complete approach to *business* architecture. As such, it is imperative reading for executives, managers, business analysts, and IT professionals that require an understanding of the structural relationships of the components of an enterprise.

BPM EVERYWHERE

Internet of Things, Process of Everything
http://bpm-books.com/products/bpm-everywhere-print

Critical issues currently face BPM adopters and practitioners, such as the key roles played by process mining uncovering engagement patterns and the need for process management platforms to coordinate interaction and control of smart devices.

BPME represents the strategy for leveraging, not simply surviving but fully exploiting the wave of disruption facing every business over the next 5 years and beyond.

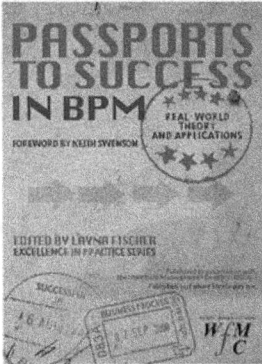

PASSPORTS TO SUCCESS IN BPM:
Real-World Theory and Applications

http://futstrat.com/Passports.php

Is your BPM project set up for success or failure?

Knowing what BPM success will look like before you even begin will help you achieve it. So will knowing what are the most common causes of failure. BPM projects fail more often as a result of missed expectations than inadequate technology.

Yet a greater number of BPM projects fail to launch at all due to the inability to be a credible business case. Discover why.

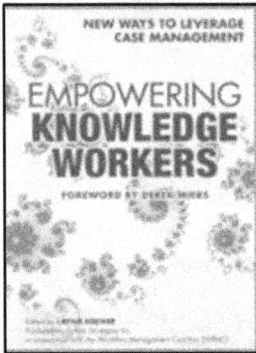

EMPOWERING KNOWLEDGE WORKERS: NEW WAYS TO LEVERAGE CASE MANAGEMENT

futstrat.com/books/EmpoweringKnowledgeWorkers.php

ACM allows work to follow the worker, providing cohesiveness of a single point of access. Case Management provides the long-term record of how work is done, as well as the guidance, rules, visibility and input that allow knowledge workers to be more productive. Adaptive Case Management is ultimately about allowing knowledge workers to work the way that they want to work and to provide them with the tools and information they need to do so effectively.

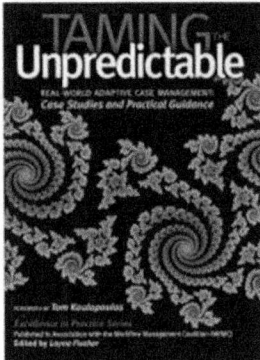

TAMING THE UNPREDICTABLE

http://futstrat.com/books/eip11.php

The core element of Adaptive Case Management (ACM) is the support for real-time decision-making by knowledge workers.

Taming the Unpredictable presents the logical starting point for understanding how to take advantage of ACM. This book goes beyond talking about concepts, and delivers actionable advice for embarking on your own journey of ACM-driven transformation.

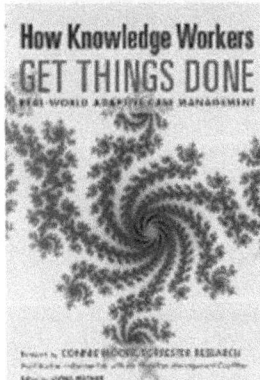

HOW KNOWLEDGE WORKERS GET THINGS DONE

http://www.futstrat.com/books/HowKnowledgeWorkers.php

How Knowledge Workers Get Things Done describes the work of managers, decision makers, executives, doctors, lawyers, campaign managers, emergency responders, strategist, and many others who have to think for a living. These are people who figure out what needs to be done, at the same time that they do it, and there is a new approach to support this presents the logical starting point for understanding how to take advantage of ACM.

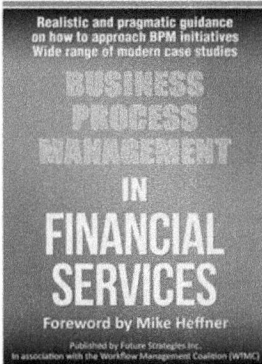

BPM IN FINANCIAL SERVICES

https://bpm-books.com/products/bpm-in-financial-services

The Financial Services industry is in the middle of a major transition to become more customer value focused, more compliant, and better-adjusted to new normal cost structures.

This book provides realistic and pragmatic guidance on how to approach BPM initiatives, along with a wide range of modern case studies developed by those who have undertaken real BPM programs.

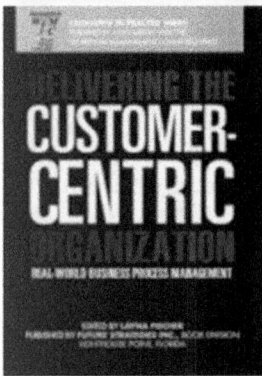

DELIVERING THE CUSTOMER-CENTRIC ORGANIZATION

http://futstrat.com/books/Customer-Centric.php
The ability to successfully manage the customer value chain across the life cycle of a customer is the key to the survival of any company today. Business processes must react to changing and diverse customer needs and interactions to ensure efficient and effective outcomes.

This important book looks at the shifting nature of consumers and the workplace, and how BPM and associated emergent technologies will play a part in shaping the companies of the future.

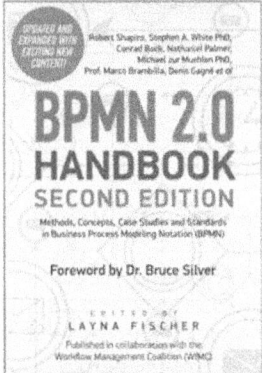

BPMN 2.0 Handbook SECOND EDITION

(see two-BPM book bundle offer on website: get BPMN Reference Guide Free)
http://futstrat.com/books/bpmnhandbook2.php

Updated and expanded with exciting new content!

Authored by members of WfMC, OMG and other key participants in the development of BPMN 2.0, the BPMN 2.0 Handbook brings together worldwide thought-leaders and experts in this space. Exclusive and unique contributions examine a variety of aspects that start with an introduction of what's new in BPMN 2.0, and look closely at interchange, analytics, conformance, optimization, simulation and more.

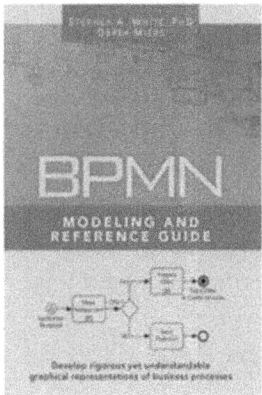

BPMN MODELING AND REFERENCE GUIDE

(see two-BPM book bundle offer on website: get BPMN Reference Guide Free)

http://www.futstrat.com/books/BPMN-Guide.php
Understanding and Using BPMN
How to develop rigorous yet understandable graphical representations of business processes.

Business Process Modeling Notation (BPMN) is a standard, graphical modeling representation for business processes. It provides an easy to use, flow-charting notation that is independent of the implementation environment.
See special 2-book offer online
http://bpm-books.com/products/bpmn-best-books-bundle

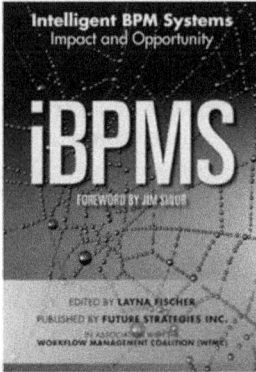

iBPMS - INTELLIGENT BPM SYSTEMS

http://bpm-books.com/products/ibpms-intelligent-bpm-systems-print

"The need for Intelligent Business Operations (IBO) supported by intelligent processes is driving the need for a new convergence of process technologies lead by the iBPMS. The iBPMS changes the way processes help organizations keep up with business change," notes Gartner Emeritus Jim Sinur in his Foreword.

The authors of this important book describe various aspects and approaches of iBPMS especially the impact and opportunity.

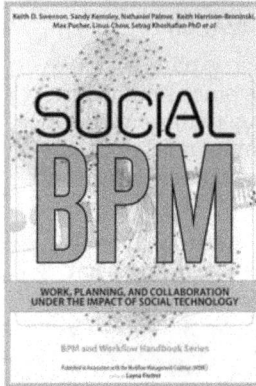

Social BPM

http://bpm-books.com/products/social-bpm-print-edition
Work, Planning, and Collaboration Under the Impact of Social Technology

Today we see the transformation of both the look and feel of BPM technologies along the lines of social media, as well as the increasing adoption of social tools and techniques democratizing process development and design.

It is along these two trend lines; the evolution of system interfaces and the increased engagement of stakeholders in process improvement, that Social BPM has taken shape.

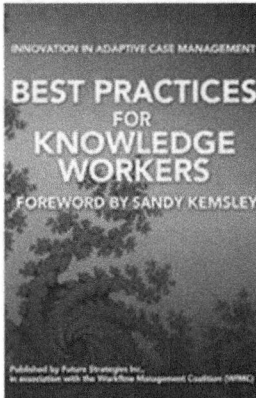

BEST PRACTICES FOR KNOWLEDGE WORKERS

Innovation in Adaptive Case Management

http://bpm-books.com/products/best-practices-to-support-knowledge-workers-print

Best Practices for Knowledge Workers describes ACM in the current era of digitization, Internet of Things (IoT), Artificial Intelligence (AI), intelligent BPMS and BPM Everywhere.

You will learn how support of adaptive, data-driven processes empowers knowledge workers to know in real-time what is happening at the edge points, and to take actions through the combination of rule-driven guidance and their own know-how.

Get **25% Discount** on ALL these Books!

Use the discount code **BOOK25** to get **25% discount** on ALL books in the store; both Print and Digital Editions (even on already-discounted prices).

Download Now - Digital Edition Benefits:

Enjoy immediate download, live URLs, searchable text, graphics and charts in color. No shipping charges. Download from our website now.

Published by Future Strategies Inc.
http://bpm-books.com

www.ingramcontent.com/pod-product-compliance
Lightning Source LLC
Chambersburg PA
CBHW080548220326
41599CB00032B/6408